INTERNALLY DISPLACED PEOPLE

Map by András Bereznay

SOLOMON
ISLANDS
30,000

UZBEKISTAN
3,500

AFGHANISTAN
900,000-1,200,000

PAKISTAN
3,000

PHILIPPINES
140,000

INDONESIA
1,300,000

RUSSIAN FEDERATION
460,000

BURMA
600,000-
1,000,000

SRI LANKA
800,000

BANGLADESH
500,000

INDIA 650,000

AZERBAIJAN
570,000

IRAQ
700,000

SYRIA
300,000

LEBANON
300,000

ARMENIA
50,000

ERITREA
57,000

ETHIOPIA
12,500

SOMALIA
400,000

KENYA
200,000

UGANDA
550,000

RWANDA
undetermined

GEORGIA
270,000

SUDAN
4,000,000

BURUNDI
475,000

ZIMBABWE
50,000

TURKEY
1,000,000

MOLDOVA
1,000

YUGOSLAVIA
330,800

ALGERIA
200,000

NIGERIA
500,000

CONGO
150,000

DEMOCRATIC
REPUBLIC
OF THE
CONGO
2,200,000

ANGOLA
4,100,000

CROATIA
22,000

BOSNIA AND
HERZEGOVINA
440,000

FYROMACEDONIA
17,000

CYPRUS
210,000

ISRAEL
200,000

PALESTINIAN
TERRITORIES
9,000-20,000

SENEGAL
6,000

GUINEA-BISSAU
2,000

GUINEA
250,000

SIERRA
LEONE
200,000

LIBERIA
80,000

COLOMBIA
2,100,000

PERU
60,000

GUATEMALA
250,000

MEXICO
10,000

INTERNALLY DISPLACED PEOPLE

A Global Survey

SECOND EDITION

Global IDP PROJECT

NORWEGIAN
REFUGEE COUNCIL

EARTHSCAN

Earthscan Publications Limited
London • Sterling, VA

First published in the UK and USA in 2002 by
Earthscan Publications Ltd

ISBN: 1 85383 952 3 paperback
      1 85383 953 1 hardback

Typesetting by JS Typesetting Ltd, Wellingborough, Northants
Printed and bound by Bookcraft, Midsomer Norton
Cover by Karen Ford
Cover photo: Huambo, Angola, March 2000: Child in an IDP camp. © Ami Vitale/Panos
Frontispiece © Global IDP Project, April–May 2002

For a full list of publications please contact:

Earthscan Publications Ltd
120 Pentonville Road
London, N1 9JN, UK
Tel: +44 (0)20 7278 0433
Fax: +44 (0)20 7278 1142
Email: earthinfo@earthscan.co.uk
http://www.earthscan.co.uk

22883 Quicksilver Drive, Sterling, VA 20166–2012, USA

A catalogue record for this book is available from the British Library

Library of Congress Cataloging-in-Publication Data

Internally displaced people : a global survey / Global IDP Project & Norwegian Refugee
Council.–2nd ed.
        p. cm.
    Includes bibliographical references and index.
    ISBN 1-85383-952-3 (pbk.) — ISBN 1-85383-953-1 (hdbk.)
        1. Refugees. 2. Migration, Internal. 3. Refugees–Civil rights. 4. Refugees–Protection.
    5. Human rights. I. Global IDP Survey. II. Flyktningerêad (Norway)

HV640 .I516 2002
325'.21–dc21

                                                                            2002012851

Earthscan is an editorially independent subsidiary of Kogan Page Ltd and publishes in
association with WWF-UK and the International Institute for Environment and Development

This book is printed on elemental chlorine-free paper

Contents

Part 1: Issues and Perspectives

Part 2: Regional Profiles

Regional overview • *Algeria* • *Angola* • *Burundi* • *Democratic Republic of Congo* • *Eritrea* • *Ethiopia* • *Guinea* • *Guinea-Bissau* • *Kenya* • *Liberia* • *Nigeria* • *Republic of Congo (Brazzaville)* • *Rwanda* • *Senegal* • *Sierra Leone* • *Somalia* • *Sudan* • *Uganda*

Regional overview • *Colombia* • *Guatemala* • *Mexico* • *Peru*

Editorial team

Managing editor
Stacey White

Editors and analysts
Andreas Danevad
Oliver Wates

Assistant
Tordis Birkeland (bibliography)
Produced by the Norwegian Refugee Council's Global IDP Project under the direction of
Elisabeth Rasmusson

Norwegian Refugee Council/Global IDP Project
Chemin Moïse Duboule, 59
1209 Geneva – Switzerland
Tel: +41 22 799 0700
Fax: +41 22 799 0701
Email: idpsurvey@nrc.ch
http://www.idpproject.org

Main contributing authors

Christophe Beau: Europe regional overview, Armenia, Azerbaijan, Bosnia and
                         Herzegovina, Croatia, Cyprus, Federal Republic of Yugoslavia,
                         Georgia, Moldova and Russian Federation

Cathy Benetti: Americas regional overview, Colombia, Eritrea, Mexico, Somalia
                         and Sudan

Andreas Danevad: Chapter 2, Asia regional overview, Bangladesh, Burma/Myanmar,
                         Kenya, Uganda and Uzbekistan

Jeroen Klok: Algeria, Ethiopia, FYRoMacedonia, Guatemala, Nigeria, India,
                         Pakistan, Peru and Turkey

Frederik Kok: Asia regional overview, Afghanistan, Indonesia, The
                         Philippines, Solomon Islands and Sri Lanka

Claudia McGoldrick: Africa regional overview, Angola, Guinea, Guinea-Bissau,
                         Liberia, Republic of Congo (Brazzaville), Senegal and Sierra
                         Leone

Bjorn Pettersson: Chapter 3

Stacey White: Chapter 1

Greta Zeender: Middle East regional overview, Burundi, Democratic Republic
                         of Congo, Iraq, Israel, Lebanon, Palestinian Territories, Rwanda
                         and Syria

Acknowledgements

The information contained in this book reflects the contributions of hundreds of different people and agencies around the world in regular contact with the Global IDP Project. It is only through their input and support that the Global IDP Project has been able to produce this book. The Global IDP Project is also thankful to the users of its database at www.idpproject.org, whose invaluable feedback has allowed its staff to continually develop and improve the compilation of information on conflict-induced internally displaced people.

The Project would like to thank Derek Miller for the graphic design work in this book and András Bereznay for his production of the maps (www.historyonmaps.com). The Project would also like to thank Lisa Alfredson, Cecilia Bailliet, Stuart Katwikirize and Derek Miller for their written contributions to text boxes in this survey. The Project is also indebted to the Office of the Representative to the UN Secretary-General on Internally Displaced Persons, Dr Francis M Deng, for its contribution of a Foreword. Assistance in identifying photos was offered by Chamrong Lo of the International Committee of the Red Cross, Anne Kellner of the United Nations High Commissioner for Refugees (UNHCR), and Barry Sandland and Bruno de Cock, both of Médecins Sans Frontières.

Special mention goes to Catherine Hubert and Simone Cosma of the Global IDP Project for their hard work in securing funds for this publication. The Global IDP Project is grateful for the financial contributions from the following donors for this and other activities of the Project:

Ministry of Foreign Affairs, Norway
Department for International Development, UK
Department of Foreign Affairs and International Trade, Canada
Swedish International Development Agency (SIDA)
Department of Foreign Affairs, Switzerland
Ministry of Foreign Affairs, The Netherlands

Acronyms and abbreviations

ACCORD	Australian Centre for Country of Origin Asylum Research and Documentation
ACF	Action Contre la Faim
ACRA	Aceh Child Rights Alliance Directory
ACT	Action by Churches Together
ACTSA	Action for Southern Africa
ADF	Allied Democratic Front (Uganda)
AFP	Agence France-Presse
AFSC	American Friends Service Committee
AI	Amnesty International
AIDS	acquired immune deficiency syndrome
AIMS	Afghanistan Information Management Service
AIS	Islamic Salvation Army (Algeria)
AP	Associated Press
ARMM	Autonomous Regions of Muslim Mindanao (The Philippines)
ASEAN	Association of South-East Asian Nations
ASG	Abu Sayyaf Group (The Philippines)
AUC	United Self-Defence Forces of Colombia
BBC	British Broadcasting Company
BERG	Burma Ethnic Research Group
BiH	Bosnia and Herzegovina
CAID	Christian Aid
CAP	Inter-Agency Consolidated Appeal (United Nations)
CARDI	Consortium for Assistance to Refugees and Displaced Persons in Indonesia
CARE	Cooperative for Assistance and Relief Everywhere
CEC	Commission of the European Community
CEH	Commission for Historical Clarification (Guatemala)
CEPED	Centre Français sur la Population et le Développement
CFSI	Community and Family Services International (The Philippines)
CGES	Commissioner General of Essential Services (Sri Lankan government)
CHT	Chittagong Hill Tracts (Bangladesh)
CHTC	Chittagong Hill Tracts Commission
CIEPAC	Centro de Investigaciones Económicas y Políticas de Acción Comunitaria
CIREFCA	International Conference on Central American Refugees

CIS	Commonwealth of Independent States
CODHES	Consultoría para los Derechos Humanos y el Desplazamiento (Colombia)
CoE	Council of Europe
CONDEG	National Council of the Displaced in Guatemala
CONGAD	Conseil des ONGs d'Appui au Développement
CPA	Centre for Policy Alternatives (Sri Lanka)
CPDIA	Permanent Consultation on Internal Displacement in the Americas
CPR	Communities of People in Resistance (Guatemala)
CSW	Christian Solidarity Worldwide
CUNY	City University of New York
DIAL	Diálogo Inter-Agencial (Colombia)
DRC	Democratic Republic of Congo
ECDFC	European Platform for Conflict Prevention and Transformation
ECGD	Export Credits Guarantee Department (UK government)
ECHR	European Court of Human Rights
ECOMOG	Ceasefire Monitoring Group of the Economic Community of West African States
ECRE	European Council on Refugees and Exiles
ELN	National Liberation Army (Colombia)
ERREC	Eritrean Relief and Refugee Commission
EU	European Union
EZLN	Zapatista Army of National Liberation (Mexico)
FAO	Food and Agriculture Organization (United Nations)
FAO GIEWS	FAO Global Information and Early Warning System
FARC	Colombian Revolutionary Armed Forces
FDD	Forces for the Defence of Democracy (Burundi)
FEWS Net	Famine Early Warning System Network
FHH	female-headed household
FIDH	International Federation of Human Rights
FIS	Islamic Salvation Front (Algeria)
FLN	National Liberation Front (Algiera)
FNL	National Liberation Forces (Burundi)
FRoY	Federal Republic of Yugoslavia
FSAU	Food Security Analysis Unit
GAM	Free Aceh Movement
GIA	Islamic Armed Group (Algeria)
Göç-Der	Immigrants Association for Social Cooperation and Culture (Turkey)
HADEP	People's Democracy Party (Turkey)
HCIC	Humanitarian Community Information Centre
HIV	human immuno-deficiency virus
HRDC	Human Rights Documentation Centre
HRFT	Human Rights Foundation of Turkey
HRW	Human Rights Watch
Human Rights Now	Human Rights Network on the Web
IACHR	Inter-American Commission on Human Rights
ICBL	International Campaign to Ban Land Mines
ICG	International Crisis Group
ICRC	International Committee of the Red Cross

ICVA	International Council of Voluntary Agencies
IDF	Israeli Defence Forces
IDP	internally displaced person/people
IFM	Isatabu Freedom Movement (The Philippines)
IFRC	International Federation of Red Cross and Red Crescent Societies
IHF	International Helsinki Federation of Human Rights
ILO	International Labour Organization
IMC	International Medical Corps
IMF	International Monetary Fund
IMTD	Institute for Multi-Track Diplomacy
IMU	Islamic Movement of Uzbekistan
IOM	International Organization for Migration
IRC	International Rescue Committee
ISAF	International Security Assistance Force (Afghanistan)
ITAP	Immediate and Transitional Assistance Programme for the Afghan People (Afghanistan)
JRS	Jesuit Refugee Service
KDP	Kurdish Democratic Party (Iraq)
KFOR	Kosovo Force
KNLA	Karen National Liberation Army (Burma/Myanmar)
LOC	Line of Control in Kashmir
LNF	Lebanese NGO Forum
LNM	Lebanese National Movement
LRA	Lord's Resistance Army (Uganda)
LRRRC	Liberian Refugee, Repatriation and Resettlement Commission
LTTE	Liberation Tigers of Tamil Eelam (Sri Lanka)
LURD	Liberians United for Reconciliation and Democracy
MCI	Mercy Corps International
MCIC	Macedonian Centre for International Cooperation
MECC	Middle East Council of Churches
MEF	Malaita Eagle Force (Solomon Islands)
MEMRI	Middle East Media and Research Institute
MENADES	Mesa Nacional sobre Desplazamiento y Afectados por Violencia Política (Peru)
MERIP	Middle East Research and Information Project
MFDC	Mouvement des Forces Démocratiques de Casamance (Senegal)
MHH	male-headed household
MILF	Moro Islamic Liberation Front (The Philippines)
MINOPS	Minimum Operational Standards for Resettlement and Return of IDPs (Angola)
MINUGUA	United Nations Human Rights Verification Mission in Guatemala
MLC	Movement for the Liberation of Congo
MNLF	Moro National Liberation Front (The Philippines)
MONUC	United Nations Mission in the Democratic Republic of Congo
MPLA	Popular Movement for the Liberation of Angola
MRRR	Ministry of Rehabilitation, Resettlement and Refugees (Sri Lanka)
MSF	Médecins Sans Frontières
MUAC	the mid-upper arm circumference test
NAFTA	North American Free Trade Agreement
NATO	North Atlantic Treaty Organization

NCCK	National Council of Churches of Kenya
NCRRR	National Commission for Reconstruction, Resettlement and Rehabilitation (Sierra Leone)
NGO	non-governmental organization
NLA	National Liberation Army (Former Yugoslav Republic of Macedonia)
NPA	New People's Army (The Philippines)
NPFL	National Patriotic Front of Liberia
NPMHR	Naga Peoples Movement for Human Rights (India)
NRC	Norwegian Refugee Council
NRCS	Nigerian Red Cross Society
NSCN-IM	National Socialist Council of Nagaland–Isak–Muivah (India)
NY	New York
OAS	Organization of American States
OAU	Organization of African Unity
ÖDP	Freedom and Solidarity Party (Turkey)
OHR	Office of the High Representative of Bosnia and Herzegovina
OLS	Operation Lifeline Sudan
OSCE	Organization for Security and Cooperation in Europe
OSCE ODIHR	OSCE Office for Democratic Institutions and Human Rights
ÖDP	Freedom and Solidarity Party (Turkey)
PAR	Programme for the Repopulation and Development of Emergency Zones (Peru)
PAROS	government-operated vulnerability assessment system (Armenia)
PCP	Principled Common Programming (Afghanistan)
PDA	Project on Defence Alternatives
PHR	Physicians for Human Rights
PLO	Palestine Liberation Organization
PKK	Kurdistan Workers' Party (Turkey)
PRODERE	UN Development Programme for Displaced Persons, Refugees and Returnees in Central America
PROMUDEH	Propuesta de MENADES al Ministerio de Promocíon de la Mujer y Desarrollo Humano (Peru)
PUK	Patriotic Union of Kurdistan (Iraq)
RCD–Goma	Congolese Rally for Democracy–Goma
RCD–Kinshasa	Congolese Rally for Democracy–Kinshasa
REST	Relief Society of Tigray (Ethiopia)
RI	Refugees International
RRA	Rahanweyn Resistance Army (Somalia)
RRAN	Resettlement and Rehabilitation Authority of the North (Sri Lanka)
RSS	Social Solidarity Network (Colombia)
RUF	Revolutionary United Front of Sierra Leone
RUFP	Revolutionary United Front of Sierra Leone (political party)
SAARC	South Asian Association for Regional Cooperation
SACB	Somalia Aid Coordination Body
SAHRDC	South Asia Human Rights Documentation Centre
SALW	small arms and light weapons
SCF	Save the Children
SFOR	Stabilization Force
SIDA	Swedish International Development Agency
SIPAZ	International Service for Peace (Mexico)

SISDES	Sistema de Información sobre Desplazamiento Forzado y Derechos Humanos en Colombia
SLA	South Lebanese Army
SPDC	State Peace and Development Council (Burma)
SPLA	Sudan People's Liberation Army
SPLM/A	Sudan People's Liberation Movement/Army
SRRA	Sudan Relief and Rehabilitation Association
SRRC	Somalia Restoration and Reconciliation Council
SRSG	Special Representative of the United Nations Secretary–General
SSA	Shan State Army (Burma)
SZOPAD	Special Zone of Peace and Development (The Philippines)
TMMOB	Union of the Chambers of Turkish Engineers and Architects
TNG	Transitional National Government (Somalia)
TOHAV	Social Law Research Foundation (Turkey)
TRNC	Turkish Republic of Northern Cyprus
TSZ	Temporary Security Zone (Eritrea and Ethiopia)
UK	United Kingdom
UN	United Nations
UN-Habitat	United Nations Human Settlements Programme
UNAMA	United Nations Assistance Mission to Afghanistan
UNAMSIL	United Nations Mission in Sierra Leone
UNCERD	United Nations Committee on the Elimination of all Forms of Racial Discrimination
UNCHR	United Nations Commission for Human Rights
UNCTE	United Nations Country Team Ethiopia
UNDOF	United Nations Disengagement Observer Force (Syria)
UNDP	United Nations Development Programme
UNDP EUE	United Nations Development Programme Emergencies Unit for Ethiopia
UNECOSOC	United Nations Economic and Social Council
UNEP	United Nations Environment Programme
UNEP DEWA	United Nations Environment Programme Division of Early Warning and Assessment
UNFICYP	United Nations Peacekeeping Mission in Cyprus
UNFPA	United Nations Population Fund
UNGA	United Nations General Assembly
UNHCHR	United Nations High Commissioner on Human Rights
UNHCR	United Nations High Commission for Refugees
UNIAC	United Nations International Advisory Committee
UNICEF	United Nations Children's Fund
UNIFEM AFWIC	United Nations Development Fund for Women African Women in Crisis Programme
UNIRIN	United Nations Integrated Regional Information Networks
UNIRIN-CEA	United Nations Integrated Regional Information Networks–Central and Eastern Africa
UNIRIN-WA	United Nations Integrated Regional Information Networks–West Africa
UNITA	National Union for the Total Independence of Angola
UNMAS	United Nations Mine Action Service
UNMEE	United Nations Mission in Ethiopia and Eritrea

UNMIK	United Nations Interim Administration Mission in Kosovo
UNMOGIP	United Nations Military Observer Group in India and Pakistan
UNOCHA	United Nations Office for the Coordination of Humanitarian Affairs
UNOGBIS	United Nations Office in Guinea-Bissau
UNOLS	United Nations Operation Lifeline Sudan
UNOMIG	United Nations Military Observer Mission in Georgia
UNOPS	United Nations Office for Project Services
UNOSOM	United Nations Mission in Somalia
UNRC	United Nations Resident Coordinator (The Philippines)
UNRWA	United Nations Relief and Works Agency for Palestine Refugees in the Near East
UNSC	United Nations Security Council
UNSG	United Nations Secretary-General
US	United States
USAID	United States Agency for International Development
USBHR	United States Bureau for Human Rights
USCIA	United States Central Intelligence Agency
USCR	United States Committee for Refugees
USDCHA	United States Bureau for Democracy, Conflict and Humanitarian Assistance
USDOS	United States Department of State
USOFDA	United States Office of US Foreign Disaster Assistance
UXO	unexploded ordnance
WCC	World Council of Churches
WCRWC	Women's Commission for Refugee Women and Children
WFP	World Food Programme
WFP VAM	World Food Programme Vulnerability Analysis and Mapping Unit
WHO	World Health Organization

Foreword

It has been four years since the Norwegian Refugee Council's Global IDP Survey published the first volume of *Internally Displaced People: A Global Survey*. Since then, it is fair to say that discernible progress has been made in addressing the plight of the internally displaced. The international profile of the problem has been raised to the extent that the needs of internally displaced persons are universally acknowledged and understood. More specifically, a normative framework is now in place for meeting the protection and assistance needs of the internally displaced, as reflected in the Guiding Principles on Internal Displacement, which are widely acknowledged as providing useful guidance to governments and other relevant actors. The international humanitarian community continues to work towards more effective international institutional arrangements for responding to crises of internal displacement and a more coordinated response on the part of the United Nations, which has culminated in the recent establishment of the Unit on Internal Displacement within the Office for the Coordination of Humanitarian Affairs. In addition, the Global IDP Database has become firmly established as a leading resource on internal displacement, reflecting the importance of information for the development of a comprehensive system of protection and assistance for internally displaced persons.

Such progress notwithstanding, as this second volume so clearly indicates, this is no time for complacency. Many of the country situations reported on in the 1998 volume continue to lack an effective solution, while at the same time the numbers of displaced persons appear to be on the increase, now estimated at around 25 million, either as a result of the deterioration of existing crises or the outbreak of new ones. And despite the efforts to foster a more effective and coordinated response on the part of the United Nations, that response remains selective and ad hoc. In short, in many parts of the world, protecting and assisting masses of displaced people living in often desperate and appalling conditions is still a neglected concern, or an unfulfilled aspiration, at best. There remains, therefore, an urgent need for all relevant actors at the national, regional and international levels to take the crisis of internal displacement very seriously and to respond commensurately.

Within this context, access to accurate information on the causes and manifestations of displacement, the degree of access of the populations affected to basic services, their protection concerns, the willingness and capacity of governments to address their needs, and the level of response of the international community, remain essential. It is for this reason that I sincerely welcome and endorse this second volume of *Internally Displaced People: A Global Survey*. Based upon the country profiles contained on the website of the Global IDP Database, this volume stands both as a stark reminder of the magnitude of the challenge by which we are confronted and as an invaluable resource and tool for all those with a role to play in responding to that challenge, in government, in civil society and in regional and international organizations.

Dr Francis M Deng
Representative of the UN Secretary-General on Internally Displaced Persons

List of maps

List of figures, tables and boxes

Figures

Tables

Boxes

List of photos

Part 1
Issues and perspectives

1

Introduction

For every person internally displaced by conflict, there is a story – 25 million different stories of fear, persecution and human suffering. Each year, hundreds of thousands of people in different corners of the world are forced from the safety of their homes and compelled to take flight. Across regions and continents, direct threats to personal security and other forms of violence oblige individuals, families and entire communities to gather what they can of their belongings – if any – and depart for uncertain destinations.

Some of these people are able to take shelter with family or friends. Others congregate in camps where they hope to find safety, food and shelter. Still others hide in forests, jungles and other inhospitable terrain, too fearful to seek assistance of any kind. The journey is often difficult and dangerous. An untold number of people are victims of violence and disease along the way.

In some cases, people move to a neighbouring village for a short period until the fighting that caused their displacement has subsided. In still other cases, chronic or large-scale insecurity compels people to make a more dramatic and permanent move, to a camp at some distance from their home or to the outskirts of a metropolitan centre. In a good many situations, however, the movement is repeated with people displaced more than once and forced to flee to a range of different localities. In some of the worst cases, people are simply dispersed, fleeing without a trace and left to fend for themselves.

The Problem of Internal Displacement

The focus of this survey is on people who take flight within the boundaries of their home countries and are, thus, identified as internally displaced people, or IDPs. These people are forced to seek safety not through asylum in a second state, but before their own governments and within the confines of national borders. The welfare of internally displaced populations has become the subject of international attention because the governments legally accountable for their care and protection are often unable or even unwilling to act on their behalf. Indeed, in many cases, the government in question is at least partly if not wholly responsible for the displacement of its citizens in the first place. Internal displacement has also become an issue of increasing international concern because the mass displacement of populations can pose serious threats to the security and stability of entire regions.

The phenomenon of internal displacement has been widely described by international observers as one of the most pressing humanitarian challenges of our time. Since the end of the Cold War, conflicts between different communities, ethnicities, religions and socio-economic groups have multiplied at an alarming rate. Intra-state conflicts have centred on secessionist demands or appeals for regional autonomy, on the persecution of groups on the basis of their ethnic, religious or socio-economic backgrounds, and on struggles over territories and the exclusive control of natural resources. A single conflict in one part of a country has often fragmented, leading to the emergence of still further communal disputes in other geographical areas of the state. At the same time, external support for one or more parties to the conflict remains a common feature of modern-day conflict, functioning to enlarge and sustain the vast majority of contemporary civil wars.

In the first part of 2002, about 25 million people were estimated to be internally displaced, up from an estimated five million in the 1970s (Schmeidl, 1998, p28).[1] Today, IDPs outnumber refugees by nearly two to one, with a particularly large number of them – an astonishing 13.5 million – on the African continent. Sudan, Angola and the Democratic Republic of Congo (DRC) currently host IDP populations in the millions. Uganda, Nigeria, Burundi and Somalia have either surpassed or are nearly reaching the half million mark.

Shocking figures of conflict-induced IDPs, however, are not limited to Africa. Across the globe, different country situations give reason for alarm. From Colombia to Indonesia, Turkey to Afghanistan, IDP statistics are in the millions. Add those countries where over half a million people remain internally displaced by conflict, and Iraq, Azerbaijan, Sri Lanka, Burma and India join the list.

Although stark figures help to gain a general understanding of the scale of the problem in a particular country or region, they certainly do not tell the whole story. In countries such as Burundi or Lebanon, for example, where IDP numbers do not reach the millions, the ratio of the displaced to the national population is still quite high, nearly 10 per cent in each of these

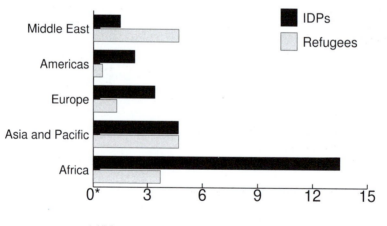

* All figures in millions

Figure 1.1   IDP and refugee figures by region

Note: Country figures for internal displacement have been reported during the first half of 2002. The Global IDP Database has not collected the country figures itself, but relies on information made available by different public sources. Where lack of humanitarian access has made it impossible to compile anything but rough estimates, the Global IDP Database has calculated a median figure using the highest and lowest available figures. Refugee statistics come from the UN High Commissioner for Refugees' (UNHCR's) provisional 2001 statistics released in May 2002.

Source: Global IDP Database, April–May 2002; UNHCR, 16 May 2002

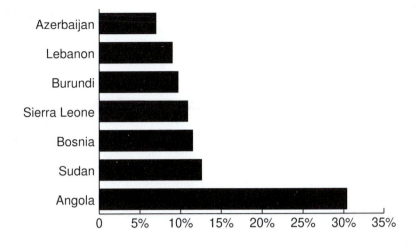

Figure 1.2   Ratio of displaced versus resident populations in selected countries (2002)

Source: Global IDP Database, April–May 2002; UN Population Fund, 2001

cases. These kind of statistics offer an indication of the limited capacity of host governments and resident populations to respond to and absorb the needs of the displaced.

Still, the well-being of IDPs is impossible to quantify as statistics rarely reflect the gravity of humanitarian needs. Over the last year, some of the most vulnerable populations have been much smaller in size. In West Africa, for instance, continued fighting in the Mano River region countries of Liberia, Sierra Leone and Guinea has been accompanied by widespread human rights abuses, putting both the internally displaced and resident populations at risk. In Liberia, a dangerous environment at the end of 2001, characterized by extra-judicial executions, torture and widespread rape, forced many civilians to hide and trek through dense forests for weeks. Human rights conditions for IDPs in the Russian Federation and, in particular, Chechnya also continue to be a subject of serious concern.

In still other countries, detailed information about the welfare of civilian populations is piecemeal at best. Only limited information is available about IDPs in Algeria, Iraq, Kenya and north-eastern India, where the human rights situations are reported to be grave.

Factors causing displacement

As documented throughout this book, the main factors leading to 'conflict-induced' displacement include armed conflict, generalized violence, the systematic violation of human rights and the forced displacement or 'dislocation' of people as a primary military or political objective of either government or rebel forces.

In each and every one of the 48 countries contained in this survey, the lack of respect for fundamental human rights and humanitarian law principles by security forces or insurgent groups – and usually both – has been a leading cause of the mass flight of civilians. Indiscriminate attacks, massacres, torture and other inhuman treatment are part and parcel of the vast majority of conflicts surveyed in this book. In many cases, civilian populations are not only exposed to the dangers of armed combat, but are even targeted as a result of their presumed affiliation with the opposing forces.

In Colombia – a country with one of the highest levels of political violence – assassinations, threats of physical harm and other forms of intimidation are the primary reasons cited by civilians for fleeing their homes. In fact, it is noted in this survey that direct confrontations between different armed groups are not common in Colombia, and that parties to the conflict more commonly seek to weaken their adversaries or gain access to territories by attacking civilians suspected of sympathizing with the 'other side'.

The 'you are either with us or against us' attitude taken by some armed forces towards civilian populations has unfortunately gained ground since the launch of the global 'war on terrorism' in late 2001. Following the terrorist attacks on the US in September 2001 and the subsequent US-led bombing of Afghanistan, various governments appear to be exploiting the global alliance against terrorism in order to strengthen their stance against insurgent groups in their own countries. In many instances, this has led to a concentration of security forces in civilian areas suspected of harbouring so-called 'terrorists'.

The example most covered by the international media in 2002 of reinvigorated state efforts to counter terrorism is the Israeli campaign in the Palestinian Territories. Following a marked rise in suicide bombings against Israeli civilians in 2002, Israeli forces have struck back, conducting military operations in direct proximity to civilian settlements during the course of the year. However, the Middle East is certainly not the only place where events appear to have been influenced by the new anti-terrorism landscape. Other governments that have intensified counter-insurgency efforts during 2002 include Colombia and The Philippines; perhaps not coincidentally, both receive significant US support.

Further to the civilians displaced as a result of direct exposure to armed hostilities, a large number of persons described in this book have been victim to forced displacement or dislocation policies and operations. In 26 of the 48 countries studied in this survey, political and military policies conducted with the single aim of displacing communities have resulted in the movement of populations. Different country-specific justifications are given for pursued policies of forced dislocation. However, the main reasons behind this kind of displacement can generally be grouped into one of four categories:

1   the forced relocation of populations by state and paramilitary forces as a means of isolating and combating insurgency movements;
2   the state-ordered grouping of civilians into 'peace villages' and other settlements with the official aim of ensuring their greater protection and access to basic services (while unofficially depriving rebel groups of local support and at the same time securing a labour base to combat them);
3   the sometimes decades-long political strategy of altering the demographic composition of a region by evicting or otherwise expelling indigenous populations considered undesirable and replacing them with other populations; and
4   the struggle for control of strategic or resource-rich territories.

The oft-cited examples of forced dislocation of civilians are Sudan and Angola, the two countries in the world that are also host to the largest number of IDPs. In Sudan, government troops have been responsible for the aerial bombing of civilian targets – in many cases, as a means of clearing areas for oil-production and the construction of oil pipelines. In Angola, both the government and the National Union for the Total Independence of Angola (UNITA) rebels have been blamed for the forced and repeated displacement of civilian populations. The government has evacuated villages in order to isolate UNITA troops; UNITA has forcibly displaced populations in order to get human and material support. In Burma, as well, hundreds of thousands of people have been forcibly relocated by government troops for the officially declared purposes of combating insurgency movements. Thousands of displaced people have been subject to forced labour in the process.

In Burundi, Rwanda and Uganda, the 're-groupment', or 'villagization', of populations has been undertaken with the official objective of protecting civilian populations from armed conflict. Operations such as these have been criticized by human rights organizations, who characterize them as involuntary movements of civilians with the undeclared aim of depriving rebel forces of local support and regaining control of territory. 'Protected villages' in the north of Uganda have been the sites of abduction and sexual violence against children.

In still other situations, so-called 'undesirables' have been evicted or expelled from their indigenous communities as a result of policies to alter the demographic composition of a particular region. This has been the case in Iraq where the government has launched an 'Arabization' policy in oil-rich Kirkuk, and in Sudan where the government has sought to 'Islamicize' the Nuba Mountains by forcing out indigenous Nuba populations.

Human rights and humanitarian concerns

Unfortunately, the targeting, persecution and marginalization of these civilian populations do not cease after their initial displacement. As noted in chapter after chapter of this book, IDPs are subject to all forms of harm during the period of displacement, whether in private accommodation, in organized camps or in makeshift shelters on the outskirts of metropolitan centres. The most reported human rights abuses against IDPs are extra-judicial executions, torture, rape, sexual assault, abductions and forced recruitment. Those responsible for these violations are largely government and rebel forces. However, in some instances, civilian members of the resident population are also to blame.

While the greatest volume of human rights violations is reported out of the continent of Africa, extremely poor human rights records in Burma and Colombia – to name just two countries – underline the fact that IDPs are at high risk across the globe. The worst violations generally occur at the height of the fighting when perpetrators are more easily able to act with impunity. However, this can also be the case in protracted low-level conflict situations where the lack of a functioning police force encourages lawlessness and criminality. Such violations have often occurred in places as unlikely as the Solomon Islands and Mexico.

Gross human rights violations and subsequent displacement are also a major element in post-conflict situations where civilian populations associated with the 'enemy' have been targeted by civilian and military abusers. In Kosovo, for example, members of the ethnic Serb and Roma communities fled en masse during the period of Kosovo Albanian return in 1999, fearful of retaliation and revenge violence. More recently, in Afghanistan, civilian members of the Pashtun community have become the target of attack due to their ethnic association with the fallen Taliban regime. In both cases, isolated incidents have led to the displacement of still others following the main crisis period.

Women and children are widely recognized as the most vulnerable of IDPs. In camp and non-camp situations, they are victim to rape, sexual assault, forced recruitment and other forms of forced labour. Some of the countries with the worst records of forced child recruitment include Sierra Leone, Angola, the DRC, Sudan, Uganda, Burundi, Afghanistan, Colombia, Burma and Iraq. In Burundi alone, as many as 14,000 children are reported to be under arms, all of them IDPs. In many instances, vulnerable women and children are forced to sell their goods and even their bodies in order to procure scarce food and other rations.

The need for improved protection for IDPs has increasingly become the focus of human rights and humanitarian organizations working with displaced populations. One of the primary obstacles before the international community is the lack of access to war-affected populations who are in most dire need of protection. In nearly all situations of internal displacement described here, access to large areas of the country is fully blocked at any one time. As a result, human rights and humanitarian aid agencies are both unable to document atrocities taking place and incapable of acting to prevent them.

Box 1.1 *Child soldiers and displacement*

Thousands of children around the world are doubly at risk of military recruitment and displacement as refugees, internally displaced persons (IDPs) or asylum seekers. Yet, the connections between child soldiers and displacement remain poorly understood, seriously impeding efforts to address affected children's needs.

Displacement and child recruitment are not merely parallel or unrelated offshoots of war; they are often deeply interrelated. In fact, whether during war or peace, there is a strong correlation between risk of recruitment during displacement, as well as risk of displacement as an outcome of recruitment. But the most serious risk arises in countries in the midst of protracted or intense armed conflict, where the numbers both of displaced persons and child soldiers may soar – providing an indication of the risk factor involved and the potential scale of the problem.[1]

Displacement may occur before, during or after a child is recruited, at any stage of armed conflict, and even during peace (for example, to escape conscription). Recruitment may affect all types of displaced children – refugees, asylum seekers, the internally displaced and those separated from their families or caregivers – who are often targeted due to their particular vulnerability. Children may be conscripted, forcibly recruited, or may 'volunteer' under extreme duress – for example, to prevent their families from being punished; because militaries may appear to be the only source of food and protection within conflict areas; because they have lost their families; and sometimes even to seek revenge for the death of family members and for atrocities perpetrated against their communities. All too often, recruitment as well as re-recruitment (of demobilized children) occurs not only in environments where children are difficult to identify and access in order to protect, but even inside refugee and resettlement camps where they are supposed to be protected. These categories and situations are far from mutually exclusive; children often become trapped in a vicious circle of vulnerability to both recruitment and displacement.

More broadly, it has been insufficiently recognized that nearly all children under the age of 18 who enlist, are conscripted or are forced to serve in armed forces or armed groups are – as soldiers – also 'separated' and displaced children. They are removed from their families and home environments.[2] They are displaced from their communities and normal way of life to live in military camps and militarized environments. They are physically relocated, often at great distances from their homes and often to dangerous zones. Not only are they not free to return to their family or community at will (or lack the knowledge or support for their right to do so where legislation on conscientious objection to military service exists), but they often lack the means to return without facing grave dangers, or because their families or communities have also been displaced or killed. Their removal from traditional structures of support and protection leaves children even more at the mercy of the armed forces and armed groups whom they serve. These groups all too often not only exploit the labour of children and endanger children's lives, but also physically, emotionally and sexually abuse them.

Notes

1   On child soldiers, see Coalition to Stop the Use of Child Soldiers, *Child Soldiers Global Report*, 2001. Recent armed conflicts that produced the largest populations of IDPs or refugees in the world, including literally millions of children, as well as largest numbers of child soldiers, include: Sierra Leone, Angola, the DRC, Northern Uganda, Sudan, Burundi, Somalia, Afghanistan, Myanmar and Colombia. The United Nations High Commissioner for Refugees (UNHCR) estimates that there are some 22 million uprooted children in the world. In the worst affected areas, children tend to remain displaced for an average of six or seven years.
2   A small number of children serve with family members or are born in a military camp.

Author: L Alfredson

In Africa, in particular, insecurity has seriously hampered humanitarian access to vulnerable displaced populations. As described in Chapter 4, the Africa regional chapter of this book, humanitarian catastrophes characterized by acute levels of disease and malnutrition have often occurred beyond the ambit of humanitarian programmes. Perhaps the most upsetting, and consequently most heavily cited, example of the problem of access is that of the DRC, where the International Rescue Committee (IRC) estimated that the majority of the 2.5 million war-related deaths in the country from 1998 to 2001 were attributable to malnutrition.

While one of the most shocking cases, the situation in the DRC is far from singular. In nearly every country surveyed in this book, lack of humanitarian access to war-affected people, many of them IDPs, has resulted in a threat to the survival of these populations. In Angola, the United Nations (UN) estimated at the end of 2001 that as many as 500,000 IDPs were in areas inaccessible to humanitarian agencies. In Somalia, the number of people in need has been nearly impossible to calculate given the long-term problem of access in the country, particularly in the southern and south-western provinces most affected by conflict and drought. Chechnya has also been an area of widespread concern. Humanitarian agencies operating there have had their activities repeatedly blocked and have been exposed to a range of security threats, resulting in their limited presence – under armed escort in the case of UN specialized agencies.

Generalized insecurity is not the only reason for humanitarian access problems. Lack of political will is also to blame in a good number of countries, including Algeria, Burma and India.

Return

Information on return is little documented in this survey. This is unfortunately due to the fact that new displacements over the last few years have heavily outweighed return movements. With the exception of the mass return of displaced populations in the Republic of Congo (Brazzaville), Eritrea and Guinea-Bissau in 2000, as well as the more recent return movements in The Philippines in 2001, Macedonia, and Afghanistan in 2002, return has for the most part been blocked by:

- continued fighting and insecurity;
- political impasse;
- difficulties in regaining lands and properties;
- the widespread presence of land mines in areas of return; and
- an understandable lack of confidence regarding lasting peace in the country.

Although all-out conflict and outbreaks of violence are responsible for the inability of millions of IDPs to return to their homes of origin, and, in a great number of cases, are to blame for the multiple displacements of populations, political stalemates over disputed territories in situations of relative peace appear to be equally obstructive to the return process. In Europe and parts of the Middle East that have quietened down over the last few years, the return of IDPs – and the children of IDPs – remains far from a reality. In both Azerbaijan and Georgia, the return of displaced populations is blocked, in part because the return of a specific ethnic group to a particular territory is perceived to have a negative effect on the decision over the ultimate political designation of that territory. A similar situation exists in Syria where populations remain unable to return without a negotiated settlement over the Golan Heights.

In many cases of protracted displacement, or 'post-conflict displacement' as these situations are sometimes termed, the return of IDPs is given little attention by governments and members of the international community, who do not necessarily give a high priority to care programmes for IDPs in the post-conflict reconstruction and economic development of the country. In many cases, IDPs are lumped into the larger grouping of vulnerable, poverty-stricken populations.

Sometimes this is appropriate; sometimes it is not. In many cases, the transition from the humanitarian to the development phase is accompanied by a redefinition of residual IDP populations. In Guatemala, but also to a certain extent in Mexico and Peru, the situation of internal displacement has been the subject of reinterpretation by some observers who no longer consider displaced populations as such, even though many of them are still unable to integrate as a result of major difficulties in recovering lands.

National and international response

The primary responsibility for the protection and assistance of IDPs rests with national governments, as is clearly expressed in the UN Guiding Principles on Internal Displacement.[2] Unfortunately, government response to conflict-induced internal displacement is, in most cases, inadequate to meet the needs of these populations. The reasons for gaps in protection and assistance vary widely. In some countries, governments have made efforts to address the needs of IDPs. Nevertheless, insufficient funding, insecurity and lack of expertise on the part of central and local authorities have meant that conditions for IDPs, both during the period of their displacement and during the course of return, have fallen well below the international standards outlined in the UN Guiding Principles.

In many cases, however, ethnic, religious and socio-economic divisions at the root of the conflicts causing displacement exist as primary hindrances to assistance for vulnerable populations during the period of displacement as well. Internally displaced people are stigmatized by governments as 'politically subversive', or are simply discriminated against as a result of their ethnic or religious identity.

In a number of situations, concerns over territorial sovereignty rest at the core of government inaction. In Georgia and Azerbaijan, where territorial disputes have been outstanding for years, national authorities have long prevented the integration of displaced persons into the communities where they are currently displaced as a way to maintain sovereignty claims on the secessionist or occupied territories from where these people originally fled. In the Russian Federation, the government has conducted policies adversely affecting the situation for IDPs in Ingushetia, presumably to induce their return to Chechnya and, therefore, to normalize the situation on its territory.

In most instances, however, lack of government action on behalf of IDPs stems from a number of different, interrelated and overlapping factors. In countries experiencing protracted conflict, the bulk of government resources is often channelled to the war effort. At the same time, state services and national infrastructure are nearly always in such a state of disrepair that governments would have great difficulty providing the proper assistance and provisions to vulnerable populations even if this were their intention. Collapsed and partially collapsed states – the textbook case being Somalia – have very little chance of responding to the needs of their civilian populations, be they displaced or not. Even for governments able to respond at the central level, through the establishment of legislative or humanitarian initiatives, lack of implementation on the ground is a major problem. Some governments – such as that of Angola – have been criticized for not 'putting their money where their mouth is', failing to follow up central legislation or policy strategies in support of displaced populations with the required funding to make their implementation a reality on the ground.

Lack of political will also lies at the core of the international community's inability to respond to the growing number of displaced persons around the world. Although donors would appear less inclined to use humanitarian assistance to exert leverage over a conflict by withholding assistance than was the practice in the 1990s, donors remain wary of procuring funding in situations where humanitarian access is poor.[3] Unfortunately, the decision to withhold funding is often taken by donors without accompanying political pressure to improve the access problem.

As has traditionally been the case, humanitarian assistance remains intricately linked to politics. Strategically significant countries such as those in south-eastern Europe in 2000 and Afghanistan in 2002 receive much greater funding per capita than African countries further afield that do not have the same politico-economic importance – a difference that cannot be accounted for solely in terms of varying relief costs or needs.[4] The uneven distribution of aid resources means that internally displaced people in 'forgotten crises' benefit from little humanitarian support and nearly always receive less than their more visible refugee counterparts across the border.

Although donor governments are generally keen to invest at the height of a crisis – as seen with the widespread and overwhelming international support for Afghanistan in 2002[5] – their approach is nearly always too short term, reducing funds too quickly and too dramatically. Donor focus on life-saving support during the worst of a humanitarian emergency is unfortunately not followed up with appropriate funding for reintegration and self-support schemes over the medium and long term. As a result, the redefinition of a situation from a humanitarian crisis to a post-conflict development situation usually takes as its victims residual IDP populations – sometimes counted in the hundreds of thousands – who, as a result, stand little chance of receiving the minimal aid required to return or resettle in dignity and in safety.

'Donor fatigue' is not the only reason for gaps in the international response to internal displacement. A lack of leadership and coordination on the part of the international humanitarian community has also been a major weakness. Although the appointment of a representative to the UN Secretary-General on internally displaced persons, Dr Francis M Deng, in 1992 has resulted in increased international awareness of the problem of internal displacement, and in the establishment of international standards for the protection and assistance of these vulnerable populations with the UN Guiding Principles on Internal Displacement, the response by humanitarian agencies in the field has remained ad hoc at best. In an effort to respond to institutional gaps in the response to internal displacement and to standardize UN efforts on behalf of these vulnerable populations, the United Nations created an IDP unit in 2002. Working under the overall direction of the UN emergency relief coordinator, this unit is expected 'to ensure a predictable and concerted response among all concerned actors to the problems of internal displacement'.[6]

In 2002, only 21 out of the 48 countries under consideration in this book were covered by a UN-coordinated annual funding programme (or UN Inter-Agency Consolidated Appeal process). As of May 2002, the average funding contributions per appeal ranged from 15 to 30 per cent. Food security and other life-saving needs were those sectors pulling in the greatest contributions.[7]

The Global Survey

This survey is the second of its kind. The first was published in 1998, at the time of the Global IDP Project's beginnings. This book provides information on internal displacement in 48 countries across the globe. It also includes chapters on the development and methodologies of the Global IDP Project electronic database on internal displacement, as well as the Project's training programme on the UN Guiding Principles on Internal Displacement.

Unlike the first volume of the Global Survey, comprising information on situations of internal displacement caused by conflict, as well as large-scale development projects, this second volume focuses exclusively on situations of conflict-induced internal displacement.

One of our continual challenges in putting together this book has been the unending job of including the most up-to-date information on IDPs in each country. We have come to accept that this is an all but impossible task, for even as the print is drying on this page, military and political events are likely to be unfolding around the world, displacing still more civilian populations not included in this book and even allowing some of them to return home.

For example, one situation of conflict-induced displacement that is not covered in this book but is now being covered by the Global IDP Database is that of Zimbabwe. Due to political violence in that country associated with the elections in 2000 and 2002 and the closure of white-owned farms, an alarming number of people have been displaced over the last two years. Information on Zimbabwe and other countries that are not included in this survey can be found on the Global IDP Database at: www.idpproject.org.

The regional chapters that follow are filled with numbers, percentages and other statistics describing, among other things, the numbers of people newly displaced, the numbers registered in camps and the numbers of food-aid beneficiaries. There are lists of countries with the highest percentage of IDPs, of ethnic groups most affected by the systematic violation of human rights and of provinces where war-affected populations are inaccessible. There are maps and graphs that attempt to illustrate the specific characteristics of the internal displace-ment problem in any one country. At its heart, however, this is a book about people – people whose full stories will never be told through the compilation of data and other statistics, people who appeal to us for critically needed assistance and a durable solution.

Endnotes

1 The figure of 25 million IDPs is not unprecedented. The total number of IDPs in the world peaked at 27 million in 1994. However, this figure was not limited to conflict-induced IDPs, and included some development-induced IDPs. See Susanne Shmeidl in Hampton (ed), 1998.

2 The UN Guiding Principles on Internal Displacement were established in 1998 following a request by the United Nations Commission on Human Rights and the General Assembly to the Representative of the UN Secretary-General on Internally Displaced Persons, Dr Francis M Deng, to prepare a normative framework for the internally displaced. The guidelines are not a binding instrument but do reflect and are consistent with existing international law. See the annotations by Kälin, 2000.

3 For further information on trends in humanitarian assistance, see the report by the Overseas Development Institute, April 2002.

4 ibid.

5 Although UN agencies did receive significant support for the return of IDPs and refugees in Afghanistan following the US bombing of the country in late 2001, by mid 2002 these funds were said to be insufficient to respond to the massive return of displaced populations, far larger in scope than had been predicted by humanitarian agencies at the beginning of the year.

6 From the 'Mission Statement of the UN Internal Displacement Unit', February 2002.

7 With the major exception of Afghanistan, which had received nearly 50 per cent of requirements as of May 2002. For more details, see UNOCHA, 2002 UN Consolidated Inter-Agency Human-itarian Assistance Appeals (summary of requirements and contributions by affected country/ region as of 17 May 2002).

2

The Global IDP Database: challenging the information gap

After publishing the first volume of *Internally Displaced People: A Global Survey* in 1998, the Norwegian Refugee Council – through its Global IDP Project – was encouraged by the humanitarian community to continue the research process by establishing an online mechanism to improve the accessibility of information on internal displacement. The outcome was the launch of the Global IDP Database on the Internet in December 1999.

The backbone of the database has been a set of comprehensive online country profiles that provide users with both updated information and direct access to source documents. Initially, the database covered only the largest and most acute situations of internal displacement. However, donations and improved capacity made it possible to gradually increase the number of countries covered. By mid 2002, the database comprised detailed information on conflict-induced displacement in 48 countries on five continents. This second volume of the *Global Survey* is entirely based on information collected by, and for, the Global IDP Database. It therefore reflects the current availability of information on internal displacement the world over.

The country profiles in the database focus on situations where people have become internally displaced because of armed conflicts, generalized violence or systematic human rights violations and have not – according to available information – durably returned to their homes of origin or permanently resettled elsewhere in the country. For example, analysis of the situation in Mozambique resulted in the omission of this country from the database as there was overwhelming evidence that all people that had been displaced by the civil war had returned to their homes or resettled following the consolidation of peace in 1994. However, in the course of research on other 'post-conflict' countries, this has not always been the case. Guatemala, Guinea-Bissau and Rwanda remained in the Global IDP Database as of 2002 because the database team did not consider information on return or resettlement conclusive enough.

The first version of the *Global Survey* included information about internal displacement related to a wider set of causes than discussed in this volume, and some readers will wonder why the focus has been narrowed to displacement caused by conflict. Internal displacement can also be related to natural and human-made disasters and misguided development projects – for example, forced evictions related to hydroelectric projects in India or people fleeing drought and hunger in the Horn of Africa. Resource constraints and information gaps have led us to the decision that coverage of displacement related to other causes than armed conflict and generalized violence should begin only when we have fulfilled our ambition with regard to global coverage of conflict-induced displacement.

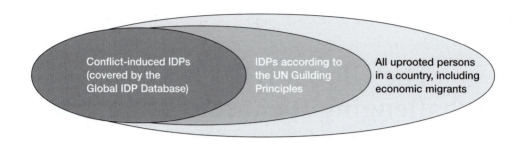

Figure 2.1   Focus of the Global IDP Database (2002)

Improving Access to Available Information

The task of collecting and analysing data on IDPs for the Global IDP Database is undertaken by a team of six information officers. The database is updated regularly, with revised country profiles posted online every three to four months. In the case of emerging conflicts or rapidly changing situations, information officers closely follow the movement of populations and include recent reports in the database as soon as they are available.

Information in the database is structured according to the UN Guiding Principles on Internal Displacement. Data for each country situation is broken down into categories such as background to the conflict, global figures, patterns of displacement, protection concerns, access to education, national and international response and so on. In this way, it is easily accessible to users who are interested in specific aspects of the situation of internal displacement. It is also easier to identify which aspects of the UN Guiding Principles are of serious concern or remain unaddressed in a particular country or region.

The information presented in the database is collected through research on government, humanitarian and academic Internet sites, as well as libraries, participation in humanitarian meetings and conferences, field visits, and personal contacts. Each and every country profile found in the database represents weeks of research, e-mail correspondence and telephone conversation. Given the fragmented nature of the information, database information officers spend much time compiling small pieces of data in order to establish a clear and reliable picture of the situation. They must also work to fill gaps as best as possible in crisis situations where information is scant and the situation ever changing.

The database actively strives to collect and include information from all sides of a conflict. Every effort is made to present information in an objective and fair manner without judgement or bias. However, the database does not include information of a political nature that does not add substantively to the understanding of the situation facing internally displaced populations. The most common sources in the database include governments, United Nations (UN) agencies, international and national non-governmental organizations (NGOs), International Committee of the Red Cross (ICRC) and Red Crescent Societies, IDP associations and groups, and academics and individuals within a country. Where information is inconsistent or even contradictory, all sources are offered, allowing the user to judge the particular situation or issue for his or herself.

While the bulk of data still comes from UN agencies and international NGOs, the database has intensified its efforts to reach out to national NGOs and individual academics in order to get independent and detailed accounts about the welfare of displaced populations, many of whom were previously beyond the range of our information collection networks. As of 2002, there were well over 4000 documents in the database, representing information from over 700 different sources around the world.

Information on Internal Displacement Remains Inadequate

It has been said more than once that updated and reliable information on IDPs is key to their improved protection and assistance. While problems relating to the availability of information on internal displacement remain a challenge, the material presented in both the database and this published volume illustrates how the quantity and quality of information has improved significantly since the 1998 version of the Survey. This allows for a much more detailed and reliable picture of country situations, as well as a more sound foundation for cross-country comparisons and the identification of trends across regions. One major reason for this improvement is certainly related to the dramatic increase in use of Internet and e-mail by humanitarian actors during the recent years.

Despite the positive developments, poor access to comprehensive and updated data on internal displacment in many countries is still one of the major obstacles to an adequate humanitarian response at both national and international levels. As continually noted by the information officers who are working on the database, reporting on internal displacement is fragmented, with major geographical and thematic information gaps. Even where access to IDPs is relatively good, publicly distributed information is often difficult to validate with regard to origin and reliability. Often the desk officer is left with nothing more than occasional reports from field assessment missions or the annual UN Consolidated Appeal – snapshots of the situation that are difficult to follow over time or compare to other situations.

Daily and weekly updates prepared by humanitarian actors in the field generally have no medium-term equivalents, leaving observers with no other choice but to make analyses based on very specific daily or weekly bulletins, on the one hand, and much more general annual reports, on the other. At the same time, common analytical tools for reporting on the human rights and humanitarian situations of IDPs are still at a nascent stage. Despite the widespread promotion of international human rights instruments, terminology varies widely. Even when terms are commonly used, they are often used differently by different actors. For example, 'return', 'reintegration' and 'resettlement' mean different things in different country settings.

The need to quantify internally displaced populations is both a major practical and methodological challenge. Even if the UN Guiding Principles may give guidance about who should be counted, local circumstances often complicate the matter. When it comes to national figures, the database uses estimates cautiously – being aware that these numbers are known to change radically over short periods of time and do not necessarily reflect the most recent situation on the ground. National figures may be understated or inflated – politicized by one actor or another. During its earliest stages, the database relied heavily on national figures produced by the US Committee for Refugees and the United Nations, nearly the only organizations publishing IDP statistics at the time. Over the last few years, however, information officers have been able to collect global estimates from other sources, extending the ability of the database to track situations of internal displacement accurately.

In situations where regular access to the displaced is possible, in Uganda and Kosovo, for example, humanitarian actors have increasingly invested in information collection and management systems. Quality data is more regularly produced, compiled and shared with partners. Unfortunately, humanitarian actors in the field often shied away from reporting on issues related to the physical protection needs of internally displaced people. The work is often considered too politically sensitive, the risks to operational programmes too high, and concerns about staff security too great. However, in recent years, protection and advocacy work has moved slowly into the realm of humanitarian action, led most notably by agencies such as Médecins Sans Frontières, or less-known, but highly dedicated, civil society groups working bravely to collect and share valuable information about some of the most vulnerable populations in the world.

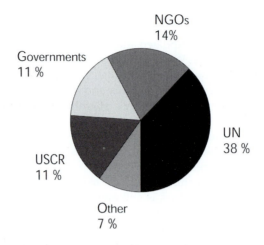

Figure 2.2   Sources for national figures on conflict-induced internal displacement
(April 2002)

Note: These ratios are based on the information available in the Global IDP Database in April 2002.

The need to let the fate of internally displaced populations be known is both a major practical and methodological challenge that must be given higher priority by humanitarian actors. It is the hope of the Global IDP Project that its information services may trigger new thinking about how best to approach the protection and assistance of the growing number of people around the world who find themselves internally displaced.

3

The Global IDP Project reflects on its training programme

Training National Authorities and Local NGOs in the Use of the UN Guiding Principles

The favourable reception of the UN Guiding Principles by the United Nation (UN) agencies and the international community at large in 1998 clearly marked a milestone in the ongoing efforts to enhance internally displaced person (IDP) protection and assistance. However, the important provisions in this instrument sharply contrasted with the deplorable situation for displaced people around the world, a reality urgently calling for concrete measures to not only develop and disseminate the Principles, but also to implement them. This could only be achieved through a targeted effort to raise the awareness, knowledge and skills of those governmental and non-governmental officials directly responsible for the well-being of the displaced population. Therefore, in 1999 the Global IDP Project responded to the calls of the Representative of the Secretary-General on Internally Displaced Persons and others for concrete training initiatives on the content and use of the UN Guiding Principles.

A modest training programme was envisaged and five training modules were developed in close collaboration with the Office of the Representative and the Office of the High Commissioner for Human Rights. A first training on the UN Guiding Principles was held in Kampala, Uganda, in March 1999, targeting national authorities, non-governmental organizations (NGOs), UN staff and the IDPs themselves. Since then, the training programme has

Table 3.1 Global IDP Project training workshops (1999–2002)

Location	Date
Colombia	2–3 July 2002
Indonesia	28 February–1 March 2002
India	28–30 November 2001
Burundi	29–31 October 2001
Liberia	23–25 October 2001
Colombia	15–17 May 2001
Sierra Leone	12–14 March 2001
Georgia	13–15 November 2000
Angola	29–31 August 2000
Thailand	28–30 March 2000
Philippines	22–24 November 1999
Uganda	29–31 March 1999

become an important component of the Global IDP Project, with more than 12 training workshops delivered in Africa, Asia, the former Soviet Union and Latin America.

National Authorities and NGOs Brought Together to Discuss the UN Guiding Principles

The Project quickly realized that national bodies in charge of both the protection and assistance of IDPs, whether they be specially designed refugee and IDP agencies or more general social welfare institutions, often have the greatest impact on the well-being of the displaced. Specialized government agencies have therefore been a favoured counterpart for, and sometimes coorganizer of, the Global IDP Project's training activities. This ad-hoc partnership has had many advantages. Most important, senior government officials' participation in the inauguration of the workshops and their stated commitment to the UN Guiding Principles have guaranteed extensive government staff participation (around 40 per cent of participants). Secondly, conclusions and recommendations coming out of the workshops have been developed with the participating authorities and are therefore more likely to be well received and followed up.

The other main target group has been those national and international non-governmental organizations working directly with the displaced communities. Many of them have long and detailed experience with internal displacement issues, and when introduced to the Guiding Principles often find that these norms effectively amount to a collective expression of some of their most urgent concerns. In addition to these two core groups, the workshops have included representatives of the displaced communities themselves and of the most relevant UN agencies.

This mix of participants has guaranteed a broad and insightful perspective on displacement, allowing for constructive differences in opinions and experiences. In several workshops, participating authorities have represented both civilian and military institutions. This has led to sometimes heated but respectful and constructive discussions on the current security situation of the displaced and the best way to implement the UN Guiding Principles. Participation by both non-governmental and governmental institutions has also provided an important space for exchange of information and socializing, which has hopefully enhanced cooperation and communication beyond the workshops.

The active participation of the displaced has also been made a priority, particularly where the IDP communities are clearly represented by identifiable leaders. In some countries, other participants, representing government and non-government agencies, have been displaced at some point themselves or, even still, consider themselves displaced. The distinction is often highly subjective.

A fourth category of participants is made up of a limited number of representatives of relevant UN agencies. Given the UN's capacity to train their own personnel, the training programme has not been aimed at including large numbers of UN staff. Rather, collaboration with key UN agencies – United Nations High Commissioner on Human Rights (UNHCHR), United Nations Commission for Human Rights (UNHCR) and United Nations Office for the Coordination of Humanitarian Affairs (UNOCHA) – has been in the area of general political support and the delivery of some workshop sessions.

The situation of IDPs analysed through the lens of the UN Guiding Principles

These diverse groups of participants have been brought together not merely to discuss a theoretical normative instrument, but rather to analyse and discuss the displacement situation in their country, through the lens of the UN Guiding Principles. Firstly, participants are provided with an introduction and background to the Principles, as well as their legal background and standing. The definition of an IDP is also discussed. Then, a number of protection provisions relevant to the specific country situation are selected for more detailed analysis. At this point, participants assess how well these Guiding Principles are adhered to in their particular region and, secondly, try to identify and discuss concrete measures for better implementation.

Given that the vast majority of participants are primarily humanitarian actors and not traditional human rights defenders, a number of basic human rights and humanitarian law concepts are explained in order for participants to better understand the content of the Principles. Such an introduction to human rights and humanitarian law also contributes to the strengthening of these humanitarian actors' ability to effectively introduce protection activities in their relief programmes for IDPs. The workshops have therefore become a contribution to recent efforts to overcome the divide between humanitarian action and protection/human rights. In Indonesia, for example, the Global IDP Project was asked by the humanitarian NGOs to specifically address the issue of protection by humanitarian actors, in addition to the protection provisions in the UN Guiding Principles.

Human rights organizations benefit from the workshops in a different way. They are, of course, very familiar with the basic human rights and humanitarian law concepts behind the Principles, but gain familiarity with a new instrument and with a human rights phenomenon (displacement), which has often been seen as the domain of humanitarian NGOs. They often come away in a better position to use the Guiding Principles as a complement to binding human rights or humanitarian law instruments in their daily advocacy activities on behalf of victims.

Customizing the workshops: each country situation requires a different focus
A core content, made up of five modules, is used for all of the workshops; but needless to say, each country situation requires a special emphasis. This is achieved through the selection of particularly country-relevant Principles for the group exercises and through the design of additional sessions on issues of particular concern to participants. These could be specialized sessions – normally facilitated by a local expert – on the government's IDP policy (Angola, Georgia, Indonesia), on advocacy possibilities when the Guiding Principles are not adhered to (Burma, Sierra Leone), on national IDP legislation (Colombia), on ways of implementing protection activities (Indonesia) or on any other subject of particular relevance to the displacement situation in a given country.

We are convinced that the objective of our workshops can only be achieved through a highly participatory methodology, and therefore try to minimize the time dedicated to formal lectures. There is certain basic information about the UN Guiding Principles and their international application that has to be conveyed through presentations by the facilitators. They are, however, always followed by extensive group exercises, group presentations and plenary discussions. Through this format we create an informal and open atmosphere in which all participants feel comfortable in sharing important information and discussing sensitive issues. Group discussion inevitably means that not every important point will be recorded in the workshop report or even shared with the larger group; but everyone is heard and a lot of learning is taking place in the groups.

Follow-up and implementation of workshop findings
One of the most challenging aspects of the training programme is to make sure that appropriate follow-up is designed and implemented. The actual implementation of follow-up activities logically falls on our counterparts and coorganizers in the specific country where the training

has been carried out. However, the Global IDP Project promotes and supports such activities. An important result of a workshop is often the identification of additional training needs and the design of country-based training activities. This is currently taking place in Burundi, where, following the Global IDP Project workshop, the Norwegian Refugee Council (NRC) Field Office is working to replicate a similar training workshop in a number of provinces. Such a follow-up has also been designed by the NRC Angola Office, but funding has yet to come through.

As a crucial tool for follow-up, workshop reports that include conclusions and concrete recommendations are always generated. These recommendations can be used as a road map by coorganizing national authorities or NGOs, as well as by individual participants when designing protection activities for IDPs. Sometimes concrete activities are suggested during the workshop. In Sierra Leone, for example, workshop participants identified the need for a simplified version of the UN Guiding Principles, as well as an audio version for radio transmission, the production of which was subsequently financed by NRC Sierra Leone.

Follow-up activities focus on the countries where the workshop is offered, but can be effectively complemented by advocacy efforts at headquarters level. For example, during the India workshop, participants expressed concern about limited access to IDPs and suggested the creation of a 'platform for dialogue' between the authorities, humanitarian organizations and IDPs. The setting up of the platform has to be pursued by participating organizations in India, but the Global IDP Project has campaigned for increased access to IDPs in India through public statements to the UN Commission on Human Rights.

Country-based Training Programmes can Increase Sustainability and Programme Coverage

In 2001, the Global IDP Project organized five training workshops on three different continents. We consider it a satisfying achievement, which we are proud of. However, it also made us realize that in order to expand our coverage, respond better to the existing training needs and make sure workshops are followed up in a sustainable fashion, there is a need to decentralize some training activities to NRC field offices. This coincides with a general development within NRC towards a more pronounced protection role for the organization, without abandoning its traditional relief efforts for IDPs and refugees. These two needs could be addressed through the hiring of training/protection officers (IDP Affairs Officers) in a number of selected NRC field offices. The IDP Affairs Officers would bring needed protection experience and skills to the organization and would ensure the effective implementation of decentralized UN Guiding Principles training programmes, as well as an increased NRC involvement in protection issues related to IDPs. The Global IDP Project has introduced this idea to NRC headquarters and field offices and offered to identify, train and technically support these officers.

A couple of NRC field offices have responded favourably to this idea and are in the process of implementing a modified version of this concept or are securing funding (Burundi and Angola). Others are assessing how this could be implemented in their respective country programmes (Indonesia and the Democratic Republic of Congo – DRC). Such decentralizing of training and protection activities will take some time. Meanwhile, the Global IDP Project will continue to directly organize training workshops in selected countries, while at the same time supporting recent field office-based training efforts.

Finally, we would like to think that our training efforts are not only making a normative instrument more widely known and used, but that they actually contribute to increased protection and assistance for IDPs. Hopefully, these activities will complement, and to some extent be incorporated within, NRC operational relief activities in the field. At the same time, we see our initiative to promote field-based training as a contribution to a much broader international effort aimed at the full implementation of the UN Guiding Principles, which should be carried out by a large number of diverse organizations committed to the rights and needs of the internally displaced.

Part 2
Regional profiles

Part 2

Regional profiles

4

Africa

Regional Overview

The African continent has more internally displaced persons (IDPs) than the rest of the world put together and the total is continuing to rise. The number of IDPs in Africa reached 13.5 million by the end of 2001 – an increase of more than 5 million since 1998. For comparison, Africa's refugee population was estimated at 3.6 million in early 2002.

Despite the generally bleak statistics, there have been some positive developments. After 27 years of civil war in Angola, the death of the National Union for the Total Independence of Angola (UNITA) rebel leader Jonas Savimbi in February 2002 paved the way for a ceasefire agreement between the two sides in April. Humanitarian access to the country's 4.1 million internally displaced persons began to improve almost immediately. With the official end of Sierra Leone's 11-year civil war in January 2002, large numbers of displaced people and refugees have been going home. And since the 2000 peace agreement between Eritrea and Ethiopia, ending trench warfare reminiscent of World War I, the return processes have accelerated dramatically in both countries.

Causes of Displacement

The magnitude of internal displacement in Africa reflects a worsening of armed conflicts during the 1990s – mostly internal in nature – that, in 2002, affected more than one quarter of the continent's 53 countries. The protracted wars in Angola, Sudan and the Democratic Republic of Congo (DRC) have, together, produced a total of more than 10 million IDPs – about three-quarters of internal displacements in the entire continent. At the beginning of 2002, upsurges in fighting in Liberia, Republic of Congo and Nigeria also displaced hundreds of thousands. In Zimbabwe, land seizures and state-sponsored violence created a growing number of IDPs in 2002.

Many of the conflicts – while intra-state – have a regional dimension and are sustained by external factors, not least cross-border support for armed groups or rebel movements active in resource-rich areas. Liberia's civil war, which started in 1989 and eventually engulfed neighbouring Sierra Leone and, to a lesser degree, Guinea, has been fuelled by competition for diamonds, timber and other raw materials. The Revolutionary United Front (RUF) rebels in Sierra Leone had been armed and supported by Liberia in return for diamonds. In the DRC, one factor that started – and sustained – the civil war that broke out in 1998 was rival claims over the country's rich natural resources, including diamonds, gold and precious metals. The war embroiled at least five other countries in the region – Angola, Zimbabwe and Namibia,

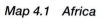
Map by András Bereznay

Map 4.1 Africa

supporting the government in Kinshasa, and Rwanda and Uganda, supporting rebel movements. Another common factor prolonging these, and many other wars in Africa – and thereby exacerbating situations of internal displacement – is the exceedingly high availability of small arms and light weapons [see Box 4.1].

Box 4.1 *Africa: small arms trade booming in Africa*

Small arms and light weapons (SALW) have been traded and sold to African tribes and states since the first days of European exploration and colonialism. Today, Europe remains the primary source of modern weapons for Africa.

The greatest number of small arms came to Africa in the last half century. The period of decolonization after World War II coincided with the decline of the UK and France as colonial powers, the rise of the Soviet Union and the US as world powers, and the globalization of Marxist doctrine. In this context of global conflict and nation-building, nascent African states served as proxy battlegrounds for the great powers. Small arms and light weapons were injected into the continent to prop up governments and gain influence. They were willingly received by many weak states in order to suppress insurgencies and gain control over unruly regions.

When the Cold War came to an end in the early 1990s, another wave of weapons came to the continent. Stockpiles of unneeded small arms in Europe and the former Soviet Union were sold off. Today's major suppliers remain countries of Eastern Europe and the former Soviet republics, as well as China. Countries throughout Africa are also recipients of illicit small arms, often supplied to insurgency groups, such as those in Sierra Leone, Angola, Sudan, the DRC and Algeria.

Africa, as a whole, is a net importer of small arms but does have some limited domestic manufacturing. In North Africa, Egypt, Sudan, Algeria and Morocco have varying levels of regular production capacity. In sub-Saharan Africa, Guinea, Burkina Faso, Nigeria, Cameroon, Ethiopia, Uganda, Kenya, Tanzania, Zimbabwe and South Africa all produce some small arms, with South Africa being the continent's largest and most sophisticated producer.

The result is an Africa awash with weapons that are fuelling and helping perpetuate civil wars and other local conflicts, and thus the mass displacement of African populations. Some efforts have been made in recent years to limit the accessibility of small arms. The 'Declaration of a Moratorium on Importation, Exportation and Manufacture of Light Weapons in West Africa' was signed by 16 countries of the Economic Community of West African States in 1998. In the south, the Southern Africa Regional Action Programme on Light Weapons and Illicit Arms Trafficking has sought to strengthen regulation and control. Neither has had much success.

Author: D Miller

The forced displacement of civilians has been a strategy used by both government and opposition forces in various countries in order to achieve different military and economic ends. This has occurred, for example, in Angola by UNITA rebels in order to procure a workforce, and, in turn, by government forces in order to isolate UNITA. In Sudan a 'scorched earth' policy was pursued by government forces to depopulate oil-rich areas; and in Burundi the government policy of 'regroupment' relocated the largely Hutu population in camps guarded by government forces, purportedly for protection from attacking rebel groups.

Competition for scarce land and water resources has also triggered conflict, leading, in turn, to sometimes massive displacement – in Somalia and Rwanda, for example, and to a lesser extent in Kenya. Severe drought conditions in the Horn of Africa in recent years have exacerbated the particular situations of internal displacement throughout the region. Internal displacement in some African countries has, to varying degrees, been linked with oil exploration and extraction – for example, in Sudan, the Republic of Congo and Nigeria.

Human Rights and Humanitarian Concerns

Internally displaced persons in Africa have often been particularly vulnerable to direct physical attacks or threats, sexual assault and forced labour. Human rights abuses including torture, mutilation and rape – inflicted on civilians by armed combatants – have been documented in recent years in nearly every African country under consideration in this book. However, as illustrated by the case of Guinea in 2000, the spotlight has sometimes been disproportionately focused on human rights abuses committed against refugees, rather than on internally displaced persons (Amnesty International, 25 June 2001). In 2002, an assessment by the United Nations High Commissioner for Refugees (UNHCR) and Save the Children–UK (SC–UK) revealed the extent of sexual violence and exploitation of both refugee and IDP children living in camps in Sierra Leone, Liberia and Guinea (UNHCR/ SC–UK, January 2002). Agency workers from local and international non-governmental organizations (NGOs), as well as United Nations (UN) agencies, were found to be among the prime exploiters.

Insecurity, as well as poor infrastructure, have seriously hampered humanitarian access to IDPs, who in many cases have not been able to find shelter in organized camps or protected areas and whose only option has been to seek refuge in host communities already exhausted by the effects of war, or to hide in the bush. There have been numerous examples in recent years of humanitarian catastrophes unfolding beyond the reach of aid organizations. In the DRC, where more than 2.2 million people remained internally displaced in 2002, the International Rescue Committee (IRC) estimated that the majority of the 2.5 million war-related deaths between August 1998 and April 2001 could be attributed to disease and malnutrition. Following the upsurge in fighting in the Republic of Congo in 2002, tens of thousands of people who fled into the forests of the Pool region near the capital were for some time completely inaccessible to humanitarian agencies. This was reminiscent of the height of the 1998–1999 civil war when the Pool region was cut off from outside help and the principal cause of death was malnutrition.

In Somalia, where malnutrition rates have been consistently alarming, chronic insecurity has rendered large areas of the country off-limits to humanitarian organizations, and the limited movement they have enjoyed has been under the protection of heavily armed militia. And in Angola, some months before the April 2002 ceasefire agreement, the UN reported that tens of thousands of newly displaced persons were believed to be on the brink of starvation, with an estimated 500,000 people in need living in areas inaccessible to international agencies. More than 200,000 were described as being in 'acute distress' (UN, November 2001, p12).

A major impediment to the ability of civilians to flee, as well as to their eventual return, has been the abundance of land mines in numerous African countries. Angola is reported to be the most heavily mined country in the world, with an estimated 8 to 10 million land mines in 2001 (UNICEF, 2001). The war between Ethiopia and Eritrea, which ended in 2000, left a legacy of land mines that has hampered the return process in both countries. Land mines used in the conflict in the Casamance region of Senegal have, according to the US Committee for Refugees (USCR), rendered 80 per cent of farmland in the region unusable. Border areas in neighbouring Guinea-Bissau have been similarly mined, adversely affecting the successful reintegration of IDPs in that country into their original communities.

National and International Response

A common problem in many African countries, despite the holding of multiparty elections, has continued to be the lack of good governance, transparency and accountability. In the most extreme case, Somalia, there has been no functioning central government at all. Therefore, at the national level, there has, in the majority of cases, been a lack of recognition by governments of their obligations to provide internally displaced persons with the necessary protection and assistance. The Angolan government, for example – despite being one of the first state authorities to adopt and use the UN Guiding Principles on Internal Displacement – has for the most part fallen far short of expectations in its assistance to the country's massive internally displaced populations, especially in the light of its huge mineral wealth. In some cases, government response has actually exacerbated the plight of IDPs. In Rwanda, the government 'villagization' process starting in 1996 aimed to move the entire rural population into grouped settlements in order to better provide basic services and access to land. Instead, living conditions in some of the resettlement sites were substantially worse than in the pre-war era. And in Uganda, the government's controversial policy of moving populations into 'protected villages' in some cases made IDPs even more vulnerable to rebel attacks.

Unlike in other regions of the world, most notably perhaps Latin America, war-torn African countries generally lack a strong civil society that can bring international attention to internal displacement in their countries. Neither do the displaced themselves tend to organize themselves into self-help or advocacy groups. Regionally, while bodies such as the Organization of African Unity and the African Commission on Human and People's Rights have at various times called for an improved response towards internally displaced persons, little has been put into action.

The impact of recent UN peacekeeping operations on situations of internal displacement in Africa has been mixed, with general scepticism about their effectiveness remaining high in the wake of the debacles in Somalia and Rwanda during the 1990s. In Sierra Leone, where hundreds of UN peacekeepers were taken hostage in 2000, the eventual full deployment of the United Nations Mission in Sierra Leone (UNAMSIL) force at the end of 2001 did help to consolidate security throughout most of the country and prompt the return of large numbers of IDPs. In some cases – such as Angola and the DRC – not all the warring parties have consented to a peacekeeping operation, posing risks to both peacekeepers and humanitarian actors trying to negotiate access and defend humanitarian principles. Regional and sub-regional forces, such as the Ceasefire Monitoring Group of the Economic Community of West African States (ECOMOG) peacekeeping force in both Liberia and Sierra Leone, have also been deployed to help restore peace and facilitate humanitarian assistance, sometimes in collaboration with the UN. They often have limited success.

International humanitarian operations have been hampered not only by the limited access to internally displaced populations, but also by an overall dearth of donor funding. Aid flows to sub-Saharan Africa on the whole have shrunk in recent years. Countries that are rich in resources and, at the same time, have UN sanctions imposed on them appear to attract particularly little donor interest. Liberia is a prime example. The 2002 Inter-Agency Consolidated Appeal, requesting some US$17 million, had received zero funding by April 2002. Donor antipathy toward the government of President Charles Taylor – accused of human rights violations both at home and in neighbouring countries, coupled with allegations of profiteering from diamonds and other natural resources – has ultimately led to a reduction in humanitarian programmes in Liberia. Taylor, meanwhile, has blamed all the problems faced by the Liberian people on the sanctions and arms embargo, and therefore on the UN. And in Angola, where despite a series of UN sanctions against UNITA, at least US$1 million of embargoed diamonds are reported to leave the country every day, the United Nations Office for the Coordination of Humanitarian Affairs (UNOCHA) warned in March 2002 that inadequate funding threatened to put millions of vulnerable people at serious risk.

Algeria[1]

Gripped by political turmoil for nearly a decade, Algeria is described by international observers as one of the most violent countries in the Middle East and North Africa. Over the last ten years, hundreds of thousands of Algerians have been forced to flee armed attacks, massacres and large-scale human rights abuses. The precise number of Algerians displaced by the political violence is impossible to assess given the information void that has surrounded the conflict since its onset. This said, some estimates have been published. The US Committee for Refugees said in 2001 that between 100,000 and 200,000 persons were believed to be internally displaced in the country (USCR, 2001, p62).

Background to the Conflict

The current violence in Algeria was triggered by an army-backed coup in 1991. This blocked the electoral victory of the Islamic Salvation Front (FIS) over the National Liberation Front (FLN), the then ruling party and political heir to the Algerian revolution. In response, the Islamic Salvation Army (AIS), an armed group affiliated to the FIS, launched an armed campaign to bring down the new government. Thousands of Algerians supported the opposition campaign against the new regime, and violence quickly spread throughout the country.

The violence reached the status of civil conflict between 1992 and 1998 as fighting intensified between the military-backed regime and an armed opposition made up of a number of often rival clandestine groups (ICG, 2000). At the height of the crisis, some 1200 persons were reported killed every month in Algeria, victims of massacres, indiscriminate armed attacks and assassinations (ICG, October 2000).[2] Women were often the most vulnerable targets of ruthless violence. In some cases they were abducted, enslaved, raped and later executed (HRW, 2000, p335). The region south of Algiers on the Blida plain was the site of some of the most heinous crimes against civilian populations and became known as 'the triangle of death'.

Protection Concerns

Since the darkest days of the conflict, the situation in Algeria has improved, albeit not to the level observers might have hoped. Although the AIS has generally respected a ceasefire since 1997 and security has returned to the larger metropolitan centres, Human Rights Watch (HRW) has reported that killings and the violation of human rights have continued unabated and unpunished in rural areas over the last few years (HRW, 2000, p335). The election of Abdelazis Bouteflika as president in 1999 raised hopes that the violence would diminish. However, President Bouteflika's government has made little effort to bring justice to the thousands of victims of the Algerian conflict, and its Civil Concord amnesty law has failed to encourage guerrillas to lay down their arms. Perpetrators of crimes, both members of government security forces and armed groups, continue to enjoy impunity in the face of the most criminal actions (Amnesty International, 21 November 2000).

A guerrilla organization notorious for its brutality, the Islamic Armed Group (GIA), is said to have been responsible for the bulk of the violence in recent years (HRW, 2000, p335). However, government security forces have also been blamed for direct abuses of human rights (HRW, 1999, p333; Cohen, 6 December 1999). Reports from April 2001 revealed that as many as 800 persons were killed as a result of political violence in the first four months of that year (BBC, 1 April 2001). Many other persons were apparently arbitrarily arrested and allegedly tortured while in detention.

Problems of Access

As for the thousands of other Algerians affected by the situation of violence and large-scale human rights abuses in the country, little is known. Throughout the whole of the conflict, the Algerian government has heavily restricted and often censored information about human rights conditions (HRW, 2000, p338). For years, all major international human rights organizations have been prohibited from visiting the country. Though some agencies were finally permitted entry in 2000, the visit of the International Federation of Human Rights (FIDH), for one, was reportedly conducted under conditions of strict surveillance. In fact, the FIDH made three requests to return to Algeria in 2001, but as of October 2001, no response was forthcoming from the government (FIDH, November 2001). As of April 2002, Algeria continued to refuse visits by UN rapporteurs and the UN Working Group on Enforced or Involuntary Disappearances. At the same time, the few human rights NGOs working in Algeria itself face continual obstacles and restrictions in the conduct of their work.

Due to the longstanding problems of access, virtually no information is available about internally displaced persons. In 1998, there were indications that persons were being displaced from Médéa, Blida, Ouled Allel and other towns south of Algiers (Dammers, 1998, p180). However, today even rough data such as this is no longer readily available. It is vaguely reported that the most recent movements of displaced persons are from vulnerable rural areas to the relative safety of metropolitan centres, that the displaced live with family and friends and not in camps or shelters, and that the level of actual population displacement is today far lower than in previous years. Whether the displaced wish to return home or not is impossible to discern. These individuals remain 'invisible' in a security situation that does not permit real choices about voluntary return.

Overall, international reaction to the situation in Algeria has been one of cautious observation. Apart from a response to major floods in the country in late 2001, external support to the ongoing political crisis in Algeria has been markedly absent. The floods of November 2001 killed 711 people and left thousands homeless (IFRC, 10 January 2002). While aid to flood victims was quickly forthcoming, the natural disaster only exacerbated discontent among the Algerian people, suggesting the possibility of even further instability for the Bouteflika regime.

Endnotes

1 It should be noted that very little information about internal displacement in Algeria is currently available. Problems of access continue to hinder the work of human rights and humanitarian organizations.
2 According to Human Rights Watch, another 4000 persons 'disappeared' during this period. See HRW, 2000, p337.

Angola

Angola bears the ignominy of having one of the largest internally displaced populations in the world, with some of the worst human development indicators, while at the same time producing vast mineral wealth that ends up on faraway foreign markets and consistently eludes ordinary Angolans.

Box 4.2 *Angola: How can one of the world's top diamond-producing countries not afford to feed its own people?*

Rich pickings. . .

- Angola is the second largest oil producer in sub-Saharan Africa, after Nigeria, and is, at times, the eighth largest oil supplier to the US.
- Angola's offshore oil industry accounts for over 90 per cent of fiscal revenue, amounting to US$3.18 billion in 2001.
- Investigations in Angola suggest that almost one third of state revenue, some US$1.4 billion, went missing in 2001.
- Angola is the world's fourth largest diamond producer, after Botswana, Russia and South Africa.
- Despite a series of UN sanctions, as of April 2002, at least US$1 million worth of embargoed diamonds were leaving Angola every day (25–30 per cent of this from UNITA-held areas, the rest from areas held by government troops).

. . .but empty coffers.

- Angola is rated 146th out of 162 countries in the United Nations Development Programme (UNDP) human development index.
- Approximately 10 per cent of all Angolans – an estimated 1.3 million people – rely on external assistance to meet their basic food requirements.
- A greater proportion of Angolans are at risk of disease and destitution than in virtually any other African country, and less than 30 per cent of the population have access to health care.
- At least 25 per cent of families in towns and surrounding areas live below the extreme poverty line, attempting to survive on US 60 cents per day.
- Life expectancy is 44 years; the under-five mortality rate is the second highest in the world, with 30 per cent of all children dying before the age of five.

Sources: BBC, 4 April 2002; Global Witness, 8 February 2002; HRW, 5 March 2002;UNOCHA, 8 February 2002; UNSC, 12 October 2001

At the end of 2001, the UN put the total number of persons displaced throughout the 26-year civil war at 4.1 million – one third of the country's 12 million inhabitants. Of the 3.59 million people who were internally displaced in the three previous years, little over one third were actually confirmed by humanitarian organizations and were receiving assistance. At the same time, the UN reported that tens of thousands of newly displaced persons in interior regions were believed to be on the brink of starvation, with an estimated 500,000 people in need living in areas inaccessible to international agencies. More than 200,000 were described as being in 'acute distress' (UN, November 2001, p12).

Background and Causes of Displacement

This dire humanitarian situation is the direct result of protracted conflict between the government of Angola and the National Union for the Total Independence of Angola (UNITA), who were bitter enemies even before the country's independence from Portugal in 1975. Some of the worst fighting broke out in 1992, following the electoral victory of the government party, the Popular Movement for the Liberation of Angola (MPLA), and its subsequent rejection by

UNITA. Hundreds of thousands of people were killed, and up to 2 million displaced. The 1994 Lusaka Peace Protocol failed to end the violence, and all-out war resumed by the end of 1998.

Both sides to the conflict have used civilian populations as pawns in their military strategies. By mid 2001, UNITA appeared to have moved away from guerrilla tactics in favour of terrorist warfare, becoming increasingly involved in kidnappings and the deliberate targeting of civilians. One stark example was the UNITA attack on 10 August 2001 on a civilian train in Cuanza Norte Province, resulting in the death of over 400 people. Witnesses reported that the train was derailed by an anti-tank mine, and that passengers attempting to escape were killed by UNITA soldiers lying in wait (Action for Southern Africa, 5 September 2001 and 5 October 2001).

UNITA has, in recent years, forcibly displaced civilian populations in order to get human and material support, while government forces have, in turn, moved civilians in order to isolate UNITA. According to Médecins Sans Frontières (MSF) in its March 2002 briefing to the UN Security Council, 'The widespread and systematic forced displacement occurring in Angola and the failure to assure proper conditions for IDPs is responsible for devastating the health and nutritional status of large civilian populations' (MSF, 5 March 2002).

The death of UNITA leader Jonas Savimbi at the hands of government troops in February 2002 gave new impetus to the peace process. After a shaky start – with fighting ongoing as peace talks between the two sides got underway in the eastern Moxico Province in March – the Angolan government and UNITA finally signed a ceasefire agreement in April 2002. This was to pave the way for the demobilization of 50,000 UNITA troops who would be absorbed into the Angolan army and police. President Jose Eduardo dos Santos, who had earlier declared he would be stepping down at the next elections, promised that free elections would be held – but without giving a date.

As reported by the BBC in April 2002, some observers were optimistic that this peace agreement would hold where others had failed due to the fact that it was achieved entirely by Angolans themselves without any foreign mediation. Indeed, the precise role of the UN in supporting the peace plan remained to be worked out (UN News Service, 8 April 2002). At the same time, humanitarian organizations warned that even in the event of lasting peace, the humanitarian challenges facing the war-ravaged country remained enormous.

Conditions of Displacement

The traditional movement of displaced populations has been from rural areas to state-controlled provincial capitals. Once there, however, the absence of sustained and effective government services has meant that resident populations – already impoverished by the effects of the war – have been forced to shoulder the burden caused by the massive levels of displacement. 'The overwhelming majority of displaced persons continue to be absorbed into host communities, placing additional strains on the coping capacities of already-poor families and intensifying competition for meagre resources, including land, employment and income-generating opportunities', says the UN in the 2002 Inter-Agency Consolidated Appeal. According to the United Nations Office for the Coordination of Humanitarian Affairs (UNOCHA) in February 2002, only 320,000 internally displaced people, a relatively small number, were living in camps and substandard transit centres.

During flight, communities and families have often been separated from each other. Movements of displaced people in Bié Province – one of the worst-hit areas in terms of internal displacement – have revealed that many women are left to flee on their own with their children since their husbands are fighting for government or UNITA forces (WFP, 12 July 2001). The UN reports that more than 100,000 children are estimated to be separated from their birth families throughout the country. Many IDPs have been displaced numerous times as a result of both military strategies and wilful neglect.

Though IDPs have found some protection in provincial capitals, both UNOCHA and the UN Commission for Human Rights (UNCHR) reported in the first half of 2001 that persons in all areas were vulnerable to attack, rape, kidnapping and forced conscription by UNITA and government forces. Women and children have naturally been the most vulnerable populations. Women have been subject to sexual harassment and forced into marriage and prostitution; children – of which the United Nations Children's Fund (UNICEF) reports 1 million are internally displaced – have been forcibly recruited and victims of kidnappings and sexual assault (UNICEF, 2001).

At the same time as peace talks between the government and UNITA got underway in March 2002, UNOCHA reported acute malnutrition in at least nine locations with high concentrations of IDPs, including the provinces of Bié, Huila, Malanje and Huambo. Vaccine-preventable diseases, as well as a sharp increase in HIV/AIDS, were also contributing to the very high morbidity and mortality rates among IDPs in these locations. Agencies estimated that 90 per cent of displaced communities were using contaminated water sources, resulting in potentially fatal waterborne diseases. Some of the worst living conditions in the country, according to UNOCHA, were in the 22 transit centres and warehouses in seven provinces that remained open, accommodating some 17,500 IDPs. The continuous new displacement throughout 2001 and early 2002 meant that instead of the substandard transit centres and warehouses being closed by the end of 2001, as planned, four new centres opened in Huambo in January 2002. According to UNOCHA, at the end of 2001, just under half a million IDPs had been resettled in temporary areas over the previous three years.

Humanitarian Response and Constraints

The Angolan government was one of the first states to incorporate the UN Guiding Principles on Internal Displacement in national policy and legislation – first to form the basis of Minimum Operational Standards (MINOPS) for Resettlement and Return of IDPs, developed in cooperation with UN agencies in the summer of 2000, and culminating in the adoption of these standards in a government decree (1/01) of 5 January 2001 as the 'Norms on the Resettlement of Internally Displaced Persons'. The government has also cooperated with the UN in developing provincial protection plans based on the Guiding Principles. However, actual compliance with the norms has been limited, according to UNOCHA (which monitors implementation at provincial level), though this increased to nearly 70 per cent by the end of 2001.

In general, the Angolan government has fallen far short of expectations in its level of assistance to displaced populations. In a rare oral briefing to the UN Security Council in March 2002, several NGOs – including MSF and HRW – reiterated their criticisms of the government (as well as UNITA) for failing to fulfil its responsibilities to populations under its control.[1]

The humanitarian operation in Angola is very large; in 2001, it comprised 10 UN agencies, 100 international NGOs and more than 340 national NGOs, as well as numerous government ministries and departments. It is also one of the most expensive humanitarian operations in the world due to exorbitantly high transport costs, mostly by air. Delivery of humanitarian aid to war-affected populations has been hampered in recent years by widespread insecurity – including the deliberate targeting of aid organizations such as World Vision and the World Food Programme (WFP) in 2001, as well as by dilapidated airstrips and dangerous roads. As a result, 60 per cent of humanitarian relief had to be transported by air (UNOCHA, 22 May 2001). However, by the time the Angolan government and UNITA signed the ceasefire agreement in April 2002, WFP reported that due to stronger army escorts and increasing prospects for peace, about 60 per cent of humanitarian aid was being delivered by road and 40 per cent by air – quite a dramatic change in a short space of time.

The UN Inter-Agency Consolidated Appeal (CAP) for Angola has been consistently under-funded. For example, of the US$233 million requested in the 2001 CAP, only 50 per cent was funded. As reported by UNOCHA in May 2001, the UN has linked the poor donor response in the Angolan context to the expectation by some donors that the government of Angola would allocate additional resources from oil revenues to social sectors. However, as of spring 2002, adequate government funding in this regard was not forthcoming.

Photo 4.1   An elderly man in an IDP camp, Mexico, Angola (June 2001)

Source: Joanna Ladomirska/MSF

Endnotes

1 HRW, MSF, Oxfam and Save the Children testified before the UN Security Council in an Arria Formula briefing. This is an informal meeting of the members of the council, rather than of the security council per se. It allows council members to hear the views of representatives of non-council members, representatives of non-state parties and NGOs in an informal and confidential setting.

Burundi

Since 1993, the ethnic war in Burundi has caused the death of at least 250,000 people, the vast majority of them civilians. The establishment of a power-sharing transitional government in November 2001, including ethnic Hutu and Tutsi representation, was seen by local and international observers as a positive step towards solving the conflict. As of May 2002, however, there was still no ceasefire between the government and the two main rebel groups operating in Burundi. Approximately 475,500 people were internally displaced, both in sites and dispersed throughout the countryside (UNOCHA, 28 February 2002, p6). Insecurity, lack of access and poor funding continued to severely constrain the capacity of the international community to respond to the needs of the displaced.

Main Causes of Displacement: Ethnic Violence and Regroupment Policy

Since its independence from Belgium in 1962, Burundi has succumbed to several waves of political and ethnic clashes. The latest round of large-scale violence has plagued Burundi since 1993, following the assassination of the first, and so far only, elected president, Melchior Ndadaye. Massive waves of displacement occurred in 1993 but also in 1994–1996 when the conflict between a new coalition government and several rebel groups escalated. During 1996–1997, in the wake of the conquest of Zaire (now the Democratic Republic of Congo – DRC) by Laurent Kabila, thousands of Burundian refugees returned to their country and became internally displaced. Clashes between government and rebel forces have since continued to cause severe displacement and, as of early 2002, approximately 7 per cent of the 6.8 million Burundians were displaced.

In addition to chronic insecurity, internal displacement in Burundi is also the result of a government policy known as 'regroupment'. The regroupment policy was implemented in 1996–1997 and again in 1999–2000 and consisted of relocating the population – mostly Hutu – into camps guarded by government armed forces. The official aim of this policy was to ensure the security of the population in areas subject to systematic destabilization by rebel groups. According to many observers, the undeclared aims were, in fact, to deprive the rebel forces of local support and to regain control of territory. In September 1999, the government forced nearly 350,000 civilians to move into 53 regroupment camps, mostly in the province of Bujumbura Rural. The displaced often suffered serious human rights violations during the regroupment process and while in the camps at the hands of both government and rebel forces (HRW, June 2000). By the end of July 2000, the regroupment camps had been dismantled as a result of international pressure. A UN assessment pointed out that the government had failed to provide assistance during the resettlement process (UNOCHA, 8 June 2000).

Latest Political Developments

The current president, Major Pierre Buyoya, took power in a military coup in 1996. In response to the coup, governments of neighbouring states imposed an economic embargo. The embargo was lifted in January 1999 after Buyoya agreed to a power-sharing agreement in the national assembly and began negotiations for a peace settlement with opposing parties and armed opposition groups. Former South African President Nelson Mandela assumed the role of facilitator of negotiations from the end of 1999 to the end of 2001. On 28 August 2000, a peace agreement was signed in Arusha between 19 different political parties, both Hutu and Tutsi.

In July 2001, following months of negotiation, Buyoya and Domitien Ndayizeye, an opposition leader, were formally endorsed as president and vice-president of Burundi for the first phase of the three-year transition. Hutu politicians were allocated 14 out of the 26 ministerial posts. South Africa committed 700 military and administrative personnel to safeguard opposition leaders returning from exile.

The transition period started on 1 November 2001 but by April 2002 there was still no ceasefire between the government and two Hutu armed rebel groups who had refused to take part in the Arusha peace process, the Forces for the Defence of Democracy (FDD) and the National Liberation Forces (FNL). Fighting even intensified in traditional zones of insecurity, such as Bujumbura Rural, Ruyigi and Cankuzo, and also in the northern provinces, which had been less affected by conflict for some time. Several UN reports indicated in February 2002 that members of rebel groups had been crossing into the eastern and western provinces from the DRC and from Tanzania, causing substantial displacement, as well.

Number of Internally Displaced Persons

In October 2001 the UN reported that 375,500 of the estimated 475,500 internally displaced were registered in 211 sites. At this time, the largest number of internally displaced resided in sites in the southern provinces of Makamba (99,500), Bururi (87,500) and Rutana (78,000), as illustrated in Map 4.2 (UNOCHA, 28 February 2002, p6). They included those displaced as a result of the 1993 violence (mainly of the Tutsi ethnic group) and those who were unable to return home due to insecurity when the regroupment camps were dismantled in July 2000 (mainly ethnic Hutus). Chronic insecurity and problems of access have made it impossible to count displaced people outside the sites. But it is estimated that an additional 100,000 persons may be dispersed in the countryside, including those who found refuge with friends and relatives following the dismantling of the regroupment sites and those who have fled their home communities over the past years.

The above statistics do not fully reflect the scope of internal displacement in Burundi, because many people have been displaced more than once and these estimates only reflect long-term displacement. Significant temporary displacement to escape government and rebel military operations has also occurred in the Burundian context.

Human Rights Situation

During a Norwegian Refugee Council (NRC) workshop on the UN Guiding Principles on Internal Displacement in Bujumbura in October 2001, the minister of human rights indicated that during displacement, violations to the right to life, physical and moral integrity, such as rape, torture and theft, were common. Since the creation of the transition government in November 2001, local and international human rights groups have continued to report widespread human rights violations both by rebel and government forces against the Burundian population. Children are particularly at risk. Up to 14,000 children, many of them displaced, have been forcibly conscripted in the civil war in Burundi since 1993, according to a report from the Coalition to Stop the Use of Child Soldiers released in June 2001.

Humanitarian Needs

Various UN reports indicated that 1 million people depended upon humanitarian aid in Burundi in early 2002. Many are internally displaced people who have been unable to gain access to their fields and depend upon international assistance for their livelihood. The Food

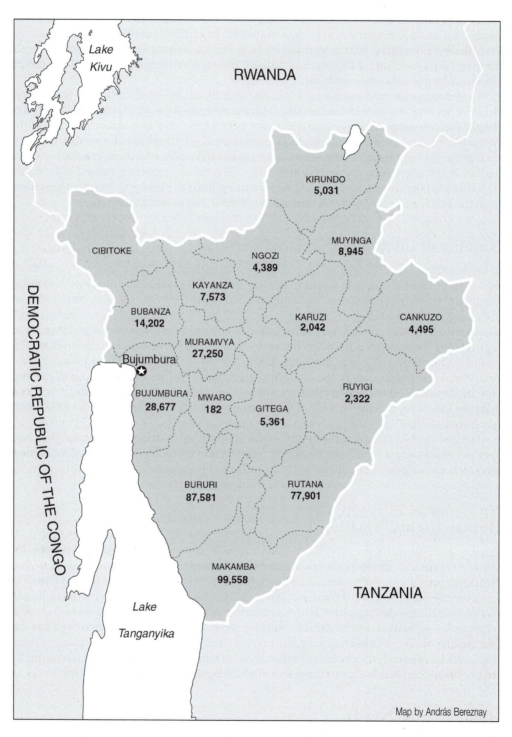

Lake Kivu

RWANDA

KIRUNDO
5,031

MUYINGA
8,945

CIBITOKE

NGOZI
4,389

KAYANZA
7,573

BUBANZA
14,202

KARUZI
2,042

CANKUZO
4,495

MURAMVYA
27,250

Bujumbura

DEMOCRATIC REPUBLIC OF THE CONGO

BUJUMBURA
28,677

MWARO
182

GITEGA
5,361

RUYIGI
2,322

BURURI
87,581

RUTANA
77,901

MAKAMBA
99,558

TANZANIA

Lake

Tanganyika

Map by András Bereznay

Map 4.2   Burundi: number of IDPs by province (January 2002)

Source: UNOCHA, 15 January 2002

and Agriculture Organization (FAO) reported in December 2001 that emergency food assistance was a continued requirement for IDPs (FAO GIEWS, 13 December 2001).

Despite a reported overall decrease of malnutrition, an August 2001 nutrition survey in seven provinces indicated a 10 per cent rate of acute malnutrition (FAO GIEWS, August 2001). In February 2002, the level of malnutrition remained particularly high in provinces suffering from insecurity or frequent drought, namely Bujumbura Rural, Gitega, Cibitoke, Rutana, Cankuzo, Muramvya and Mwaro. The ongoing conflict has resulted in the destruction and lack of maintenance of health centres, water and sanitation facilities and schools. UNICEF has reported that only 12 per cent of the displaced population in sites had access to potable water in 2000 (UNICEF, 1 March 2001). The situation had apparently not improved six months later (UN, November 2001, p25).

HIV/AIDS is the leading cause of mortality in Burundi, with 40,000 killed by the disease in 2000 alone, according to the director of Burundi's national AIDS programme. HIV rates are particularly high in IDP sites due to the prevalence of sexual violence and the breakdown of family structures. The number of malaria cases rose dramatically at the end of 2000 when an unprecedented epidemic broke out. While the number of cases has now stabilized, malaria was still affecting nearly half of the Burundian population in 2001 (IMC, 25 March 2002).

Land Issues

Available land has become very scarce in Burundi, and local observers have noted that parcels allocated to the displaced are often not sufficient to cover their needs. The government of Burundi conducted in January 2002 a national survey of available land to be allocated to internally displaced people and refugees upon their reinstallation in their communities of origin. Some of the displaced have been resettled into planned 'villages', where the government aims to provide social services. Planned villages mark a change in the way of life for the displaced, as traditionally the population has been living in houses scattered in the hills. In a country where 85 to 90 per cent of the population live on subsistence farming, disputes over land have worsened considerably over recent years due to massive population displacement and growing poverty.

Humanitarian Response

The capacity of aid agencies to reach the displaced has remained severely constrained by insecurity. The US Agency for International Development (USAID) reported in 2001 that humanitarian access was at best intermittent in 70 per cent of the country (USAID/BHR/OFDA, 3 July 2001). According to the UN, people dispersed in the countryside are beyond the reach of humanitarian assistance. Recent attacks on humanitarian workers, such as the November 2001 killing of the World Health Organization (WHO) representative to Burundi and the kidnapping of several NGO workers in May 2001, illustrate the obstacles faced by the humanitarian community.

In 2000 and 2001, the UN Representative on Internally Displaced Persons and other UN observers highlighted the need to improve existing coordination mechanisms to better protect and assist the displaced. A UN inter-agency mission also noted that the majority of humanitarian agencies focused their activities on the provision of assistance, while inadequate attention was given to the protection needs of the displaced.[1] Following the visit of a team from the UN Senior Inter-Agency Network on Internal Displacement, several measures were taken to improve the response to the needs of the displaced. An important step was the creation, in February 2001, of a framework of consultation between the government and the humanitarian community to discuss issues related to the protection of the displaced and to support the implementation of the UN Guiding Principles on Internal Displacement. At a donor conference in December 2001, US$830 million was pledged for the overall reconstruction of Burundi, including the resettlement of the internally displaced. But as long as there is no durable ceasefire in the country, the resettlement of thousands of Burundian citizens remains but an elusive hope.

Photo 4.2   School for IDP children, Burundi (1998)

Source: Giacomo Pirozzi/Panos Pictures

Endnotes

1 The UN Representative on Internally Displaced Persons, the Senior Inter-Agency Network on Internal Displacement, and the Special Rapporteur on the Human Rights Situation in Burundi have all highlighted the need to improve existing coordination mechanisms to better protect and assist the displaced. See UNCHR, 6 March 2000; UN Senior Inter-Agency Network on Internal Displacement, 23 December 2000; UNCHR, 19 March 2001.

Democratic Republic of Congo

Despite a ceasefire between the primary armed groups in the Democratic Republic of Congo (DRC) since January 2001, fighting continued in the north and north-east of the country, where most of the 2.2 million internally displaced persons are located.[1] The humanitarian situation remains desperate, and due to insecurity and lack of funding, the international response is far from sufficient to cover the needs of the displaced. It is estimated that over 2.5 million people died in the DRC between 1998 and 2001 in the context of the war, the majority from disease and malnutrition (IRC, April 2001).

Historical Background

The dramatic situation of internal displacement in the DRC is the result of an armed power struggle between various groups – both external and internal – accompanied by inter-ethnic rivalry in the central and eastern regions. The present conflict started in October 1996 when a rebel army, supported by Rwandan and Ugandan troops, launched an attack on the regime of President Mobutu Sese Seko. It resulted in the fall of Mobutu and the coming to power of Laurent Kabila. By mid 1997, about 150,000 people were estimated to be displaced in the country (USCR, 1998, p61). In 1998, a major rebellion against the new regime, supported by Kabila's former allies, Rwanda and Uganda, started in the east and developed into a new civil war. Continued hostilities between Kabila's forces, armed contingents from several African nations, and three rebel factions resulted in large-scale massacres and massive displacement. At the same time, clashes between the rebels and armed groups such as the Mai Mai traditional warriors also forced people to flee their homes. Competition for control of the DRC's rich natural resources, including diamonds, gold and precious metals such as coltan, has sustained the war.[2]

Under the auspices of the government of Zambia, Kabila's government, with allies Zimbabwe, Angola and Namibia, signed a ceasefire with Rwanda and Uganda on 10 July 1999 in Lusaka, Zambia. The UN Security Council (UNSC) then authorized in November 1999 the deployment of a UN mission (MONUC) to support the Lusaka Accord. However, the ceasefire was not respected. In January 2001, the assassination of Kabila and the rise to power of his son, Joseph Kabila, led to a new momentum in the peace process. The ceasefire finally took hold, and by the end of 2001, the disengagement of forces from the front lines was largely complete. The Lusaka agreement also provided for an 'Inter-Congolese Dialogue' to discuss the establishment of a transitional government. Meetings between Congolese armed rebel movements, civilian political parties and organized civil society took place, but by April 2002 had not resulted in concrete steps toward the creation of such a government. On 15 June 2001, UNSC Resolution 1355 extended the mandate of MONUC for another year and strengthened it to include a civilian police force component.

As of 2002, the country remained de facto divided into three main parts: the government of Kinshasa controlled the western part, supported by Angola, Zimbabwe and Namibia; the Movement for the Liberation of Congo (MLC) controlled much of the Equateur Province and parts of Orientale in the north, with support from Uganda; the Congolese Rally for Democracy–Goma (RCD–Goma) controlled the east and south-east, that is North Kivu, South Kivu, Maniema, Orientale, and Katanga provinces, supported by Rwanda. Each party had to contend with opposition groups, such as the Mai Mai and the Rwandan and Burundian Hutu groups in the east. The situation in the Kivus and in Maniema continued highly unstable, with significant operations by the RCD and the Rwandan army against armed group activity. In the Orientale Province in the north-east, fighting between the MLC and another group, the Rally for Democracy–Kisangani, intensified in early 2002. At the same time, ethnic clashes in the province caused hundreds of killings and 20,000 displaced in February 2002 alone (UNOCHA, 28 February 2002, p16).

Numbers of Internally Displaced People

The majority of the over 2.2 million internally displaced in the DRC are located in the east, particularly in North and South Kivus, Orientale Province and northern Katanga, the areas most affected by the war. As Figure 4.1 illustrates, the number of internally displaced people remained stable from mid 2001 to early 2002 in most provinces, except for an increase of 210,000 registered IDPs in South Kivu and of 20,000 in Orientale Province.[3]

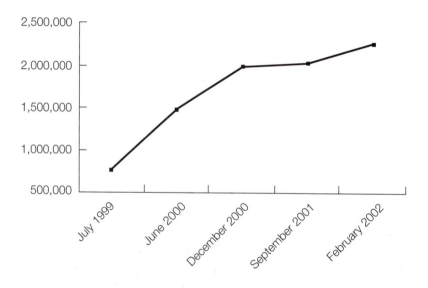

Figure 4.1   Number of IDPs in the DRC from 1999–2002

Source: UNOCHA, 28 February 2002; UNOCHA, 30 September 2001; UNOCHA, 31 December 2000; UNOCHA, 11 July 2000; UNOCHA 15 July 1999

These numbers probably underestimate the true extent of displacement in the DRC. Internally displaced people are difficult to count due to a high degree of dispersion and limited access. The global estimates do not reflect the fact that people who fled their villages a first time may have had to flee again to escape violence or natural disasters. In January 2001, many people who had been displaced by conflict and who had found refuge in Goma were forced to flee once more when the Nyiragongo volcano erupted. The eruption caused the destruction of around 15 per cent of Goma town, and approximately 120,000 people lost their homes (UNOCHA, 28 February 2002, p14).

Human Rights Situation

The human rights situation is critical in the DRC. UN agencies, as well as NGOs, regularly report widespread killings, torture and other human rights abuses against civilians by armed groups on all sides. Amnesty International (AI) reported in June 2001 that the rape of women and girls had been used extensively by all armed groups (AI, 19 June 2001, p4). In October 2001, UN Secretary-General Kofi Annan reported that internally displaced women had often been preyed upon by armed elements and subjected to torture, sexual assault and other abuses, as well as ethnically motivated killings (UNSC, 16 October 2001).

Displaced children are easy targets for forced recruitment by armed groups. More than 10,000 children remained under arms in the DRC as of mid 2001, recruited by all parties to the conflict (Oxfam, 6 August 2001, p14). Girls are recruited as well, often falling victim to forced labour and sexual abuse. Both the DRC government and the RCD–Goma have pledged to cease child recruitment and to demobilize child soldiers under their command, but this commitment has been slow to take form. In December 2001, President Kabila demobilized a first group of 300 child soldiers enlisted in the government army.

Humanitarian Situation

The civilian population of the DRC continues to suffer tremendously, especially in the central and eastern regions of the country. According to the International Rescue Committee (IRC), an estimated 2.5 million people died in the context of the war between August 1998 and April 2001, the majority due to disease and malnutrition.

Several reports suggest that the displaced and the general war-affected population share the same needs. The health care system, already in a weak state when the second stage of the present conflict started in August 1998, has degraded even further due to looting, the flight of staff and lack of resources. Humanitarian agencies on the ground report that up to 70 per cent of the population may now be excluded from basic health services. The system has been unable to cope with the sharp increase of diseases such as malaria and cholera. The situation is particularly worrying in Goma, where the volcano eruption caused the destruction of five health facilities and further reduced the capacities of health authorities. The internally displaced suffer great exposure to HIV/AIDS infection as a result of the conflict, since they have no means of protecting themselves from this infection and no access to information about its transmission. Most IDPs have not sought shelter in camps but have integrated within host communities, whose abilities to cope with the influx are seriously overstretched.

In mid 2001 it was reported that 16 million people (33 per cent of the population) had critical food needs as a result of prolonged displacement and other factors (UNSC, 8 June 2001). Oxfam reported in February 2002 that approximately 64 per cent of people in eastern DRC were undernourished and that this was the highest ratio in the world (Oxfam, 2 February 2002).

Humanitarian Response

Access to government-controlled regions has improved since the Kinshasa government approved freedom of movement for international humanitarian personnel in March 2001. In the past, humanitarian agencies have been frequently forced to suspend operations in rebel-held territory because of insecurity and localized violence, particularly in certain parts of the Kivus, Maniema, northern Katanga and Ituri (UNSC, 15 February 2002). Refugees International (RI) reported in September 2001 that RCD–Goma authorities, in search of new sources of revenue following a drop in the price of coltan, had started to tax humanitarian supplies, jeopardizing the humanitarian effort (RI, 4 September 2001).

Despite the numerous security and political constraints, many UN agencies and NGOs continue to assist the internally displaced in government- and rebel-held territories. They provide food and non-food items to the displaced, health care, emergency education, and support child protection and reintegration activities. Several humanitarian agencies have recently opened sub-offices in the field to get closer to displaced communities living in isolated locations.

Photo 4.3 Women in MSF feeding centre, North Kivu, DRC centre (October 2001)

Source: Chris Keulen/MSF

Endnotes

1 Figures are from February 2002.
2 For more information on the exploitation of natural resources in the DRC, see UNSC, 12 April 2001, and UNSC, 13 November 2001.
3 UNOCHA, 28 February 2002, p13; UNOCHA, 30 September 2001, p2.

Eritrea

Internal displacement in Eritrea stems from a combination of war and drought, recurrent themes in the Horn of Africa. More than 1 million people were forced to flee their homes during a ferocious border conflict with Ethiopia that erupted in 1998. Most were able to return following a ceasefire two years later, and by early 2002 only 57,000 people remained displaced (UNSC, 8 March 2002). The destruction caused by the fighting was exacerbated by a devastating three-year drought in south-western Eritrea, and the need for food aid remained strong.

Background

Eritrea was formally annexed by Ethiopia in 1962, but the armed struggle against Ethiopian rule had begun the previous year. Ethiopian forces were finally expelled after a 30-year struggle; in 1993, following a referendum, Eritrea became an independent state. At this time, the Ethiopian–Eritrean border was – in line with the Organization of African Unity (OAU) principles on integrity of colonial boundaries – that which Italian colonials had established in 1890. The Italians, however, never clearly demarcated the frontier, and it has remained the subject of discord ever since.

In May 1998, fighting broke out between the two over disputed frontier zones in Debub, Gash-Barka and northern Red Sea districts. It resulted in the deaths of some 19,000 fighters and an unknown number of civilians and forced 1.1 million people to flee from their homes near the border (IFRC, 1 January 2002).

A ceasefire was agreed in June 2000 and the Algiers Peace Agreement followed six months later. A demilitarized Temporary Security Zone (TSZ) was established along the 1000km Eritrea–Ethiopia frontier in April 2001 and 5000 peacekeeping troops were deployed under the auspices of the United Nations Mission in Ethiopia and Eritrea (UNMEE) to monitor the ceasefire.

The border issue was resolved in April 2002 by a ruling of the Independent Boundary Commission in the Hague. Both Eritrea and Ethiopia accepted it, though a final demarcation of the key town of Badme, where the present conflict first flared up, would appear to remain unclear (UNIRIN, 22 April 2002).

Return

The displaced returned rapidly to the regions of Gash-Barka, Debub and the southern Red Sea after the June 2000 ceasefire and the partial withdrawal of Ethiopian troops from border areas. Six months later the total number of IDPs had fallen from 1.1 million at the height of the crisis to about 210,000, sheltered in 24 camps in Gash-Barka, Debub and North Red Sea zones. Another 100,000 were thought to be hosted by local communities (USCR, 2001, p77).

By November 2001, the numbers had fallen further, to an estimated 50,000 in camps and 23,000 among host communities (UN, November 2001, pp24–31). By early 2002, the total number of displaced had dropped to 57,000.

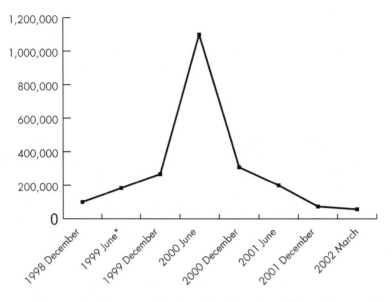

* Estimate produced by averaging December 1998 and December 1999. Actual data unavailable.

Figure 4.2   Eritrea: number of IDPs from 1998–2002

Source: UN, January 2000; UNHCR, July 2000; USCR, 1999, pp64–65

The returnees required substantial assistance to rebuild and re-establish their livelihoods, especially in the war-ravaged Debub and Gash-Barka zones where infrastructure was completely destroyed. An additional problem in Gash-Barka was a three-year drought that had severely depleted local water sources in this traditionally fertile area (UN, November 2001, p29). The presence of about 1.5 million land mines and 3 million items of unexploded ordnance (UXO) has been another major factor hindering the return of farming and pastoralist communities.

Humanitarian Needs

The burden has been a heavy one for host communities, who in spite of harbouring up to five IDP families for each of their own, reportedly received less assistance than the IDPs. Indeed, assessments have shown that the nutritional status of children returning from IDP camps was better than that of non-displaced children (GoE Ministry of Health and SCF, August 2001).

Although humanitarian needs are not comparable to those at the height of the crisis, Eritrea nevertheless remains in need of considerable emergency assistance. Three years of drought and the loss of nearly two-thirds of south-western Eritrea's livestock as a result of the conflict have had serious repercussions on food security in the country. In 2001, pastoralists were reported to be selling or eating their dying livestock as a last resort. Malnutrition was as high as 30 per cent, with 3.5 per cent severe malnutrition in drought-prone areas (UN, November 2001, pp41–65). The UN expected that 800,000 vulnerable people would require food aid in 2002.

Humanitarian Response

The government of Eritrea has played an important role in coordinating humanitarian operations through the Eritrean Relief and Refugee Commission (ERREC). UN activities have been coordinated by UNOCHA, supported by a joint government/UN Information and Coordination Centre. A mechanism to coordinate humanitarian assistance in the TSZ was established in April 2001.

The mass return of civilians since 2000 has resulted in a corresponding reduction of humanitarian aid in the country. However, as in many post-conflict situations, the decrease in humanitarian aid could be characterized as 'too much, too fast'. As a result of reduced funding, the World Food Programme (WFP) has been forced to cut its food ration by 40 per cent resulting in a considerable increase in malnutrition (FEWS Net, 7 February 2002). In addition, projects in the non-food and agricultural sectors have been particularly hard hit, as they received less than 10 per cent funding in 2001 (UN, November 2001, p7). However, delivery of humanitarian aid stabilized the humanitarian situation in 2001 and efforts continue to promote the reintegration of returning populations and the rehabilitation of infrastructure and social services.

Ethiopia

More than 300,000 people were displaced by a military confrontation between Ethiopia and Eritrea, which flared up out of a border dispute in May 1998. Most of them were able to return home after a ceasefire was declared in June 2000, and by early 2002, no more than 12,500 remained displaced, according to available information. But another 60,000 returnees were still unable to resume their traditional farming practices because of limited access to land.

Background

The area of the bitterest fighting was Badme, but there were also intense clashes in other areas such as Tsorona-Zalambessa and Bure. Within a year, the war had forced nearly 316,000 Ethiopians from their homes (UNDP, 19 February 2002). Most of the displacement was from the Tigray region as a result of Eritrean shelling; but approximately 29,000 people were also displaced in the Afar region further east (UNDP, 12 April 1999, p4). According to aid agencies, women and children constituted 75 per cent of the displaced population (UNCTE, 28 January 2000, p34).

A major Ethiopian offensive in May 2000 was halted by a ceasefire agreement one month later. This facilitated the return of the majority of IDPs. It also triggered the return of some 60,000 Ethiopian refugees from Eritrean territory, most of whom returned to the Tigray area and became part of the same resettlement process as returning IDPs (GoE, 17 November 2000).

The return process was further encouraged by the signing of a permanent peace agreement in December 2000, the establishment of a demilitarized Temporary Security Zone (TSZ) and the deployment of a United Nations Mission in Ethiopia and Eritrea (UNMEE), mandated to monitor the ceasefire. Although disagreement over the border of the TSZ stalled some returns, available information in early 2002 suggested that only about 12,500 IDPs were still unable to return to their areas of origin. In addition to this figure, there were some 63,000 who had returned but were unable to start agricultural activities because of limited access to farming lands (WFP, 8 February 2002).

An Independent Boundary Commission based in the Hague issued a ruling on the border issue in April 2002, and it was accepted by both Eritrea and Ethiopia. The final demarcation of the key town of Badme, however, appeared to remain unclear (UNIRIN, 22 April 2002).

Protection and Living Conditions

The main protection concern for IDPs has been the extensive presence of mines and unexploded ordnance in areas close to the border, especially between the front lines. The World Bank, among others, has supported a major project to de-mine areas of return.

The Ethiopian government encouraged the internally displaced to integrate into communities outside the conflict area. However, some camp-like settlements did sprout up in areas with high concentrations of internally displaced people, especially at locations along Tigray's northern belt. The majority of the IDPs were completely dependent on relief assistance due to their inability to gain access to farmland, livestock and productive assets. Other IDPs, in the Afar region, for example, were able to keep their animals and household goods, maintaining their nomadic livelihoods during the period of displacement (UNDP, 12 April 1999). In some cases, displaced people were even able to maintain business activities.

By the end of 2001, many civilians had returned to their communities of origin. Others remained displaced and continued to require basic support, including the provision of water, shelter, health care and education (UNOCHA, 26 November 2001).

Humanitarian Assistance

The government has attempted to provide assistance to the internally displaced through existing infrastructure. Special efforts have also been made to set up temporary health services in areas of return. A major government actor has been the Relief Society of Tigray (REST).

The UN has pursued a recovery strategy based upon existing long-term development programmes in the affected areas. An example of such assistance has been the Emergency Recovery Programme of the World Bank, which focuses on the recovery of farming and non-farming activities, as well as on housing rehabilitation and reconstruction.

Because of the return of a significant number of displaced persons to their places of origin, the target group of food assistance at the end of 2001 narrowed significantly to include only those with the most urgent needs. A population of 75,000 persons is still dependent upon aid. Many persons who have been able to resettle still lack access to cropping or pasture land (WFP, 8 February 2002).

International NGOs have not played a major role in assisting the conflict-induced displaced persons in Ethiopia. In many cases, national structures have replaced direct partnerships between the UN and NGOs. However, several national NGOs have been actively supporting the internally displaced, often under a tripartite arrangement between a UN partner, the NGO and the government.

Guinea

The influx of half a million refugees from the civil wars sweeping Liberia and Sierra Leone had already created ethnic tensions and economic decline in Guinea during the 1990s. Then, in 2000, violent cross-border attacks from both neighbouring states was followed by fighting in a border region, and thousands of people were displaced inside Guinea itself. At the beginning of 2002 the government put the total of internally displaced at 359,000, though estimates by international aid agencies were as low as 200,000. The security situation stabilized during 2001 and remained calm in 2002, though tensions were raised by renewed armed conflict in northern Liberia in early 2002, with new influxes of refugees.

Background and Causes of Displacement

The complex regional conflict was started by warlord Charles Taylor in Liberia in 1989. Guinea was a founding member of the West African peacekeeping force (ECOMOG), established in an attempt to restore order in Liberia in 1990. At the same time, Guinea became the base for Liberian dissidents, many of them refugees, who would later form an armed rebel group in opposition to Taylor.

Border attacks on Guinea from both Liberia and Sierra Leone began in 2000 in the Parrot's Beak area, where the three countries meet. These were violent raids, where the attackers would kill, burn and loot. Local populations soon turned against the refugees living in their midst. Guinea's president, Lansana Conté, was quick to blame Taylor, who had been elected president of Liberia three years earlier. Indeed, it became clear that Taylor's forces were launching cross-border attacks against Liberian rebel bases near Macenta in the Parrot's Beak. It also became apparent, however, that a Guinean rebel group and the Sierra Leonean Revolutionary United Front (RUF) insurgents were also responsible for the mayhem (BBC, 13 February 2001).

The Guinean government responded with helicopter gunships and heavy artillery in the border areas. Yet, the attackers still managed to strike the important towns of Macenta and Guéckédou, forcing residents to flee and leaving buildings in ruins. The crisis inside Guinea itself escalated in September 2000, when fighting broke out in the Parrot's Beak and thousands of Guineans became internally displaced.

The situation in Guinea eased with the ceasefire agreement of May 2001 between the government of Sierra Leone and the RUF. The rebels disarmed and withdrew from Kambia District, which had provided a base for launching cross-border attacks. Further improvements came with the official end of Sierra Leone's civil war at the beginning of 2002, and – in March – an agreement between Guinea, Liberia and Sierra Leone to strengthen security along their borders and restore their latent economic grouping, the Mano River Union.

In January 2002, the government of Guinea reported that the official number of IDPs in the country was 359,000, with the largest concentrations remaining in the area of the Parrot's Beak and in and around the towns of Kissidougou, Guéckédou and Macenta. But international organizations, including the World Food Programme (WFP) and the International Committee of the Red Cross (ICRC), estimated the total number of IDPs to be much lower – between 200,000 and 250,000.[1]

Conditions of Displacement

To a large extent, internally displaced persons in Guinea have integrated with resident populations. Most of them originate from rural areas and have had to leave their lands for shelter in urban and peri-urban environments. As was the case with many Sierra Leonean and Liberian refugees displaced by the fighting in Guinea, it became apparent that Guinean IDPs also suffered human rights abuses during flight. According to an Amnesty International (AI) report published in June 2001, Guinean civilians were killed, beaten, raped and abducted by armed political groups, including the RUF, in cross-border attacks from Sierra Leone (AI, 25 June 2001). Women and children, estimated by the UN to make up 60 per cent of the IDP population, have been at particular risk (UN, November 2001, p13).

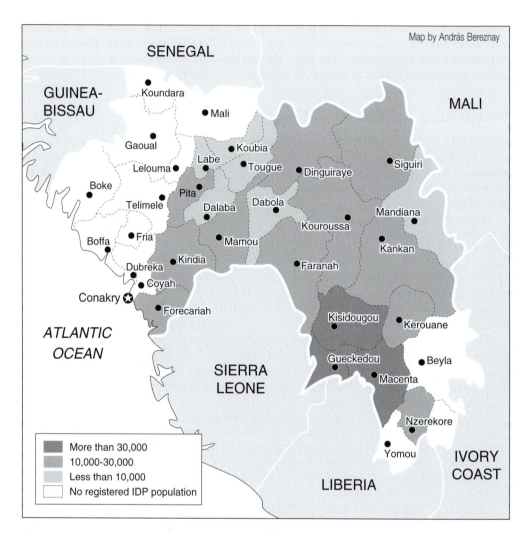

Map 4.3   Guinea: concentrations of IDPs by province (1 February 2002)

Source: UNOCHA, 1 February 2002

While figures on the return of internally displaced persons in Guinea have been lacking, it has been apparent that return has been difficult due to the destruction of many villages, and some towns, in the south-east of the country. The issue of return was further exacerbated by the destruction caused by the floods of September 2001 in Upper Guinea – an area hosting thousands of IDPs from border areas.

Humanitarian Response and Constraints

At the height of the fighting, humanitarian agencies were able to provide only intermittent aid to both refugees and IDPs, particularly in the Parrot's Beak region, which was closed off to aid organizations for a significant period of time. As areas began to open up again in 2001, humanitarian organizations found acute subsistence needs among all vulnerable populations – namely refugees, IDPs and host communities. In March 2001, the UN reported that many IDPs had lost everything while fleeing, and were living either in overcrowded households or in abandoned buildings unfit for human survival (UN, 23 March 2001, pp161–164). Lack of access to basic health care and minimal food were causing outbreaks of disease and high levels of malnutrition.

The overall humanitarian response to IDPs in Guinea, as well as host communities, has been described as less than adequate. In the 2002 Inter-Agency Consolidated Appeal (CAP) for Guinea, the UN declared:

> UN agencies and their partners in Guinea have been unable to fully address the needs of IDPs and host communities, as most donors have limited their contributions to refugee programmes. The resulting disparity between assistance for refugees and assistance for vulnerable groups of Guinean origin remains a major source of concern, and a significant potential source of tension between host communities and refugees (UN, November 2001, p2).

At the same time, the UN identified key problems facing UN agencies and their partners in responding to the situation of internal displacement: 'a scattered population, hard to identify, mingling with host populations, its demographic and socio-economic profile unknown' (UN, November 2001, p11).

A further impediment to the humanitarian response in Guinea has been under-funding. The 2002 CAP – based on a 'more systematic and coordinated approach' than the 2001 CAP, according to the UN – called for just under US$58.5 million in donor funds. However, according to UNOCHA's web-based financial tracking system, of the US$35.6 million requested in the 2001 CAP, a mere 21 per cent was received. While food aid was relatively well funded, protection, coordination, security, water and sanitation, and economic recovery were particularly poorly funded or not funded at all.

Endnotes

1 Guineans have also become internally displaced as a result of natural disasters. Following flash floods in Upper Guinea in September 2001, the government reported that more than 200,000 people were affected to varying degrees – although numbers of IDPs were unclear. The same region suffered drought in March and April 2002. Also in April 2002, the local authorities in the prefecture of Yomou, near the Liberian border, reported that a tornado had damaged 158 houses in the area, affecting over 1200 people.

Guinea-Bissau

Although the instability prevailing in Guinea-Bissau following the civil war of 1998–1999 has improved slightly, the political situation at the end of 2001 remained 'dangerous and volatile' (UNSC, 14 December 2001). Nearly all the 300,000–350,000 persons initially displaced by the conflict in 1998 were thought to have returned to their homes; but a string of political crises in 2001 and early 2002 continued to threaten peace and democracy in the country.

Background and Causes of Displacement

Civil war erupted in Guinea-Bissau in June 1998 when units of the armed forces mutinied against the government. The mutiny was sparked by an attempted government witch hunt of the army general staff for alleged collaboration with Senegalese rebels of the separatist Mouvement des Forces Démocratiques de Casamance (MFDC). The outbreak of war and the subsequent dispatch of Senegalese and Guinean forces to the nation's capital in support of the then President Joao Bernardo Vieira led to the internal displacement of over 300,000 civilians (Manley, November 1998).

Intermittent fighting plagued the country for the remainder of 1998; but by early 1999 a relative calm had returned to the capital, Bissau. West African peacekeeping forces (ECOMOG) were deployed to the capital starting in December 1998, and by March 1999 all Senegalese and Guinean troops were withdrawn. The calm in Guinea-Bissau was short-lived, however, and another bout of fighting commenced in May 1999. The clashes, lasting for two days, prompted a new exodus from the capital and resulted in the take-over of the government by the Junta Militar.

Following the fighting of May 1999, a fragile calm returned to the country. Presidential elections in January 2000 resulted in the successful transition of the government from military to democratic rule and brought President Kumba Yala to power. However, more trouble lay ahead. In November 2000, in an episode well-documented by Amnesty International, the government made several hundred arrests following an attempted coup by Brigadier Ansumane Mané, a former leader of the Junta Militar, who was killed by forces loyal to the government later that month.

Since that time, the political situation in Guinea-Bissau has remained in crisis. The low points of 2001 – as documented by UN Integrated Regional Information Networks (UNIRIN) – included President Yala's dismissal, in September, of two supreme court judges and their subsequent detention on dubious charges of corruption; in December, an alleged coup attempt by some members of the military, resulting in numerous arrests; and, during the inauguration in December of the country's third prime minister in less than two years, the president's warning that any politician who plotted with the military to overthrow his government would be shot.

Although security along the border with the Casamance region of Senegal improved somewhat towards the end of 2001, UN Secretary-General Kofi Annan, in his December report to the UN Security Council, stated that occasional incursions into Guinea-Bissau by MFDC rebels had occurred, and that while no major factional fighting had been reported, armed attacks against civilians were continuing. The secretary-general cited the wide circulation of small arms inside the country and the unresolved issue of reintegration of demobilized former combatants as potential security threats.

Conditions of Displacement

It has been widely reported that nearly all of the 300,000–350,000 persons forced to flee their homes during the war in 1998 have completed their return home – the inference being that a residual IDP population has not yet returned. No data is readily available for this group.

The US Committee for Refugees (USCR) reported that some 50,000 persons were still internally displaced in Guinea-Bissau at the end of 2000, but that for the most part these IDPs were able to return home over the course of the year. Although there were new displacements in the capital in November 2000, following an outbreak of violence between the government and elements of the military, these skirmishes did not last long and residents returned to their homes shortly afterwards. The US State Department, in its country report of 2000, also indicates that all areas of Guinea-Bissau were open to returning citizens during the year, and that virtually all of the 350,000 persons internally displaced by the conflict had returned to their homes. The 2001 report made no further reference to internally displaced persons.

While general information points to the near complete return of IDPs in Guinea-Bissau, there is no specific data on how these persons are coping in their regions of origin. According to the UN Security Council, over 80 per cent of the citizens of Guinea-Bissau live in poverty and few opportunities for employment exist. The abundance of land mines, particularly in areas around the border with Casamance, is another factor that may adversely affect the successful reintegration of IDPs into their original communities.

Humanitarian Response

Information is scant about international aid to IDPs in Guinea-Bissau. In 1999, the International Committee of the Red Cross (ICRC) and the local Red Cross provided non-food aid to people living in houses damaged during the hostilities. It was estimated that some 18,000 persons were living in 2500 such homes throughout the capital. The ICRC also delivered messages on behalf of displaced persons and their families (ICRC, 31 August 2000).

In 2001, the African Development Fund put up a US$6.22 million loan and a US$1.05 million grant with the objective of rehabilitating and facilitating access to basic community infrastructure, increasing the income of the poor and integrating marginalized people and ex-servicemen into production networks. The UN Security Council reported in May 2001 that there were as many as 12,000 former combatants awaiting reintegration into society. At the end of 2001, this issue remained unresolved.

The World Bank and the International Monetary Fund (IMF) have also remained 'constructively engaged' with Guinea-Bissau – especially in the key sectors of demobilization, reinsertion and reintegration, and public finances (UNSC, 14 December 2001).

With regard to de-mining, activities have focused on the most heavily populated areas. By 31 May 2001, mine-clearing operations led by Humaid Demining, an NGO, had resulted in the destruction of over 2000 mines. It is estimated that US$2 million would be needed to remove the estimated 5000 mines remaining in, and around, the capital. As reported by the UN secretary-general at the end of 2001, a Centre for Anti-Mine Action, newly established by the Guinea-Bissau government, estimated that about 20,000 mines still remained in the country.

The UN Office in Guinea-Bissau (UNOGBIS) has had a wide-ranging mandate in support of the country's peace-building process, based on promoting and supporting good governance, human rights and economic development (UNSC, 14 December 2001).

Kenya

Internal displacement in Kenya came to international attention during the 1990s with the reintroduction of multiparty politics and an associated escalation in communal violence. By 2001, more than 200,000 Kenyans who had fled their homes in the Rift Valley during this time were thought to remain displaced (Mbura Kamungi, March 2001, fn70). Reliable estimates are difficult to make, however, as there has never been a systematic registration of IDPs. In addition, return and resettlement movements have largely occurred spontaneously, and there have been additional small-scale displacements in recent years.

Causes of Displacement

The violence that uprooted Kenyans during the 1990s was related to historical migration patterns and unresolved land issues between different communities. In the early 1990s, existing tensions between various ethnic groups erupted into violence, forcing people to take flight.

The feuding was exploited by various politicians who took advantage of the situation to establish loyalist constituencies along ethnic lines.

Recent ethnic clashes and associated displacement have been related to competition over scarce water and pasture, but local human rights organizations have also pointed to an escalation of violence associated with the general elections, scheduled for the end of 2002.

Major Cases of Displacement

A first wave of violence occurred in the Rift Valley prior to the 1992 elections. By 1993, 300,000 people had been forced to flee their homes, most of them belonging to ethnic groups connected with the political opposition (HRW, June 1997, p36). Reports suggest that the majority of these people had resettled by the mid 1990s. However, additional displacements also occurred in the Rift Valley during the 1993–1995 period and later in the decade. Several thousand people fled during the first half of 1998 when Kikuyu communities were attacked in several districts. Clashes between sub-tribes of the same Kalenjin group have forced thousands of people to leave their homes since 1997 in Pokot and Marakwet areas in the northern Rift Valley.

In the Mombasa area, as many as 100,000 people fled ethnic violence prior to the December 1997 election, but later reportedly returned (Mbura Kamungi, March 2001, p8). In Wajir District in north-eastern Kenya, several armed attacks between 1998 and 2001 forced out pastoralist communities. In the Tana River district several thousand people were displaced when tensions between settled farmers and pastoralist communities erupted into violence in November 2001.

Protection concerns

One major protection problem in Kenya has been the participation of the security forces in support of the armed gangs behind the violence and displacement in the country. A further protection issue has been the rapid dissolution of camp-like settlements where IDPs have taken refuge. Local authorities have often closed these settlements without notice or the support necessary for the IDPs to integrate elsewhere. As a result, families are, in effect, forcibly displaced once again. In 2001, for example, 3000 IDPs temporarily resettled in the Kyeni forest in Thika District were forced out once again without any support. They congregated in make-shift shelters in difficult conditions while they waited for more permanent resettlement opportunities (UNOCHA, 31 August 2001).

Protection has also been compromised by the lack of an international presence. During 1993–1995, Kenyan authorities declared large areas of the Rift Valley closed security zones, allegedly to curb violence. However, these measures have hindered access for outside human rights observers (Article 19, October 1997, sect2.3).

Displaced Kenyans who have been unable to return home live in very poor conditions (Galava, 29 October 2000). Many of them have sought shelter in poor urban areas where they lack the skills to gain their livelihoods. For the most part, IDP families lack the resources to pay school fees for their children (Kamungi, March 2001). A study of the situation of IDP women in 2001 revealed very weak coping mechanisms and close linkages between displacement, social disintegration and sexual violence (UNIFEM, January 2002).

Return and Resettlement

While many people – the best available estimate is more than 200,000 – displaced from the Rift Valley during the 1990s remain so, large numbers returned to their home communities or resettled elsewhere at some stage (USDOS, 4 March 2002, sect1d). Many have chosen to resettle rather than return to their homes as a result of continued insecurity and destroyed property. Land entitlement issues have also been a major stumbling block for people seeking to regain their properties. In many cases, property owners displaced during the early 1990s lack land title documents; in other cases, their land has been nationalized by the government. There have also been instances where farmers have been pressured to sell their lands at below market value (HRW, June 1997, pp71–72).

National and International Response

Assistance to IDPs generally falls under the responsibility of the relief department at the Office of the President. However, no government agency has been specifically charged with supporting IDP populations. The government policy with regard to return has been ambiguous, at best. By 2002, there existed no clear strategy for the return of remaining IDPs from the Rift Valley, even though President Daniel Arap Moi had already declared in 1999 that 'maximum security' should be created to enable these populations to return (UNIRIN, 11 November 1999). Senior government officials have openly expressed their reluctance to encourage people to return to their original homes, and the national parliament actually voted against a resettlement proposal in November 2000 (Owino, 23 November 2000).

Although often confronted with problems of access, national NGOs and church organizations have provided support to IDP populations with minimal resources. Reconciliation efforts have been limited to local initiatives, and the National Council of Churches of Kenya (NCCK) has been particularly active in assisting resettlement and peace-building in the Rift Valley (Kathina Juma, May 2000).

International attention to the problem of displacement in Kenya has been limited. The United Nations Development Programme (UNDP) implemented a major IDP project during 1993–1995 and assisted a substantial number of people to resettle. It was, however, phased out prematurely in response to the forcible expulsion of 2000 IDPs from the Maela camp by Kenyan authorities in 1994.

Liberia

Five years after the end of a brutal civil war that killed an estimated 200,000 people and forced more than half the country's population to flee their homes, lasting peace and stability in Liberia remained a pipe dream in 2002. Since 1999, the country has become mired in yet more fighting – this time largely between Liberian security forces and armed insurgents in the north of the country. By early 2002, the fighting had spread southward, at times coming dangerously close to the capital Monrovia and prompting successive waves of population movements. In March 2002, humanitarian organizations estimated the total number of internally displaced in the country to be about 80,000 – 36,000 of them in Bong County (north-east of Monrovia) and 35,000 in the greater Monrovia area. Four camps were being used as 'emergency influx zones' (ICRC, February 2002). Arriving IDPs, who had been forcibly displaced several times, were said to be in a deteriorating physical condition and often completely destitute.

Background and Causes of Displacement

The internal displacement of civilians began in Liberia with the civil war that started in 1989. Charles Taylor, leading the National Patriotic Front of Liberia (NPFL), launched an armed rebellion against the Samuel Doe regime in the north of the country. Fighting quickly reached the capital. In 1990 the Economic Community of West African States deployed a Nigerian-led peacekeeping mission (ECOMOG) to Liberia to restore order. ECOMOG's control did not extend beyond Monrovia, however, and the rest of the country was ruled by Taylor and other insurgents battling over the country's rich natural resources.

Eventually, in 1996, the four main Liberian warlords signed a peace agreement that stuck. It provided for disarmament of the warring factions, followed by presidential and parliamentary elections in 1997. Taylor won a landslide victory in the presidential contest. More than half of Liberia's 2.8 million people had fled their homes during the fighting, 1.2 million of them as internally displaced persons, the remainder as refugees in neighbouring states (USDOS, 1998, Liberia, sect2d).

Peace was short lived. In 1999, armed dissidents, believed to have crossed the border from Guinea, attacked the town of Voinjama in northern Lofa County (Guinea subsequently accused Liberian forces of entering its territory and attacking border villages). Intermittent fighting – largely between Liberian security forces and a newly formed rebel movement known as Liberians United for Reconciliation and Democracy (LURD) – spread and intensified, forcing tens of thousands of people to flee their homes. The situation was, however, complicated by reports of in-fighting between various pro-government militias in the region, and military claims on all sides were often unverifiable. The conflict was centred in the gold- and diamond-rich area close to where Liberia, Sierra Leone and Guinea meet.

In December 2001, government forces launched a fresh offensive when the rebels came to within 60km of the capital. Fighting followed fleeing populations from one temporary location to another. At the end of January 2002, the UN was 'deeply concerned' about reports of the forced displacement of some 10,000 IDPs from the temporary camp at Sawmill. They joined thousands of other newly displaced persons in Klay Town near Monrovia. The government restricted aid agencies to the greater Monrovia area, while blocking IDPs from entering the capital, where many people who had been previously displaced continued to shelter in unfinished and war-damaged buildings.

Further attacks on Klay Town, less than 50km from the capital, prompted Taylor to declare a state of emergency in February 2002, restricting movements and requiring exit visas for everyone leaving the country, including UN staff. Sceptics believed that Taylor's government may have state-managed the crisis in order to 'create a humanitarian crisis on the doorstep of Monrovia that would draw the eyes and the sympathy of the world' (Tostevin, 14 February 2002). The president had long complained that he could not deal with the security situation properly because of a UN arms embargo.

Conditions of Displacement

Since the upsurge of fighting in 2000, IDPs from the north have been completely unprotected against increasingly widespread human rights abuses by both Liberian security forces and LURD fighters. Amnesty International (AI) documented human rights abuses in a 2001 field assessment, in which displaced northerners spoke of extra-judicial executions, torture and rape (AI, August 2001). Rape has been so widespread, according to AI, that it could be described as a weapon of war. Other aid agencies reported that many IDP women who were raped during flight were pregnant in the camps. Forced recruitment has also been a major problem. It is widely believed that many men and boys have been denied freedom to move out of Lofa County, and have, instead, been forcibly recruited.

AI further warned that the state of emergency imposed in February 2002 was being used as 'a justification by the security forces to abuse power and commit human rights violations against the civilian population' (AI, February 2002).

Civilians forced to flee their homes have hidden and trekked through dense forest for days – and sometimes weeks – before reaching relative safety. But even transit centres such as the one at Sawmill proved to be unsafe. The World Food Programme (WFP) reported that since the January 2002 attack on the Sawmill camp, many IDPs were on the move for the fourth successive time. Numbers were hard to estimate because the serious insecurity was restricting humanitarian access to all the displaced. According to WFP, the newly displaced were living in partially destroyed buildings, warehouses, or simply in the open air. Many were said to be physically weak after their flight.

Humanitarian Response and Constraints

International scepticism of the Taylor administration has remained high since the 1997 elections. The government has been accused of increasing human rights violations at home, and of backing armed insurgencies in neighbouring countries. The UN Security Council tightened an arms embargo on Liberia in March 2001 to curb arms trafficking to the Revolutionary United Front (RUF) in Sierra Leone, and two months later imposed further sanctions, including travel restrictions on senior government officials and a ban on diamond exports.

As a result, funding for Liberian humanitarian programmes has been extremely poor. By March 2002, there was still no response to the 2002 Inter-Agency Consolidated Appeal requesting US$17 million. Donor antipathy has forced NGOs to scale down their reconstruction and development activities, and reduce the level of support they have been providing to IDPs and other vulnerable populations (UN, November 2001, p12).

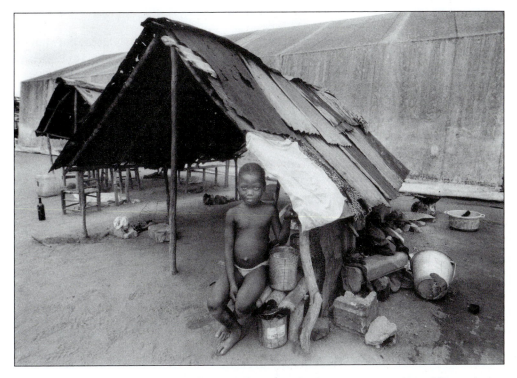

Photo 4.4   Young girl in the Fumba camp for displaced persons, Near Monrovia, Liberia (1999)

Source: Heldur Netocny/Panos Pictures

At the national level, responsibility for the coordination of humanitarian assistance and return of IDPs lies with the Liberian Refugee, Repatriation, and Resettlement Commission (LRRRC), although it, too, suffers from limited technical, financial and logistical capacity. The National Humanitarian Task Force, chaired by the Liberian first lady, was launched in February 2002 – although its operational structures were yet to be established.

International humanitarian operations have been hampered not only by a lack of resources but also by lack of access to many areas of the country where fighting has been taking place – including Lofa, Bomi, Gbarpolu and Grand Cape Mount counties.

Nigeria

Internal displacement is not a new phenomenon in Nigeria. During the Biafran war of 1967–1970, some 2 million people were killed and another 10 million internally displaced. Since that time, populations in Nigeria have continued to take flight, albeit on a significantly smaller scale than the late 1960s. In the current context, internal displacement is caused by several separate low-level conflicts. The scale and breadth of displacement is hard to estimate as many IDPs return spontaneously to their homes or resettle in a haphazard manner among family and clan members in other towns and communities. But available figures in late 2001 suggested a total of 400,000 people (UNIRIN, 29 October 2001). The most significant displacement occurred in October 2001, when some 500,000 persons were forced out as a result of ethnic clashes and army attacks in central Nigeria. At the beginning of 2002, communal fighting in Nasarawa and Plateau States, as well as ethnic clashes in Lagos, also displaced thousands of people.

The roots of conflict and displacement have existed for some time in Nigeria; but military regimes, and especially the authoritarian rule of General Sani Abacha from 1993 to 1998, kept underlying tensions in the country in check. With the election of Olusegun Obasanjo as president in May 1999 and the introduction of democracy, however, these tensions were finally expressed, resulting in a rise in inter-ethnic or inter-communal conflicts. The conflicts that have broken out since 1999 have been associated with five often interwoven factors: ethnic rivalry, religious tensions, land disputes, new administrative boundaries, and disputes linked to oil production.

Rivalries between some of the 250 ethnic groups in the country have been a major cause of conflict and displacement in Nigeria. Militant groups affiliated to specific ethnic groups have emerged, playing an important role in setting off communal violence. For example, violence in central Nigeria between the Tiv and Jukun groups gave rise to massive displacement of some 500,000 people during October 2001. Religious tension has occurred mainly in the north between Muslims and Christians and has often been related to the introduction of the Islamic legal system, Sharia, in several northern states.

Successive governments have implemented policies favouring large-scale agricultural projects, forcing small farmers away from their land. This has resulted in communal violence, often of an ethnic character, over borderlands and fishing waters. As a result of increasing desertification on Nigeria's northernmost fringes, many pastoral people have started pushing southward in search of grazing land, giving rise, to a certain extent, to conflict between the Tiv and the pastoral Hausa-Fulani peoples. Existing ethnic tensions have sometimes been exacerbated by the creation of new administrative boundaries. Displacement in the Niger Delta has often been linked to oil exploration, which is associated with state violence, communal disputes, environmental pollution and a worsening economic and material situation in the communities (Ibeanu, 1998, p49).

Major Waves of Displacement

There have been numerous cases of conflict-induced internal displacement since the beginning of 2000. The major waves are noted as follows:

- February–March 2000: religious violence in Kaduna caused the displacement of more than 100,000 persons.
- October 2000: ethnic clashes in Lagos between a militant Yoruba group and the Hausa-Fulanis displaced some 20,000 people.
- June 2001: ethnic fighting between Tivs and Hausa-speaking Azaras in Nasarawa State displaced some 50,000 people. Fighting spread to Taraba State in July 2001, creating a further 25,000 displaced.
- July–August 2001: religious clashes in Bauchi State resulted in the displacement of 23,000 people.
- September 2001: religious violence between Hausa-Fulani Muslims and indigenous Christians in Plateau State displaced 60,000.
- October 2001: ethnic clashes between the Tiv and Jukun groups and army violence displaced some 500,000 in Nigeria's central region. Most were resettled by March 2002.
- January 2002: land clashes in Mambilla Plateau between local farming communities and the Fulanis displaced thousands.
- January 2002: revenge attacks on Christians in Plateau State caused the displacement of some 3000 persons.
- January 2002: at least 1000 people moved into Benue State after threats of reprisals were issued against Tiv settlements in Taraba State.
- January 2002: communal clashes in Nasarawa State over fishing rights displaced thousands.
- February 2002: ethnic clashes in Lagos between Yorubas and Hausa-speaking northerners displaced more than 2000 people.[1]

Protection Concerns

The physical security of internally displaced people has, in some cases, been undermined by government authorities. There have been reports of the military and the police restricting the movement of the displaced. Moreover, the affiliation of officials to certain ethnic groups has sometimes led to reprisal attacks against other ethnicities. Finally, authorities have occasionally used force to coerce people to leave camps and return to their home areas, according to an NGO source in August 2001.

The extended family system has been crucial in covering the subsistence needs of the displaced; but this resource has, however, been overstretched. The special needs of women and children are often not taken into full consideration, with men tending to control relief items. Also, food needs are often aggravated by the destruction of crops.

Often the displaced head for villages where they have family or where their ethnic groups are in the majority. Many displaced are also sheltered in camps, especially those who do not have family or ethnic relations in the vicinity. A common characteristic with regard to the composition of the groups of displaced in IDP camps is the under-representation of male adults. Fear of the destruction of property and crops often forces them to stay in their villages to watch over family belongings.

In many cases, return is spontaneous and unplanned; but fear of further violence impedes the majority of displaced from returning to their communities of origin. Because many internally displaced turn to social networks and relocate to other towns and communities to

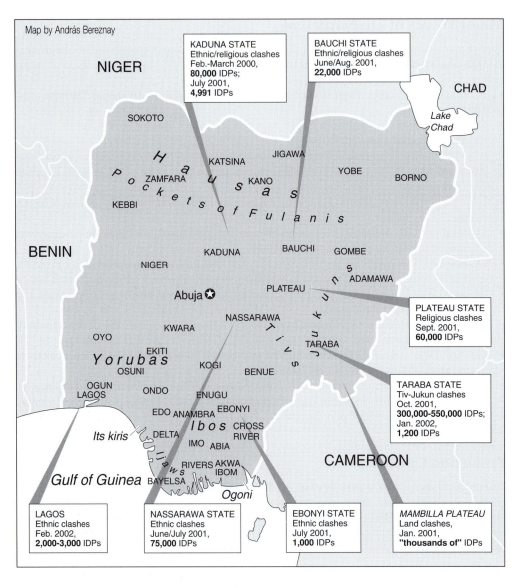

Map by András Bereznay

KADUNA STATE
Ethnic/religious clashes
Feb.-March 2000,
80,000 IDPs;
July 2001,
4,991 IDPs

BAUCHI STATE
Ethnic/religious clashes
June/Aug. 2001,
22,000 IDPs

NIGER

CHAD

SOKOTO

Lake Chad

H a u s a s
P o c k e t s   o f   F u l a n i s

KATSINA

JIGAWA

ZAMFARA

KANO

YOBE

BORNO

KEBBI

BENIN

KADUNA

BAUCHI

GOMBE

NIGER

ADAMAWA

Abuja ✪

PLATEAU

PLATEAU STATE
Religious clashes
Sept. 2001,
60,000 IDPs

NASSARAWA

KWARA

OYO

EKITI

Yorubas

OSUNI

KOGI

TARABA

TARABA STATE
Tiv-Jukun clashes
Oct. 2001,
300,000-550,000 IDPs;
Jan. 2002,
1,200 IDPs

BENUE

OGUN

LAGOS

ONDO

ENUGU

EDO ANAMBRA EBONYI

Ibos CROSS

Its kiris

DELTA

RIVER

IMO ABIA

RIVERS AKWA

Ijaws

IBOM

CAMEROON

Gulf of Guinea BAYELSA

Ogoni

LAGOS
Ethnic clashes
Feb. 2002,
2,000-3,000 IDPs

NASSARAWA STATE
Ethnic clashes
June/July 2001,
75,000 IDPs

EBONYI STATE
Ethnic clashes
July 2001,
1,000 IDPs

MAMBILLA PLATEAU
Land clashes,
Jan. 2001,
"thousands of" IDPs

Map 4.4   Main areas of conflict and displacement in Nigeria (2001)

Sources: Global IDP Database, 2002, adapted from Marin, *Le Monde Diplomatique*, 1999

join family and clan members, the scale and breadth of displacement and population movements on the whole are difficult to estimate (Ibeanu, 1998, p51).

Response

For the most part, the government of Nigeria has provided the primary assistance to IDPs, donating money and relief supplies to affected areas. However, the Nigerian Red Cross Society (NRCS) and the International Committee of the Red Cross (ICRC) have also offered crucial support to those populations. For example, during the Nasarawa crisis in July 2001, ICRC and the NRCS assisted 7000 internally displaced in Benue with non-food items, and the local and federal government provided food, shelter and health care (ICRC, 16 August 2001). UN assistance to the displaced has often been limited to urgent aid from a single agency, such as UNICEF support during the Nasarawa crisis in 2001, instead of a coordinated multisectoral approach by several UN agencies. Some NGOs, such as Catholic Relief Services and Médecins Sans Frontières (MSF), have also been instrumental in getting critical aid to IDP populations over the last years.

Endnotes

1   Sources for figures are from: UNDP, 21 August 2001; UNIRIN, 15 March 2002; UNIRIN, 'Weekly Updates' (various from 2001–2002). For further details, see Nigeria page of IRIN website at www.irinnews.org.

Republic of Congo (Brazzaville)

The Republic of Congo's slow recovery from seven years of political violence, which left its infrastructure severely damaged and its people deeply impoverished, suffered a setback in March 2002 with a new outbreak of fighting. Since a peace agreement was signed in December 1999, a tenuous peace had held in the country and the majority of the estimated 800,000 persons previously displaced by conflict had returned home. By 2001, estimates of remaining IDPs ranged anywhere from zero to 150,000 (USDOS, 2001, Republic of Congo, sect2d; USCR, 2 October 2001). However, at the end of March 2002, renewed fighting between government forces and Ninja militias broke out in the Pool region surrounding the capital, Brazzaville. Early reports by UN sources indicated that about 15,000 people were displaced in Pool, and at least 65,000 displaced in Brazzaville, although some subsequently returned.

Background and Causes of Displacement

Congo has suffered intermittent civil strife since the country's first democratic elections brought Pascal Lissouba, a southerner, to power in 1992. Disputed parliamentary elections the following year led to violent, ethnically based clashes between government forces and the opposition. While peace was restored by 1995, this was short lived and full-scale civil war broke out in 1997. Lissouba and his prime minister, Bernard Kolélas, were deposed by forces loyal to Denis Sassou Nguesso, a northerner who had the backing of Angolan government troops.

Despite efforts to restore peace to the country after the 1997 civil war, violence erupted once again in September 1998. The three key players – Sassou Nguesso, Lissouba and Kolélas – relied on different militias that formed when the army fractured along ethnic lines: respectively the Cocoye, or Zulu, the Cobra, and the Ninja. But ethnicity was not the only factor fuelling the fighting; the lure of Congo's considerable offshore oil wealth was also a key issue.

By the time President Sassou Nguesso's government and rebel forces signed a peace agreement in December 1999, the two bouts of civil conflict had exacted a toll of tens of thousands of Congolese dead and hundreds of thousands internally displaced. The situation of internal displacement reached crisis proportions during the 1998–1999 conflict, when various UN and NGO sources estimated that some 800,000–810,000 people had been forced to flee their homes – most of them from the southern provinces of Pool, Niari, Bouenza and Lekoumou, but also from Brazzaville. The UN reported that several towns, including Dolisie (80,000) in Niari Province and Nkayi (60,000) in Bouenza Province, were completely emptied of their populations (UN, November 1999, p3).

Sassou Nguesso won a landslide victory in presidential elections in March 2002 – Congo's first since 1992. Lissouba and Kolélas had, however, been declared ineligible under the revised constitution. Both were living in exile abroad, having been tried and convicted in absentia for crimes allegedly committed during the civil conflict in the1990s. Soon afterwards, government forces claimed that several military positions in the Pool region had been attacked by Ninja militias. In early April, tensions between the two sides escalated into heavy fighting in the Pool region surrounding the capital. The UN reported that tens of thousands of people were fleeing into forests or seeking the protection of military posts.

Conditions of Displacement

During the 1998–1999 war, combatants on all sides committed widespread human rights violations. Amnesty International (AI) reported that women and girls were raped, and that people fleeing were used as human shields (AI, 2001). Thousands of IDPs chose to hide in the forests of the Pool region, where they were completely without aid or shelter. As a result, they were extremely vulnerable to death and disease. UNICEF reported in October 2000 that some 70 per cent of IDPs were 'severely malnourished' at the height of the emergency in Congo. MSF confirmed that the principal cause of death during the war was malnutrition (UNICEF, 12 October 2000; MSF, 27 November 2000).

Immediately following the ceasefire at the end of 1999, relative stability was restored and a massive return of IDPs took place. Agencies estimated that as many as 500,000–600,000 IDPs returned home in the first four months of 2000. According to ICRC, return was so swift and widespread that the four remaining IDP camps in Brazzaville at the beginning of 2000 were already closed by April.

By the end of 2001, information about any remaining concentrations of IDPs in Congo had become increasingly sparse. Few public documents existed with any reference to IDPs, and news out of Congo centred on reconstruction and poverty eradication. However, various agencies believed that even before the new wave of displacements, starting in April 2002, there may still have been as many as 150,000 IDPs remaining in the country. Most of the remaining IDPs were said to reside in Brazzaville and to no longer require life-sustaining assistance. At the same time, however, the UN reported that at least some of these IDPs were unable to find formal or informal work in the city. In addition to the residual caseload of IDPs from the 1998–1999 war, there was also a smaller caseload of some 30,000 people who were temporarily displaced from Mindouli, south-east of Brazzaville, in May 2001. These people were forced to flee their homes as a result of isolated clashes between army soldiers and armed supporters of exiled former Prime Minister Kolélas (USCR, 2 October 2001).

Humanitarian Response

During the conflict in 1998–1999, the UN humanitarian coordinator for the Republic of Congo argued that while the country was experiencing the worst humanitarian crisis in the world, it was receiving the lowest level of emergency relief per capita.

Since that time – with the focus shifting more from emergency relief to rehabilitation – the government of the Republic of Congo has initiated various post-conflict projects aimed at reconstruction and poverty eradication, which have won some support from international donors. The European Union (EU), for example, donated 750,000 Euros in 2002 for the reintegration of ex-combatants (an estimated 18,000) and the collection of weapons.

While some optimism for the country's prospects could be seen in the UN's decisions to close down the UNOCHA offices in Congo in June 2001 and to reopen the World Health Organization (WHO) Africa Regional Office in Brazzaville in October, the UN Development Programme (UNDP) reported that overall lack of funding was continuing to hamper its efforts to support the country during the post-war recovery phase. It also meant that UN agencies were not in a position to respond adequately to new emergencies (UNDP, August 2001).

Rwanda

The problem of internal displacement was officially over by the end of 2000, six years after the Rwandan genocide. But a year later, some 70 per cent of the Rwandan population were living below the poverty line and approximately 192,000 families were still in inadequate shelters (Government of Rwanda, November 2001, Annex 4 III). Most of these families were resettled during 1998–1999 by the Rwandan government under the auspices of the 'villagiz-ation' process. Some UN agencies and NGOs reported that this resettlement was not always voluntary; but since the end of 2000 both the UN and the Rwandan government have considered these people permanently resettled and report that there are no more internally displaced people in Rwanda (UNOCHA, 18 December 2000).

Causes of Displacement

Over the last decade, Rwanda has fallen victim to repeated waves of conflict and displacement. In the wake of the genocide of 1994, up to 2 million people were displaced. Many stayed within the country, but the majority fled to neighbouring Zaire (now the Democratic Republic of Congo – DRC), Burundi and Tanzania. In 1997 members of the army and Interahamwe militia who had fled in 1994 launched an insurgency against the Rwandan government in the northern prefectures of Ruhengeri and Gisenyi. The conflict between government forces and insurgents led many inhabitants to flee their homes at the end of 1997. Later, in 1998, the government moved hundreds of thousands of people into supervised camps in the north-west as part of its effort to suppress the insurgency.

At the end of 1998, the government ordered the dismantling of camps in the north-west and the relocation of the displaced into new villages. A similar resettlement process had already taken place in several provinces to accommodate the needs of returnees and homeless genocide survivors. Since December 1996, the Rwandan government had made this process of villagiz-ation, or *imidugudu*, a national habitat policy and called for houses to be constructed in government-created villages, rather than in the traditional scattered homesteads.

The ultimate objective of this policy was to move the entire rural population into grouped settlements. The government maintained that basic services could be provided in a more cost-effective way in villages, that land could be distributed more rationally and that villages inhabited by different social groups could help to promote reconciliation. In the north-west, the government justified the villagization process by pointing out that traditional scattered settlements left people exposed to the action of rebel groups. Grouped settlements in the north-west were also seen as a way to deprive the insurgents of hideouts and covert support (Government of Rwanda, November 2001). By the end of 1999, the Rwandan government had largely put down the insurgency in the north-west but continued to resettle people in new villages as late as mid 2000 (HRW, 2000, p66). In 2002, Rwanda still maintained a military presence in the DRC to prevent rebel attacks into the north-west of Rwanda.

Some UN agencies and international NGOs charged that the process of villagization was not always voluntary. For instance, the UN special representative for Rwanda reported in 2000 that some coercion occurred during the resettlement process (UNCHR, 25 February 2000). Furthermore, Human Rights Watch (HRW) indicated that tens of thousands of people had been moved against their will and that many families had been compelled to destroy their homes (HRW, May 2001). It was reported in 1999 that local Rwandan authorities in several communes had recognized that more than half of the resettled population in the north-west would have preferred to have gone back to their original homes as security improved. Since that time, the people remain where they were resettled as the Rwandan government still does not allow these individuals to go back to their original homes, despite the quelling of the insurgency in the north-west.

Until December 1999, the UN included 150,000 people recently relocated into new villages in the north-west in its statistics of internally displaced and noted that these were the people receiving direct humanitarian assistance (UNOCHA, 24 December 1999). The following year, it stopped counting these people as IDPs and stated that 'while conditions of return and resettlement are often yet inadequate, governmental and international efforts to stabilize the situation through durable solutions have advanced beyond the threshold of what still could be called internal displacement' (UNOCHA, 18 December 2000). Such an analysis of the situation has been rejected by other international observers. The US Committee for Refugees (USCR), for example, stated in June 2000 that the relocation process in the north-west could be considered a new phase of displacement and gave the figure of 600,000 internally displaced persons in the country (USCR, 2000, p107).

National and International Response

The situation for resettled populations remains difficult. In 2001, the UN Special Rapporteur on the Human Rights Situation in Rwanda expressed concerns that the reintegration needs of large numbers of Rwandans had still not been sufficiently addressed and that there was a danger that people who were in desperate need would not be reached (UNCHR, 21 March 2001).

Launched in January 1999, the Brookings Initiative brought together multilateral agencies, NGOs, donor and recipient governments to discuss the gap between humanitarian assistance and long-term development. In October 2001, a multi-agency mission, including UN, donor and Rwandan government representatives, examined the conflict-related needs not fully addressed by humanitarian assistance in Rwanda, such as human settlement and access to land. It estimated that 192,000 families in resettlement villages lived in inadequate shelters, covered by old pieces of plastic sheeting or banana tree leaves, compared to 370,000 families in 1999. The habitat situation in the north-west was substantially worse than in the pre-war era, and 73 per cent of vulnerable households were now in the north-western provinces of Ruhengeri and Gisenyi. Many of the resettlement sites lacked adequate basic services, such as access to water and latrines. The families who did not have adequate shelter were among the most vulnerable in Rwanda. Many of these families consisted of woman- or child-headed households (Government of Rwanda, November 2001).

The Rwandan government is attempting to remedy some of the errors of early resettlement efforts. It has allocated the equivalent of US$1.9 million for the resettlement and reintegration of IDPs during the period of 1998–2002. It has provided social services to the new villages with the help of the international community and has encouraged mixing in villages originally inhabited by either Hutu or Tutsi groups. At the national level, it has elaborated a new land system that will permit private ownership of land on a wide scale, and should mitigate future land disputes (Government of Rwanda, November 2001).

Many donors were reluctant to support villagization programmes during the resettlement process beyond the emergency phase, stating that the internally displaced were resettled in an unplanned manner, in the absence of popular consultation, and without the required social infrastructure. Nevertheless, donors still contributed tens of millions of dollars to the resettlement programme in Rwanda. In 2000, the UN community adopted a 'Framework for Assistance in the Context of the Imidugudu Policy', a joint approach to assist the Rwandan government in the context of villagization (UN, February 2000).

Rwanda no longer attracts the level of financial support it received in the aftermath of the genocide despite an immense need for shelter and infrastructure, especially in the resettlement sites. In its country cooperation framework with the Rwandan government for 2002–2006, UNDP states that there is considerable concern about the slowdown in financing of the government resettlement programme and that UNDP will take the lead to promote the conclusions of the task force of the Brookings Initiative regarding resettlement (UNDP, 20 September 2001). In 2002, NGOs such as Oxfam and the International Rescue Committee (IRC) were addressing the water and sanitation needs of the relocated people.

Senegal

Despite being hailed as a relatively peaceful and stable country in the African context, Senegal has been the scene of intermittent clashes between government forces and rebels of the separatist Mouvement des Forces Démocratiques de Casamance (MFDC) since the early 1980s. Due to the fact that the southern province of Casamance is virtually cut off from the rest of the country by the Gambia, most people fleeing the violence have sought refuge there and in Guinea-Bissau. According to the US Committee for Refugees (USCR), the insurgency forced as many as 40,000 Senegalese to flee their homes at the height of fighting during the 1990s – both inside Senegal and across borders to neighbouring countries. By mid 2001 a total of 18,000 Senegalese were estimated to be still uprooted. Some 3000 of them had been forced to flee their homes in the first few months of 2001. Of the 18,000, approximately one third were internally displaced (USCR, August 2001). Specific figures on internal displacement in the Casamance context have often been lacking, however, and estimates have differed widely.[1]

Background and causes of displacement

Although the separatist movement has been alive in Casamance Province since before Senegal's independence from France in 1960, the first large demonstration for provincial independence did not occur until late 1982 when the MFDC organized a march on the provincial capital, Ziguinchor. Violent demonstrations continued throughout the 1980s until the MFDC officially declared its armed struggle for Casamance independence in 1990. At this time, it initiated its first organized attacks on military and civilian targets in the region (Manley, November 1998). In response to the separatist attacks, the Senegalese military arrested and tortured hundreds of people, as documented by Amnesty International (AI) in February 1998 (AI, 17 February 1998). Since then, rebel incursions and government counter-measures have established a cycle of sporadic violence that has continued to plague the southern province.

In mid May 2001, another round of violence broke out in the region. The Senegalese army and MFDC forces engaged in heavy fighting, particularly in the department of Bignona. The army shelled certain parts of the southern province and burned houses in pursuit of rebel forces. This intensification of fighting came only two months after a peace agreement was signed between the newly elected President Abdoulaye Wade of Senegal and MFDC Secretary-General Diamacoune Senghor, calling for inter alia the return of refugees and IDPs. The peace agreement was the third of its kind since the early 1990s.

Conditions of Displacement

During the successive waves of violence in Casamance, large numbers of people from the countryside have fled to the provincial centres of Ziguinchor and Kolda. While there has been no information available about the conditions in which the IDPs have been living, it is clear that inhabitants of the region, on the whole, are particularly vulnerable to food insecurity since Casamance Province is virtually cut off from the rest of Senegal by the Gambia. Furthermore, as documented by the World Food Programme (WFP) in its 2001 Country Strategy for Senegal, the minimal transport infrastructure has limited the capacity of its inhabitants to cope with natural, economic or social traumas.

As a result of political unrest in Casamance, inhabitants of the region have found themselves subject to harassment and human rights abuses by both sides in the conflict. The Senegalese army and gendarmerie have arrested hundreds of people in their attempt to quell the insurgency. AI has reported that many of the persons arrested by the government have been tortured or killed, or have simply disappeared. Individuals of the Diola ethnic community have apparently been at particular risk because government authorities suspect them of being sympathetic to the independence movement (AI, 17 February 1998).

The MFDC is also guilty of human rights abuses in Casamance. As documented by AI, witnesses have reported that rebel soldiers often raid villages and force civilians to give them food and money to support the armed incursion. Those who refuse to make a financial contribution to the separatist movement have been beaten and had their homes burned (Manley, November 1998). AI has further cited evidence that at least some of the acts perpetrated by the MFDC have been committed on the basis of ethnic criteria, with members of the Manjak, Mandingo, Balante and Mancagne ethnic groups disproportionately targeted.

Land mines have also posed a major threat to the security of inhabitants since the early 1990s. USCR claims that land mines have rendered 80 per cent of farmland unusable in some areas of Casamance (USCR, 2001, p100). Roads and tracks around Zinguinchor, as well as areas of Oussouye and Bignona, have been riddled with mines during the course of the conflict (Manley, November 1998).

By July 2001, the UN High Commissioner for Refugees (UNHCR) reported that as many as 2000 of the 3500 refugees who had fled Casamance for the Gambia in May and June 2001 had returned voluntarily to their homes just across the border to farm their lands – the implication being that many of those people internally displaced at the same time may also have returned.

Humanitarian Response

In response to the fighting in Casamance, the government of Senegal has provided punctual resettlement assistance to some families forced to flee their homes in the region (USDOS, 2001, Senegal, sect2d). At the local level, UNIRIN reported in 2001 that the Ziguinchor chapter of the CONGAD, an NGO umbrella organization, was actively managing aid efforts for refugees and IDPs affected by fighting in the region. The local unit, chaired by the governor of Ziguinchor, included representatives of humanitarian NGOs, security forces and other state bodies.

The ICRC and the Senegalese Red Cross Society have provided continual assistance to civilians affected by the conflict in Casamance over the years. According to the ICRC in 2001, their activities included regular IDP registration, evaluating needs and conducting ad hoc distributions of food aid as required.

In early 2001, WFP identified six departments in Casamance – Bignona, Oussouye, Ziguinchor, Sedhiou, Kolda and Vellingara – as highly vulnerable and targeted them as priority intervention areas. Various NGOs have been active in the province – for example, as of 2001, Catholic Relief Services and World Vision, both of which were running multisectoral projects, including agriculture, health and sanitation.

Endnotes

1 Senegal has also suffered internal displacement as a result of acute climatic conditions. In January 2002, humanitarian agencies reported that floods in the north of Senegal had destroyed close to 20,000 homes, affecting more than 179,000 people.

Sierra Leone

In January 2002, President Ahmad Tejan Kabbah of Sierra Leone declared that his country's 11-year civil war was finally over. Just a few days earlier, the UN Mission in Sierra Leone (UNAMSIL) declared that more than 45,000 former fighters had handed in their weapons, marking the end of the government's disarmament programme.

What had begun in 1991 as a small incursion from neighbouring Liberia by the Revolutionary United Front (RUF) grew into a brutal campaign of terror against civilians that cost an estimated 50,000 lives and, at its height, forced almost half of the country's 4.5 million people to flee their homes. (According to some UN agencies, there were as many as 2 million internally displaced persons in Sierra Leone at the end of 2000, as well as several hundred thousand refugees in neighbouring countries.)

By 2001, significant gains in the peace process resulted in improved security throughout the country, boosted by the full deployment of UNAMSIL peacekeepers in November 2001 and continued military support from the UK to the reformed national armed forces. This allowed the return of some 45,000 IDPs to their homes in 2001. At the same time, humanitarian access increased greatly, and recovery efforts began in the north and east of the country. However, fighting in neighbouring Guinea, and more particularly in Liberia, led to the premature repatriation of Sierra Leonean refugees who, upon their return, remained displaced in their own country. According to the UN in the 2002 Inter-Agency Consolidated Appeal, many IDPs who had returned to areas 'safe for resettlement' found a critical lack of basic community services and infrastructure, causing some to drift back to major urban centres.

While the UN cited the relatively small figure of 247,590 registered IDPs in Sierra Leone as of November 2001 – the majority residing in managed camps – it was widely believed that the real number could be much higher, with many non-registered IDPs living in host communities (UN, November 2001, p29).

Background and Causes of Displacement

The conflict, initiated by the RUF, was initially confined to the southern and eastern areas of Sierra Leone; but by 1994 it had spread throughout the country. Rebel forces twice entered the capital – first in May 1997 when RUF and renegade government troops established a military junta for nine months, and then in January 1999 when the rebels terrorized and looted the capital before being driven out by Nigerian-led ECOMOG (Ceasefire Monitoring Group of the Economic Community of West African States) forces. A violent retreat by the rebels caused a new influx of IDPs and, according to the UN Security Council, hindered humanitarian access to most of the country. The Lomé peace agreement signed by the warring parties in July 1999 failed to end the violence – culminating, instead, in an escalation of hostilities by the RUF in May 2000, including hostage-taking of UN troops and further atrocities against civilians.

The conflict spread during the second half of 2000 across the border to Guinea, with the RUF attacking Guinean villages and camps hosting Sierra Leonean refugees. This, in turn, led to armed activities by Guinean troops inside Sierra Leone. An outcome of this fragile security situation was additional internal displacement, as well as a return flow of Sierra Leonean refugees. Many of these ended up in a situation of internal displacement as their home areas remained exposed to RUF terror.

Towards the end of 2000, the rebels gradually signalled a willingness to re-enter the peace process. In November 2000, the government and RUF signed a new ceasefire agreement in Abuja and it was reiterated in May 2001.

The completion of disarmament in January 2002, marking the official end of the civil war, paved the way for preparations for the country's parliamentary and presidential elections on 14 May. Although the RUF registered as a political party (RUFP), the National Electoral Commission declared that its leader, Foday Sankoh, was ineligible to contest the presidential elections because he was not a registered voter. As of early 2002, Sankoh remained in prison on murder charges related to an incident in May 2000, when a peaceful demonstration outside his Freetown home turned violent and at least 20 people died.

In March 2002, Sierra Leone's parliament ratified the creation of a UN-sponsored special court to prosecute those people bearing 'the greatest responsibility' for serious violations of international humanitarian and national law during the civil war (AFP, 21 March 2002).

Indeed, the widespread human rights abuses committed, to differing degrees, by all sides to the conflict have been the main cause of internal displacement in Sierra Leone. The civilian population has, throughout the conflict, been targeted deliberately by the rebel groups, and severe atrocities have been well documented by organizations such as Amnesty International (AI) and Human Rights Watch (HRW). Various organizations have also reported that counter-insurgency operations by troops loyal to the government have caused additional displacement and civilian suffering. Reflecting the cyclical nature of this conflict, many Sierra Leoneans have been displaced and returned home several times as the rebel forces have advanced or withdrawn.

Conditions of displacement

Improvements in the security situation in many parts of Sierra Leone by the beginning of 2001 coincided with insecurity in neighbouring Liberia and Guinea, resulting in large movements of IDPs, returnees and ex-combatants. The strategy for dealing with the flow of displaced from the border areas, as documented by the UN Office for the Coordination of Humanitarian Affairs (UNOCHA), has been to assist communities in hosting the displaced, rather than to add to already overstretched camps or to create new ones. However, numerous humanitarian agencies have expressed concern at the limited capacity of host communities to absorb more people, in view of the poor infrastructure and lack of basic services. Even with the war over, shelter remained a priority need, with up to 90 per cent of houses destroyed in many areas. According to the UN and NGOs such as Médecins Sans Frontières (MSF), the population, in general, is the most vulnerable to ill health in the world, with high levels of malnutrition and wide-ranging medical needs.

Another major cause for concern has been the lack of adequate protection of Sierra Leone's internally displaced populations. One reason for this is the collapse of the national law enforcement system. Large parts of the country had, for a long time, been without a police presence, and the national army was disbanded after its involvement in the 1997 military coup. Civilians outside rebel-held areas received some protection from civil defence militias and the West African ECOMOG forces. However, as reported by HRW, the merciless atrocities by the rebel forces in January 1999 against civilians in Freetown revealed a situation of inadequate protection of civilians throughout the country. During the 1999–2000 period when the 'peace process' was still intact, there were reports of rebel abuses against IDPs even within areas apparently under government control (HRW, 3 March 2000).

The RUF rebels regularly abducted children, and both Amnesty International (AI) and Save the Children (SCF) reported that the use of children as combat soldiers by both RUF and pro-government forces continued during 2000. According to SCF, children constitute about 60 per cent of the IDPs, and as many as 1.8 million children may at some time have been displaced since the outbreak of the war – making them extremely vulnerable. More than 5000 parents reported their children missing in the wake of the rebel attack on Freetown in January 1999 (UNOCHA, 6 December 2000). However, there have been positive developments since the Abuja Meeting in 2001, with no further reports of large-scale abduction or conscription of children, and a total of 2378 children demobilized or released by the RUF and civil defence militias by the end of 2001.

Women have also been exposed to grave human rights abuses by fighters on all sides of the conflict. A study by Physicians for Human Rights (PHR), published in January 2001, revealed the extent of war-related sexual abuse against IDPs (PHR, 2002).

Humanitarian Response and Constraints

At the end of 2001, the humanitarian community in Sierra Leone consisted of nine UN agencies, in addition to the human rights and civil affairs sections of the UN Mission in Sierra Leone's (UNAMSIL's) peacekeeping mission, some 46 international NGOs, over 200 national NGOs and hundreds of community-based organizations, as well as government bodies – principally the National Commission for Reconstruction, Resettlement and Rehabilitation (NCRRR).

Overland delivery of humanitarian aid was extremely difficult during the conflict. Looting of aid supplies was widespread, especially when rebel forces twice entered Freetown. The rebel offensive at the beginning of 1999 made delivery of humanitarian aid nearly impossible outside of the capital. The July 1999 peace agreement improved humanitarian access and enabled the UN and NGOs to undertake aid delivery and assessment missions to previously inaccessible areas. Following the signing of the peace agreement, the UN Security Council (UNSC) deployed a peacekeeping force to Sierra Leone (later referred to as UNAMSIL), part of whose mandate has been to facilitate the delivery of humanitarian assistance (UNSC, 22 October 1999).

However, in March 2000 UNOCHA reported that there was safe access to only 5 of 12 districts – excluding about half of the population from humanitarian assistance. Escalated rebel activities in May 2000 further restricted delivery of humanitarian assistance, and humanitarian operations in most areas of the northern and eastern provinces ceased as the conflict worsened. Towards the end of 2001, gains in the disarmament process and the full deployment of UNAMSIL – a total of 17,500 troops – contributed to the creation of new opportunities for humanitarian organizations, as well as the government of Sierra Leone, in previously inaccessible areas. In March 2002, UNAMSIL's mandate was extended for a further six months.

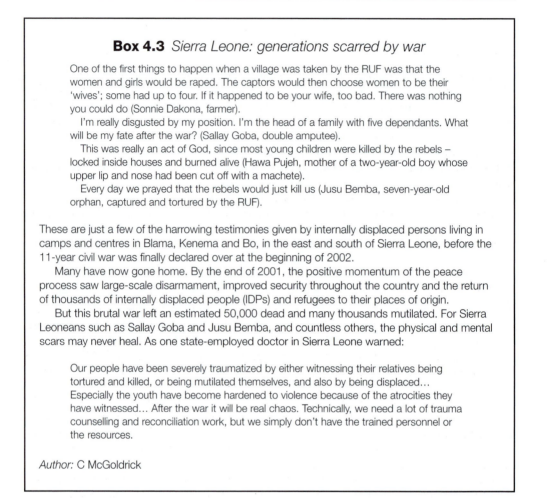

Box 4.3 *Sierra Leone: generations scarred by war*

One of the first things to happen when a village was taken by the RUF was that the women and girls would be raped. The captors would then choose women to be their 'wives'; some had up to four. If it happened to be your wife, too bad. There was nothing you could do (Sonnie Dakona, farmer).

I'm really disgusted by my position. I'm the head of a family with five dependants. What will be my fate after the war? (Sallay Goba, double amputee).

This was really an act of God, since most young children were killed by the rebels – locked inside houses and burned alive (Hawa Pujeh, mother of a two-year-old boy whose upper lip and nose had been cut off with a machete).

Every day we prayed that the rebels would just kill us (Jusu Bemba, seven-year-old orphan, captured and tortured by the RUF).

These are just a few of the harrowing testimonies given by internally displaced persons living in camps and centres in Blama, Kenema and Bo, in the east and south of Sierra Leone, before the 11-year civil war was finally declared over at the beginning of 2002.

Many have now gone home. By the end of 2001, the positive momentum of the peace process saw large-scale disarmament, improved security throughout the country and the return of thousands of internally displaced people (IDPs) and refugees to their places of origin.

But this brutal war left an estimated 50,000 dead and many thousands mutilated. For Sierra Leoneans such as Sallay Goba and Jusu Bemba, and countless others, the physical and mental scars may never heal. As one state-employed doctor in Sierra Leone warned:

Our people have been severely traumatized by either witnessing their relatives being tortured and killed, or being mutilated themselves, and also by being displaced... Especially the youth have become hardened to violence because of the atrocities they have witnessed... After the war it will be real chaos. Technically, we need a lot of trauma counselling and reconciliation work, but we simply don't have the trained personnel or the resources.

Author: C McGoldrick

The humanitarian community remained concerned, however, that new, large-scale influxes of people fleeing the fighting in Liberia could create a source of instability, partly because of the likelihood of their settling in still volatile areas with limited humanitarian access, and partly because their arrival would seriously strain the capacity of relief organizations to address their needs (UN, November 2001, p9).

The UN Consolidated Appeal for 2002 called for a total of just over US$88 million in funding – targeted primarily at the resettlement and reintegration of displaced populations; the rehabilitation and reconstruction of the infrastructure of basic social services; the continued provision of relief assistance to existing vulnerable groups; and ensuring the timely and integrated delivery of emergency relief to potential population influxes. The amount requested represented a 10 per cent increase on funds appealed for in 2001 due to improved accessibility to the north and east of the country where critical humanitarian needs were found (UN, November 2001, p9). The 2001 Consolidated Appeal was relatively well funded – a total of 80 per cent of the US$74 million requested.

Somalia

Since the 1970s Somalia has drifted from one emergency to another, running the whole gamut of repression, civil war, invasion, fragmentation, drought and famine. Conflict in Somalia has centred on control of land, aid and the livestock trade. It is unusually hard to give meaningful figures for displacement in a country where four-fifths of the population traditionally led a nomadic or semi-nomadic existence. But it is estimated that at the height of fighting in 1992, up to 2 million people were displaced (USCR, 1998, p92). By mid 2002, rough estimates indicated that more than 400,000 people remained or were newly displaced (UN, November 2001, p5).

After a somewhat hopeful start in 2001, an upsurge of factional fighting and a third consecutive year of drought have pushed Somalia back onto the miserable path it has followed for over a decade. New displacements are on the rise, and levels of distress in the country remain unparalleled, even for Africa.

From Dictatorship to Warlordism

A military coup in 1969 installed a dictatorial regime, whose divide-and-rule policy succeeded in polarizing grievances into clan-based wars and eventually splintered its own support base. It was finally overthrown in 1991, but the loose anti-government coalition quickly fell apart and proved incapable of changing pre-established war patterns. Since the early 1990s, various warlords have fought to establish hegemony over Somalia's most fertile lands – between the Jubba and Shabelle rivers – and key ports such as Mogadishu.

The US-led military operation in Somalia (UNOSOM) to protect the delivery of relief supplies ended in fiasco and was finally abandoned in 1995. Though there were high hopes for a Transitional National Government (TNG), established in October 2000 after long negotiations, the new government has found it increasingly difficult to assert control over the country, or to gain broad-based recognition.

During the latest cycle of unrest, trouble has spread to the historically calmer regions of Puntland and Somaliland in the north – Puntland runs as an autonomous administration and Somaliland as a self-proclaimed independent state.[1] Somaliland Republic has been somewhat more successful in promoting grassroots peace processes and institutional change, and brought in a multiparty system in 2001. But in both Somaliland and Puntland, leaders' reluctance to hand over political power at the end of their terms has fuelled conflict. Furthermore, in April 2002, the Rahanweyn Resistance Army (RRA) set up a new regional administration in the Bay and Bakool regions of south-western Somalia.

Causes of Displacement

Somalis have fled war-induced famines and generalized violence for decades. Warlords have deliberately looted and destroyed food stocks, mined watering places, grazing lands and major trading roads, and destroyed medical and administrative infrastructures in order to prevent people from another clan from sustaining a livelihood. Armed factions waged battles in order to claim clan sovereignty over their supposed 'native territories'.

The most ravaged regions have been in the South – Gedo, Bay, Bakool, Lower and Middle Juba, as well as the main ports of Mogadishu and Kismayo, where the livestock trade is concentrated. Violent clashes have flared up since July 2001. Clans opposed to the transitional government and warlord factions grouped under the umbrella of the Somali Restoration and

Reconciliation Council (SRRC) have taken up arms against the TNG forces and allied militias, resulting in heightened fighting in the capital and other parts of southern Somalia. Bloody confrontations over the control of Kismayo port and in Lower and Middle Juba forced many people to flee. Similarly, in Bay and Bakool, conflict between TNG and SRRC forces claimed hundreds of lives, and since March 2002, acute violence in Gedo has forced tens of thousands of people to flee the region.

In addition to the conflict, Somalis have been affected by drought and other natural calamities, which have pushed many to move in search of water, food and medical assistance. As a result of a third consecutive year of drought in 2002, water reservoirs in the traditionally most fertile regions of Bay, Bakool, Gedo and Hiran became seriously depleted and crop production severely reduced. At the end of 2001, populations were forced to move to the Lower Shabelle areas of Mogadishu and Merka (UNIRIN-CEA, 9 July 2001; UNICEF, 7 September 2001).

Many IDPs come from the farming Bantu and Bajuni communities, as well as the Rahanweyn clan, who have had a low social status in Somalia and have suffered a long history of discrimination and land dispossession.[2] While protection is granted through clan affiliation, the Bantu and Bajuni groups, politically less organized, have been particularly exposed to serious human rights abuses (Menkhaus, November 2000, p9).

Patterns of Displacement and Living Conditions

Tracking displaced populations in Somalia is particularly difficult as virtually all Somalis have been displaced by violence at least once in their life. Furthermore, 80 per cent of Somalis live a nomadic or semi-nomadic lifestyle, traditionally moving with their herds to and from grazing lands and water sources. Wars and severe droughts have complicated and hampered these seasonal migrations, and since the 1990s families have increasingly moved to towns in search of humanitarian assistance.

Scattered in overcrowded urban areas, IDPs mingle with other indigent groups and refugees who are returning in waves, especially to the north, where there is some degree of stability. IDPs tend to congregate in Hargeysa (Somaliland), where there are four different camps, and in Bosasso (Puntland). Between 100,000 and 250,000 displaced persons in Mogadishu live in approximately 200 camps and squatter settlements. Since 1999, few IDP camps have remained in the country, and the displaced are increasingly dispersed (UN, November 2001, p3).

Renewed fighting and drought mean that conditions in the few existing camps are more crowded than ever, with associated high levels of disease. Cerebral malaria is the main killer in Somalia, reflecting the high levels of dislocation to zones where people are not immune to the different types of malaria parasites. Diarrhoea and dehydration are the second cause of death, reflecting the fact that less than 20 per cent of Somalis have access to safe drinking water and proper sanitation is lacking (US Fund for UNICEF, 6 September 2000; UN, March 2001, p27). Outbreaks of cholera have been reported especially in Mogadishu (UNIRIN-CEA, 8 April 2002). As concerns the nutritional status of IDPs, food security reports conducted during 2001 show overall malnutrition rates as high as 37 per cent (FSAU, 2002, p1)

An intermittent livestock import ban imposed by the Gulf States since 2000 has also had an adverse effect on cattle-herders, who are unable to earn a living.[3]

Humanitarian Assistance

As there is no recognized central government to provide citizens with social services and protection, the delivery of humanitarian assistance is extremely difficult in Somalia. In 1993,

Photo 4.5 Burdhuba region on the river Jubba, Somalia (1997): more than 1800 persons died in Somalia during the 1997 floods and tens of thousands were displaced

Source: Marc French/WCC

the Somali Aid Coordination Body (SACB) was set up to coordinate rehabilitation and development. It includes under its umbrella the UN Country Team, the NGO Consortium and the Red Cross Movement. There is no single agency focusing specifically on IDPs, but they have been included in wider programmes.

The Somali Red Crescent is the only humanitarian institution represented across the nation since 1991, providing health care, disaster preparedness and relief. The NGO Action Contre la Faim (ACF) has been the most active in assisting IDPs in Mogadishu, and was also one of the only organizations still present in Mogadishu during the 2000 confrontations. Islamic organizations have also assisted IDPs in Mogadishu.

Problems of Access

Insecurity has been so acute in southern Somalia that it has been difficult to plan assistance or deliver it in time. The lack of a permanent international presence in the country is telling. UN staff are based in Nairobi and fly in on short missions. It is debatable how much such cross-border operations achieve in proportion to their costs.

Humanitarian access has always been obstructed by unpredictable political dynamics and violence. The 2001 upsurge in fighting has reportedly reduced it to its lowest point since the departure of UNOSOM forces in 1995. Gedo, Lower and Middle Juba and Middle Shabelle, as well as the ports of Bossaso, Mogadishu, Merka and Kismayo, have experienced some of the most intense clashes in years. The populations are in urgent need of assistance but the regions are off-limits to humanitarian workers. In Mogadishu and other seriously insecure regions, humanitarian workers are regularly kidnapped or even killed by militias, and the ambush and looting of humanitarian vehicles are common occurrences. As a result, many agencies are forced to pull out.

With the considerable access problems and donor fatigue, funds received for humanitarian assistance in 2001 decreased by 22 per cent (UN, 29 April 2002). Although the people of Somalia are extraordinarily resilient, they have little chance of surviving with the low level of assistance currently allocated to the country.

Endnotes

1 Unlike Somaliland, Puntland does not consider itself independent but a merely regional, auto-nomous administration, willing to join a united Somalia as soon as peace allows it to do so.
2 In 1999, in Baidoia (Banadir region), Aideed's militias committed human rights violations mostly against the Rahanweyn minority group. During the first half of 1999, 20,000 people were internally displaced and 30,000 fled across the border. See USCR, 2000, pp115–116.
3 Livestock accounts for 80 per cent of Somalia's exports, and 80 per cent of Somalis depend almost entirely upon livestock trade. Furthermore, following unverified accusations of abetting terrorism, the Al-Barakaat Bank and the Somali Telecommunications systems were closed. Al-Barakaat Bank was the primary channel for remittances in Somalia, and Somali Telecom-munications was one of the few successfully functioning business in Somalia. See SCF–UK, January 2002.

Sudan

More than 30 years of civil war and tribal conflicts have caused tremendous suffering for the civilian Sudanese population and generated one of the worst IDP situations in the world. Since the conflict escalated in 1983, there have been at least 2 million war-related deaths, while most sources have commonly estimated that 4 million people have been internally displaced since the mid 1990s (UN, November 2001, p52). With the recurrence of war and no significant large-scale returns reported, the US Committee for Refugees (USCR) estimated that this total was actually 4.4 million in 2001 (USCR, 2 October 2001). Quantifying IDP populations is complicated in Sudan by traditional nomadic migration patterns, as well as movements related to people searching for emergency assistance, compounded by sustained drought and other natural calamities. But available statistics showed some 1.8 million IDPs in Khartoum State, 500,000 in the east and the 'transition zone', and 300,000 in the southern states, for government-controlled areas. In the Sudan People's Liberation Movement/Army (SPLM/A)-controlled territories, there were about 1.4 million IDPs (UNCHR, 5 February 2002, para6).

Causes of Conflict-induced Displacement

The civil war in Sudan is commonly depicted as one of the Muslim north versus the Christian and animist south. In reality, there are complicating factors, with several armed factions and militias, as well as various ethnic groups, partly at war, partly in alliance with the government or fighting each other. The main parties are, on the one side, the SPLM/A and, on the other, the Sudanese army and the Popular Defence Forces, composed of various tribal militias. The civil war has no single battlefront, thus creating a very complex and fluid displacement situation. Direct exposure to military activities, often with a clear intent to displace civilians, is the main cause of displacement in Sudan. Control of territory and the appropriation of civilians' goods, as well as the denial of resources to the opposing side, have been dominant war patterns.

The government has commonly used ethnic divide-and-rule tactics to weaken the southern-based opposition, notably by sowing tensions between and among Nuer and Dinka ethnic groups. This is particularly true in the oil-rich Unity State (Western Upper Nile) and Upper Nile, where displacement has become closely linked to major geopolitical and economic interests (CAID, 17 May 2001; Harker, 2000). The strategy of depopulating the oil-rich areas by extremely violent means has forced tens of thousands of civilians to flee, increasingly so since 2001. In addition, civilians are often caught between the fire of rival armed groups seeking to establish themselves in the oilfields (ICG, 2002, pp132–136).

The Nuba Mountains – once Sudan's breadbasket – has long been the theatre of armed conflict. The government has, since the early 1990s, created so-called 'peace villages' where indigenous Nuba communities from contested areas have been forcibly moved. During the first half of 2001, for example, the government launched an offensive in the Nuba Mountains, systematically ransacking and burning homes.[1] By May 2001, 50,000 Nuba people were estimated to be displaced, and more were forcibly relocated to the so-called peace villages (UNIRIN-CEA, 23 July 2001). Over the past years, the international community has expressed its concern about the protection of Nuba IDPs in these peace villages, particularly in light of reports of forced Islamization of these non-Muslims by authorities.

Abduction of civilians is another and most extreme form of displacement in Sudan, which has continued despite several initiatives to stop it. Displacement of civilians has also been accompanied by the recruitment of child soldiers. Although the SPLM/A handed over 3500 child soldiers to UNICEF in February 2001, there were still between 4000 and 6000 children to demobilize and return to their families (UNICEF, 29 August 2001; UN, November 2001 p82).

Health and Nutrition

As a result of population movements and heightened insecurity, many areas remained short of food in 2002. The situation had deteriorated during 2001, with malnutrition rates of 15–30 per cent common in the IDP-hosting states of Bahr al Ghazal, Upper Nile, Eastern Equatorial and Unity. Further nutritional degradation was expected by the end of 2002.

Surveys conducted in September 2001 in IDP camps of northern Bahr al Ghazal reported a dramatic under-five mortality rate of 6.5 per 10,000 every day. In addition, a shortage of safe drinking water and a critical lack of access to health facilities were common in IDP camps.

Most displaced persons remain scattered outside camps, and although much of the general population is in need of humanitarian assistance, the internally displaced are often marginalized in comparison with other war-affected people. This is particularly notable during food distribution, especially for those groups not accompanied by their traditional leaders. As a result, IDPs tend to suffer higher malnutrition and mortality rates than the resident populations.

IDPs in Khartoum

The UN estimates that about 1.8 million IDPs have sought refuge in the Greater Khartoum area (UNCHR, 5 February 2002, para6). In 2000, it was reported that only 260,000 were settled in the four official IDP camps, while the remaining displaced were living in various planned and unplanned areas (UN, November 2000, p143). Several reports describe a bleak humanitarian situation facing the latter category of IDPs, including regular outbreaks of disease, chronic food insecurity and limited access to safe drinking water. Reports indicate that the displaced from the Christian southern regions of Sudan face discrimination for access to assistance and land allocation compared to those from Muslim areas. In addition, the slums where the displaced congregate have been destroyed more than once in order to remove 'undesirable elements' from the city. In May 1992, up to 600,000 IDPs were forcibly evicted. Despite these hardships, these uprooted populations preferred to stay in Khartoum rather than go back to remote war zones where pastoral lands were ravaged by drought (Pérouse de Montclos, 2001, pp23, 47).

Protection in Danger

The government has been criticized for not protecting displaced populations. Access to areas such as the Nuba Mountains, Bahr al Ghazal, Western Upper Nile/Unity State, Eastern Equatoria and southern Blue Nile is difficult for aid organizations, restricting the flow of humanitarian assistance. There are regular reports of IDPs being exposed to gross violations of fundamental human rights and humanitarian law. Since 1998, there have been regular reports of the government bombing civilian targets, including hospitals caring for IDPs, food-aid drop zones and IDP camps. During 2001–2002, human rights observers have reported an increase of such gross violations of international humanitarian law in Equatoria, Bahr al Ghazal and in the oil-rich Western Upper Nile. Notably, in February 2002, Akuem was bombed by government planes during a World Food Programme (WFP) food distribution to 18,000 civilians (WFP, 13 February 2002), and aerial bombings on Nimme, and later on a relief centre in Bieh, killed scores of civilians, including Médecins Sans Frontières (MSF) staff.

In 2001, the UN noted a general lack of awareness about human rights and humanitarian law on the part of government officials and criticized the absence of an IDP focal point in Sudan, both factors deterring potential outside funding for the humanitarian crisis in the country. However, the government agreed to develop a national policy for the displaced and to establish a department within the Humanitarian Aid Commission (federal level), focusing on IDP issues. Later developments concerning government initiatives toward IDPs, however, were not encouraging. In March 2002, the government cancelled the mission of the UN Senior Inter-Agency Network for IDPs, during which camps in southern Sudan, the Nuba Mountains and South Darfur were to be visited. Similarly, in May 2001, a mission of the Representative of the UN Secretary-General on Internally Displaced Persons, which included a workshop on internal displacement, was cancelled due to the government's concerns over infringements of national sovereignty (UNCHR, 5 February 2002, p6)

Complex Emergency Response

The main mechanism for humanitarian aid in Sudan is Operation Lifeline Sudan (OLS), under the overall coordination of the UN Humanitarian Coordinator in Khartoum. A network of 44 national and international NGOs works under the OLS umbrella and carries out relief and rehabilitation activities in partnership with UN agencies. NGOs have been operating in a very complex conflict environment and had to overcome many impediments. In March 2000, a disagreement with the Sudan People's Liberation Movement (SPLM), which threatened NGOs' control over the use of their vehicles and equipment, forced several agencies to pull out of southern Sudan, impairing the delivery of humanitarian assistance. Some have since returned.

Photo 4.6   A fighter with the SPLA Mainstream, southern Sudan (1995): Deng Ding (16); his father was killed by the SPLA United faction, and the family's cattle were stolen; Three of his brothers and sisters have since died of starvation

Source: Crispen Hughes/Panos Pictures

The UN estimates that most of the 3 million or so beneficiaries of its humanitarian pro-gramme are IDPs (UNIAC Sudan, December 2001). Despite the sheer number of IDPs in a state of chronic emergency, the UN appeal for Sudan was under-funded during 2000 and 2001. While three-quarters of requested food aid had been provided, only one third of the non-food sector was funded. As a consequence, long-term projects for IDPs in sectors such as resettle-ment or women's health were not implemented or were phased out.

Denial of Access

Humanitarian access continues to be a major problem despite efforts during recent years to negotiate an improvement of the situation. Since mid 2001, security has been a severe problem for humanitarian workers. Problems include denial of flight permission, intensified government bombing of civilian and humanitarian targets, and changing political alliances. As of March 2002, up to 45 locations were at times off-limits to aid agencies, depriving 170,000 people of food aid (UNIRIN-CEA, 4 March 2002).

In December 1999, a tripartite agreement signed by the UN, the government and the SPLM/A, included guarantees for protection of civilians and for 'free and unimpeded access' to vulnerable populations. It also bound the SPLM/A to 'customary human rights law', and contained the commitment by both parties not to enforce illegal relocations of civilians (OLS, 15 December 1999). This agreement was not fully implemented and areas most affected by conflict continued to suffer chronic access denials. In addition, needs assessments and operat-ional activities in government areas continued to be limited to sites that had been agreed by the government. In 2001, the UN reached an agreement with the government and the SPLM/A to be granted four Days of Tranquillity per month and designated Zones of Peace to facilitate access to war-affected people.

Government flight denials have obstructed the opportunity to assist civilians in Western Upper Nile, Bahr al Ghazal and Eastern Equatoria. As a result, during June 2001, WFP was only able to deliver two-thirds of food rations to southern Sudan, and over 150,000 IDPs were out of reach of WFP in Bahr al Ghazal (UNIRIN-CEA, 12 July 2001). The UN is also concerned that systematic access denial jeopardizes health programmes, especially vaccination campaigns.

In 1999, the government of Sudan for the first time allowed the UN to conduct humanit-arian assessments in the Nuba Mountains, on the basis of which a multi-sectoral programme targeting 454,000 war-affected persons was launched in 2000. In November 2001, government forces shelled one of the few airstrips in the area, while WFP planes were on the ground. Similar incidents, together with flight denials, made the Nuba Mountains inaccessible in mid 2001. As a result, the Nuba Mountains multi-sectoral programme of assistance and rehabilitation was still not operational by end 2001.

Endnotes

1   It is estimated that 2500 homes were ransacked and burned during this operation. See UNIRIN, 23 July 2001.

Uganda

Internal displacement in Uganda has been caused by separate armed conflicts in northern and western areas, as well as violent looting and cattle raids in the east since the mid 1990s. Conflict has affected about one quarter of the country's 45 districts, and about 550,000 people remained internally displaced as of February 2002 (UNOCHA, 31 March 2002).

Historical Background to the Conflict

Violent attacks by the Lord's Resistance Army (LRA), starting in the mid 1990s, forced about three-quarters of the ethnic Acholi population to flee their homes in the Gulu and Kitgum/ Pader districts of the north. The LRA soon gained a reputation for abducting children in order to forcibly conscript them, make them carry looted supplies, and sexually exploit them. A relative calm in the area during 1999 allowed for some return of displaced populations. But an escalation of LRA attacks since the beginning of 2000 has forced an increasing number of people to seek refuge in 'protected villages' or, alternatively, in the towns of Gulu and Kitgum. After a period of some stability, the LRA intensified its raids during the first months of 2002. With the consent of the Sudanese government, the Ugandan army launched an offensive operation against the LRA inside Sudan starting in March 2002 (UNIRIN, 5 April 2002).

The other main area of displacement in Uganda is in the Ruwenzori Mountains on Uganda's western border with the Democratic Republic of Congo (DRC). This region has been an arena for violent attack by the rebel group Allied Democratic Front (ADF) since November 1996. The ADF violence intensified between 1998 and 2000 and included the abduction of school children, as well as attacks on IDP camps. Bundibugyo, Kasese and Kabarole were the worst affected districts, but the violence also spread to the Bushenyi, Mbarara, Hoima and Kibaale districts. Since the beginning of 2001, the situation improved as a result of a weakening of the ADF by Ugandan security forces. District authorities were, by March 2002, actively planning the return of displaced populations in all affected areas (UNOCHA, 31 March 2002).

In eastern Uganda, internal displacement has been caused by the violent raiding of villages by Karamojong pastoralists in search of local goods and cattle. The situation in eastern Uganda, most notably in the districts of Katakwi, Soroti, Kumi, Kitgum and Lira, was particularly bad during the first months of 2000. Although the situation normalized, to some extent, by the end of 2000, about one third of the population in the Katakwi District remained displaced and housed in poorly equipped IDP camps by early 2002 (UNOCHA, 28 February 2002, p34). In December 2001, the government finally initiated a disarmament exercise of the Karamojong. However, as voluntary disarmament had only limited success, the Ugandan army began forcibly disarming the Karamojong in February 2002.

Displacement Patterns and Protection Concerns

Over the last few years, civilians in conflict areas have been fleeing their homes and returning according to the changing intensity of the conflict. Towns have become major centres of refuge. During periods of relative security, the displaced have often continued to farm their lands during the day and have returned to safe areas during the night. IDP settlements in all conflict areas have been exposed to armed attacks, abductions and looting of food aid. The government response to chronic insecurity in the north has been to gather large numbers of the population in 'protected villages'. This has been a controversial policy, and some have argued that these villages have been established primarily as a military tactic. The protected villages have not, in fact, provided adequate physical protection to internally displaced people and have even been regular targets for LRA attacks. Displaced adolescent girls have been particularly vulnerable to abduction and sexual violence (WCRWC, 2001).

Subsistence Needs

Food security has been seriously undermined by ongoing conflicts – even in areas with high potential for agricultural production such as the north. In the Karamoja area, the increasingly violent cattle raids have depleted a major source of income and food. The World Food

---

Box 4.4 *Uganda: female-headed IDP households need special attention during return*

Displacement, disease and social disintegration, reinforced by the conflict in the northern Uganda districts of Gulu, Pader and Kitgum, have placed a heavy burden on women who have often become the sole caretakers of families. As many as one out of every five households is headed by a widow, and at least 44 per cent of the total households are headed by females (widows, single women and girl children). Even with an improved security situation that would enable mass return, it is unlikely that the overall situation for these vulnerable groups will improve – indeed, their situation may actually worsen if the particular needs of female-headed households (FHHs) are not given careful attention during the return process.

According to a study conducted in Gulu District in 2001, FFHs have limited sources of income and limited access to required farm inputs compared to male-headed households (MHHs). FHHs have weak labour and may not be able to open up sufficient cultivable land upon resettlement. In addition, they lack granary construction skills and their disadvantaged economic status does not allow many of them to have one built. As a result, 20-40 per cent of female-headed households experience post-harvest handling losses. In order to limit such losses, there is a high propensity among FHHs to sell their produce during the immediate post-harvest period.

A number of factors suggest that during resettlement, more FHHs than MHHs will be vulnerable to disease. Displaced FHHs are among the poorest, and adult female illiteracy rates are more than double those of males. At the same time, only 7 per cent of FHHs have house construction skills, meaning that during resettlement, female-headed households are likely to dwell in highly substandard housing and may not even have sanitation. In addition, limited food production and post-harvest handling losses and sales may translate into poor nutrition among FHHs. The number of displaced MHHs keeping some form of livestock is more than double that of FHHs, and the number of MHHs who acquire new life-sustaining skills during displacement also nearly double. It would therefore follow that in times of severe stress – for instance, during reconstruction – more MHHs will have some form of fallback that their FHHs counterparts will not.

Author: S Katwikirize

Programme (WFP) has found it necessary to target more than 500,000 IDPs for food aid in 2002 (WFP, December 2001, p10). Overall, nutrition surveys indicate that malnutrition is more prevalent among displaced children than the population at large; but there have been signs of improved nutrition levels since the late 1990s (UN, November 2001, p43). Poor health among the displaced population has also been linked to congested camps with inadequate water and sanitation facilities, as well as a breakdown of social structures (Oxfam, 8 February 2002). As of 2002, the living conditions and health situation in Katakwi IDP camps were among the worst in the country. On the whole, conflict and displacement in Uganda have undermined community support systems, and there has been an increase in crime and in alcohol and drug abuse since the 1990s.

Although there have been positive developments with regard to access to primary education – especially in the north – high drop out rates among girls have remained, and there has been limited capacity to offer traumatized children special care.

Improved Opportunities for Return During 2002

Since the beginning of 2002, most insurgent groups have been weakened and opportunities for return have opened up in some areas of the country. Often the displaced have preferred a gradual return, by which they first take advantage of improved security to resume farming in their home areas, only later moving back to their homes on a permanent basis. However, physical security has not been the only factor determining the pace of the return process. Many displaced have been discouraged from returning because of the lack of public services and education facilities in home areas. Others have faced problems of destroyed properties and loss of land rights. The conflict has led to an increased number of female-headed households that have a limited capacity to manage the return process (Katwikirize, December 2001).

Humanitarian Access and Response

The delivery of emergency assistance has been constrained by lack of security throughout the conflicts in Uganda. There have been several instances of attacks on aid vehicles and the killing of Ugandan humanitarian staff. In many cases, it has been necessary to use military escorts when transporting and distributing food aid. Nonetheless, the access situation has, in general, been better than in other African countries experiencing armed conflict, and substantial humanitarian assistance has reached displaced populations. In addition to food aid, projects in the areas of food production and education have been successfully implemented. The government has, since 2001, launched several offensive operations to combat the rebel groups. In 2002, it was also developing a National Policy on Internal Displacement.

5

The Americas

Regional Overview

Although only 10 per cent of the world's internally displaced people (IDP) are found in Latin America, the number of persons internally displaced by conflict is by no means insignificant. By mid 2002, some 2.2 million persons were IDPs in the region – nearly four times the number of refugees. The large majority of these persons were found in Colombia, a country producing as many as 300,000 IDPs a year and considered one of the worst situations of internal displacement in the world. IDP populations were also present in Guatemala, Mexico and Peru.

With the notable exception of Colombia and, to some extent, Mexico, conflict in the Americas has, by and large, abated. While civil wars in Guatemala, El Salvador, Nicaragua, Honduras, Haiti and Peru displaced as many as 2 million people during the 1980s and early 1990s, the restoration of peace in these countries has been accompanied by large waves of returns.[1] Even in Mexico, Peru and Guatemala – all countries still hosting IDP populations – some degree of peace in these countries has allowed for a significant decrease in the number of IDPs from the height of the conflict.[2]

Still, even with successful conflict resolution throughout many parts of the Americas, the total number of displaced persons in the region has almost doubled since 1996, due entirely to the acute escalation of fighting and violence in Colombia.[3]

Background and Causes of Displacement

Strong economic disparities in Latin America – characterized most notably by inequitable ownership and access to land – have been at the heart of many of the conflicts there. In most instances, it has been indigenous or black communities who have been marginalized. In fact, poor peasant peoples, such as the Maya in Mexico and Guatemala and the Quechua-speaking people of Peru, have often found themselves persecuted and displaced. In response to economic inequalities, landless farmers with powerful indigenous support have posed serious challenges to governments. Sometimes these challenges have taken the form of armed guerrilla movements.

Latin American society has often been polarized between the indigenous under-classes, labelled 'leftist subversives', and large landowners associated with the ruling elite. In an effort to safeguard the economic interests of large landowners, governments in the Americas have often used military means to solve political problems related to land disputes. This approach has blocked agrarian reform, and its military component has resulted in the repression and mass displacement of populations. In Colombia and Peru, violence related to insurgency and counter-insurgency operations has caused mass displacement.

Map by András Bereznay

Map 5.1   The Americas

The forced displacement or dislocation of civilian populations in Latin America is not merely a by-product of armed confrontations but an end in itself. Forced dislocation for the control of territories rich in oil or mineral resources, in particular, is a major cause of conflict and displacement. In Mexico, the 1994 uprising in Chiapas coincided with the signing of the North American Free Trade Agreement (NAFTA), seen by many as a further step towards socio-economic disenfranchisement.

In Colombia, in particular, but also elsewhere in the Americas, internal displacement is heavily attributed to the activities of paramilitary forces whose strong connection with government security forces and the land-owning elite allows them to commit human rights abuses against indigenous populations with impunity. In some cases, paramilitaries have labelled indigenous people as guerrilla supporters in order to have a reason to uproot them and appropriate their lands for illicit crop cultivation or to serve the interests of large landholders. In Colombia – by far the most violent country in the Americas – the head of the paramilitary umbrella organization, the United Self-Defence Groups of Colombia (AUC), publicly declared that the organization would target social workers and trade unionists considered agents of the insurgency (UNCHR, 16 March 1999, p16).

The proliferation of drug cartels in Colombia and Peru considerably complicates the overall political landscape in these countries. Tripartite alliances between security forces, drug traffickers and wealthy landowners finance paramilitary groups to defend their interests. At the same time, guerrilla movements create and manage their own networks for the use of drug-trafficking profits for armed activities. Residents of coca cultivation zones may be forced by one or more of the parties to the conflict to participate in illicit activities, under threat of violence or expulsion from their homes.

Conditions of Displacement

Due to the traditional class struggle present in most countries of the Americas, landless indigenous populations have generally been stigmatized as politically subversive. As a result, these populations have often been the target of violent counter-insurgency reprisals by military and paramilitary groups, conducted without respect for human rights and humanitarian principles. In Guatemala, Mayan IDPs were widely considered to be associated with the uprising in that country and were consequently forced from their homes into camps controlled by the army, or were required to join counter-insurgency defence patrols. Similarly, in Peru the displaced were obliged to join defence patrols or face prison sentences for suspected ties with the terrorist group Sendero Luminoso (Shining Path).

The stigma associated with being displaced in the Americas, as well as the fear of being the target of further attacks, has meant that IDPs regularly do not register with authorities or request assistance. Even for those who would wish to register, the lack of identity documents – either because they were confiscated or because they were not issued at birth – prevents people from gaining access to social services and other assistance.

IDPs in the Americas are, for the most part, dispersed as opposed to grouped in organized camps. IDPs of indigenous origin have fled to mountainous regions and other rugged terrain, living in often desperate conditions with little food and nearly no medical supplies. Other displaced populations have found shelter with host communities where cultural ties have provided some social support. In Colombia, the stigmatization of IDPs is so strong that resident communities have been reluctant to play host to people displaced by conflict. As a result, many IDPs have been forced to find minimal shelter in urban slums with impoverished populations. There they live in abject poverty, often with no sources of income, no proper water or sanitation, and no access to medical care and education. In addition, they often face particularly intense discrimination: blacks, Indians and other non-Spanish speaking groups are considered undesirable neighbours by the authorities and resident populations alike.

National and International Response

Governments in the Americas have increasingly acknowledged the problem of internal displacement in their respective countries and have taken some steps to address it. In Colombia, national legislation concerning IDPs is more advanced than anywhere else in the world, although important parts of it remain to be implemented. Many of the peace agreements in the region have included provisions relating to the return and reintegration of the displaced; but these provisions have often never been realized. For example, even though the return of IDPs was an integral part of the 1996 peace agreements in Guatemala, the government has failed to carry out all of its commitments in this regard, and the national land agency has been reluctant to allocate land to the displaced. In Peru, the government's Project in Support of Repopulation (PAR), which has focused on the resettlement of IDP populations, has not established any programmes to integrate those people wishing to stay in urban centres.

A strong civil society in the Americas has been influential in organizing the displaced into self-help and advocacy groups. A vast network of solidarity and civil society associations has encouraged the development of IDP organizations capable of articulating claims, bringing their governments to the negotiating table, and drawing international attention to their plight. Some of the most powerful of these groups have been the National Council of the Displaced in Guatemala (CONDEG), the Reconstruction and Development Association of the Andean Communities in Peru, as well as a number of influential non-governmental organizations (NGOs) in Colombia. IDPs in both Peru and Colombia have formed national coordination bodies.

Regionally, there are various noteworthy initiatives in Latin America aimed at tackling the problem of internal displacement. These include the 1989 International Conference on Central American Refugees (CIREFCA) and the UN Development Programme for Displaced Persons, Refugees and Returnees in Central America (PRODERE) – both focused on the reintegration of uprooted populations. In addition, the Inter-American Commission on Human Rights of the Organization of American States (OAS) appointed a special rapporteur for IDPs in 1996. The commission was, in fact, the first regional body to endorse the UN Guiding Principles and apply them to its work. However, under-funding seriously limits its impact. The creation, in 1992, of the Permanent Consultation on Internal Displacement in the Americas (CPDIA) is yet another initiative, providing technical assistance to government, as well as support to displaced persons' associations.

Among international humanitarian agencies, the International Committee of the Red Cross (ICRC) has often been the most active in providing for the displaced. Its strict neutrality, mandate to safeguard international humanitarian law, and care for civilian victims of war at large place it in the best position to gain access to affected IDPs in all sides of conflict zones. In Colombia and Mexico, the ICRC is one of the few international organizations working directly with IDPs.

Endnotes

1 Conservative figures from the Brookings-CUNY Project on Internal Displacement and the US Committee for Refugees estimate that 1 million people were displaced during the 1980s in Guatemala, El Salvador, Nicaragua and Honduras, in addition to 600,000 IDPs in Peru, and 250,000 in Haiti. See Cohen and Sanchez-Garzoli, May 2001.

2 At the height of conflict in Mexico, Peru and Guatemala, IDP figures reached 40,000, 600,000 and 750,000 respectively.

3 The US Committee for Refugees (USCR) estimated at end 1996 that the number of IDPs in the Americas was 1,220,000; the Norwegian Refugee Council (NRC) estimates the number in 2002 to be 2,260,000.

Colombia

The displacement of populations in Colombia has been an endemic feature of the country's almost 40-year civil war. The deep-seated and complex conflict pits varying armed groups against one another – each with different interests and different affiliations. Although the armed factions have changed over the years, they are commonly described in one of three categories: armed insurgents, paramilitary groups, and the official military and police. During the course of the unrelenting conflict, people forced to flee their homes have often remained silent, fearful of being the target of further attacks. Extreme levels of political violence, serious human rights abuses and use of terror by all sides have worked to marginalize and threaten Colombian civilians in nearly every corner of the country.

Figures

Colombia is rated among the countries with the largest internally displaced population in the world, after Sudan, Angola and the Democratic Republic of Congo (DRC). Over 2 million people are estimated to have been displaced as a result of violence since 1985. According to local NGOs, 1 million of these people are children displaced over the past five years (Solivida/ IOM/Defensoria del Pueblo, 2002). Since 2000, the numbers of new displacements have been unprecedented. In 2001 alone, 342,000 persons were said to have been newly displaced, and in 2000 some 317,000 (CODHES, 1 January 2001 and 15 February 2002). These numbers are disputed by the Colombian government, whose estimates are considerably lower: 190,000 IDPs for 2001 and 125,000 for 2000 (UNCHR, 11 March 2002).[1]

Reliable figures are nearly impossible to establish due to under-registration and the multiple waves of displacement in the country. Nevertheless, observers agree that the annual number of new displacements has increased significantly since 1995.

According to the UN High Commissioner for Refugees (UNHCR), indigenous and black populations constitute one third of the IDP population even though they make up only 11 per cent of the national population (USDOS, 2001, Colombia, sect1g). Their disproportionately high numbers can be explained by the proximity of indigenous communities to designated reserves containing 95 per cent of the nation's natural resources.

Background to the Conflict

Colombia is burdened with a long history of violence characterized by economic margin-alization and socio-political exclusion of low-income farmers by wealthy landowners. In Colombia, possession of land has always been at the heart of the war. It is estimated that 3 per cent of landowners own more than 70 per cent of arable land in the country. Strong ties between landowners, government officials and paramilitaries have blocked any serious agrarian reform.

Armed guerrilla movements first emerged in Colombia during the 1960s in reaction to the monopoly on power established by the Liberal and Conservative parties in 1957. The most notable of the groups were the National Liberation Army (ELN) and the Colombian Revolutionary Armed Forces (FARC), both initially engaged in armed struggles for land and social equity. By 1999, guerrillas were operating in 30 of the nation's 32 departments. At the same time, paramilitaries – who have the tacit support of the army and are opposed to the guerrillas and anyone suspected of sympathizing with them – were active in 40 per cent of the country. Violence in the countryside has become commonplace and, recently, has increasingly spilled over into urban centres.

Further embedding violence in the social fabric of Colombia are the narcotics industry and counter-measures launched to combat it. In response to Colombian narcotraffic, the US government launched Plan Colombia in 2000, a package worth US$1.3 billion aimed at eradicating illegal drug activities in the Caqueta and Putumayo departments. 80 per cent of US anti-drug funding has come in the form of military assistance. This has led to a rise in generalized violence in the targeted regions, with further arms proliferation. Human rights organizations say that clashes between army-backed paramilitaries and FARC insurgents in these areas have intensified and the humanitarian situation worsened since 2000.

Causes of Displacement

Forced displacement of civilians in Colombia is not merely a by-product of confrontations between armed groups. Assassinations, intimidation and personal threats are the main reasons given by IDPs for fleeing. Indeed, direct confrontation between different parties to the conflict is rare. Instead, parties to the conflict settle scores by attacking civilians suspected of sympathizing with the 'other' side. Displacement in Colombia is a deliberate strategy of war wielded to establish control over strategic territories, to expand the cultivation of illicit crops, and to take possession of land and private properties.[2]

Peace negotiations between the government and FARC ended in January 2002, and the military took over the so-called 'de-militarized zone' between the departments of Meta and Caqueta, which had been granted to FARC in the 1998 peace agreement. Since then there has been a significant increase in displacement.[3] Paramilitaries have launched punitive raids against populations in the former de-militarized zone for their presumed affiliation with FARC guerrillas. In this, as in other areas of Colombia, civilians find themselves in a lose–lose situation. Whether they remain or flee, their actions are interpreted by one faction or another as a political choice, for which they often pay with their lives.

Due to the tight control of the armed groups and their networks, civilians find it difficult to escape persecution. For this reason, they often flee discreetly, in small groups and families, or as individuals. One notable exception to this pattern was the mass displacement of 10,000 people in Magdalena between January and mid February 2002. The British Broadcasting Company (BBC) correspondent who reported on the displacement estimated that it was the most serious population movement since 1998. The exodus was caused by a regional conflict involving several right-wing paramilitary groups, allied under the umbrella United Self-Defence Groups of Colombia (AUC).

As in many war-affected countries, flight in Colombia is generally from rural areas – where state presence is weak and where armed insurgents are active – to urban and semi-urban centres, triggering an accelerated urbanization process. Tens of thousands of Colombians forced to flee their homes have attempted to fit into the overcrowded slum dwellings of Bogotá, Barranquilla, Medellín, Cali and Cartagena. Paradoxically, in their search for safety, humanitarian aid and work, displaced populations in the cities are often even more exposed to crime and violence.

By the end of 2001, the departments with the most IDP arrivals were: Antioquia, Cauca, Bolívar, Nariño, Cesar, Magdalena, and Valle del Cauca. The main departments of IDP expulsions were Magdalena, Norte de Santander, Cordoba, Sucre, Bolivar, Meta and Caqueta and Putumayo. As of March 2002, a total of 816 of the 1100 Colombian municipalities were affected by forced displacement, up from 480 municipalities in 2000 (BBC Monitoring, 24 March 2002).

Protection and Living Conditions

Colombia is one of the most dangerous places in the world, with thresholds of violence beyond comparison. The precariousness in which displaced persons live places them at particular risk of human rights abuses. Many people who have fled to metropolitan slums are displaced once again from this minimal refuge, victims of unidentified squads who purge major cities of 'undesirable' residents, including IDPs and other poverty-stricken populations. As a result of the high level of violence against them, both during and after flight, displaced Colombians have been reluctant to register with authorities or even to seek humanitarian assistance.

Living conditions for IDPs are extremely poor, particularly in urban slums where they tend to congregate. Given the circumstances in which displacement occurs, people rarely have time to make provision for their flight and have to find the most basic shelter in dilapidated structures, or in makeshift constructions. They lack proper access to water and sanitation, often living next to streams of waste. In 2001, human rights organizations estimated that only 34 per cent of IDPs had access to health services (USDOS, 2001, Colombia, sect1g). This is complicated by the fact that many IDPs lack identification papers – a requirement when receiving medical assistance. In 2001, Médecins Sans Frontières (MSF) reported that among 36,000 beneficiaries of health projects in 26 different 'barrios', approximately 11,000 were internally displaced and only 275 of these possessed IDP cards (González Bustelo, December 2001, p69).

Legal Provisions

Despite the fact that Colombia has probably the most advanced IDP legislation in the world, the proliferation of institutional and legal arrangements pertaining to the displaced does not accurately reflect the reality on the ground. The government has pursued numerous measures to address the problem of internal displacement, but they have been widely criticized for their arbitrariness and inherently bureaucratic nature. Indeed, government humanitarian activities tend to be limited to handouts or three-month emergency packages, with little realistic assessment of needs or vulnerability.

To respond to the scope of displacement in the country, the Colombian government and parliament have adopted a number of IDP-specific laws and decrees. The centrepiece of Colombian IDP legislation is Law 387, promulgated in 1997. It provides for comprehensive coverage of the protection and assistance needs of the displaced during the various stages of displacement. The law also addresses ways of preventing displacement and stipulates the specific responsibilities of the various government agencies and institutions. On 12 December 2000, the government issued Decree 2569 to regulate and complement the provisions of Law 387, outlining the responsibilities of the Social Solidarity Network (RSS) – the government agency coordinating the National System of Comprehensive Assistance to IDPs. Some issues covered by the decree include government responsibility with regard to prevention and assistance, registration and the criteria for considering a person no longer displaced. An additional Law 589 – passed in 2000 – formally criminalized the displacement of civilian populations.

Map 5.2   Colombia: concentrations of IDPs by province (February 2002)

Sources: UNRC, 19 January 2001; CODHES, 5 and 15 February 2002

To strengthen the implementation of already existing legislation, the Colombian government promulgated Presidential Directive No 6 in October 2001. This directive confirms the
constitutional court's opinion that the UN Guiding Principles on Internal Displacement are
above national legislation and on the same level as the Colombian constitution. In addition,
the directive mandated the Social Solidarity Network to issue 'humanitarian orders' to
appropriate government officials for prompt action (within ten days) to prevent forced
displacement, and to protect and assist displaced persons.[4]

National and International Humanitarian Response

Despite security risks, local human rights and humanitarian agencies have been increasingly
active in providing IDPs with services such as legal advice, psycho-social support, food and
medical assistance. In 2000, IDP representatives formed a national coordinating body to lobby
for better government assistance. The targeted persecution of civil society leaders remains a
major obstacle to the work of national NGOs. As noted by the UN Representative on Internally
Displaced Persons, 127 leaders of indigenous displaced communities were assassinated
between 1998 and 1999.

While the largest international NGOs present in Colombia coordinate their operational
and advocacy activities under the umbrella organization DIAL (Diálogo Inter-Agencial), the
UN specialized agencies are coordinated by the UN High Commissioner for Refugees

Photo 5.1   A health promoter with a family displaced by war, Soacha, Colombia
(July 2001)

Source: Gervasio Sanchez/MSF

(UNHCR) and the UN Office for the Coordination of Humanitarian Affairs (UNOCHA). The International Committee of the Red Cross (ICRC) has the largest international presence in the country, providing emergency assistance and campaigning for the respect of international humanitarian law through 17 different field offices. The Office of the UN High Commissioner for Human Rights (UNHCHR) has also been particularly active on behalf of war-affected civilians, including IDPs. In April 2002, the European Union (EU) granted 8 million Euros for improving minimum standards of living for IDPs. Aid is to be provided as close as possible to areas of origin in order to prevent further displacement to urban centres.

Only a small percentage of IDPs are officially registered as such. This makes it difficult for humanitarian agencies to identify the most vulnerable populations and plan relief delivery. In an effort to remedy the situation, UNHCR has provided support to the Registrar's Office to promote the issuing of personal identification documents, which indirectly facilitates the effective and safe access by IDPs and other vulnerable groups to state benefits.

Access remains a major problem in Colombia. High levels of violence have impeded the delivery of assistance to many localities where IDPs concentrate. Guerrilla and paramilitary groups have commonly blocked the delivery of goods, including food rations and medicines, to areas inhabited by IDPs. The blockage of food supplies has been a strategy used by parties to the conflict to manipulate the movement of populations in and out of different areas.

Endnotes

1   The government does not consider displaced people as such after two years, and some have been displaced for over ten. (USDOS, February 2001).
2   Indeed, studies estimate that 70 per cent of IDPs have lost their lands. This phenomenon is further aggravated by the lack of identification papers required upon land titling and land reclamation (WFP, 8 September 1999)
3   This noted increase follows an already sharp rise in the level of displacement by 40 per cent from 2000 to 2001 (BBC, 24 March 2002)
4   The first humanitarian order was issued on 3 February 2002 in response to the humanitarian crisis in the region of Catatumbo, Norte de Santander.

Guatemala

UN agencies consider the IDP problem caused by Guatemala's 36-year civil war to be over, following the 1996 peace agreement. Other experts disagree, arguing that 250,000 people displaced by the war were still unable to return to their homes as of the end of 2001 (Bailliet, 10 December 2001). For the most part, these people receive little, if any, humanitarian assistance.

History

The struggle between reformers calling for economic and political changes and Guatemala's military government turned into a guerrilla war during the early 1960s. Over the following decades, an estimated 200,000 people were killed or disappeared, and about 1 million fled the country or became internally displaced (CEH, 1998, para1; USCR, 1999, p265). The indigenous populations in the departments of Petén, Quiché and Huehuetenango – viewed by the military as supporters of the insurgency – suffered particularly badly during the early 1980s. The internally displaced were scattered throughout the country, the vast majority finding refuge in the capital or on the southern coast. Some 50,000 indigenous people, calling themselves the Communities of People in Resistance (CPR), sought refuge in areas not under army control. The conflict finally ended when the government and representatives of the insurgency movement signed a number of peace accords in 1996. But some elements, such as the reintegration of the displaced, have been only partially implemented.

Figures

Current estimates of internal displacement vary between 0 and 250,000 persons. In 1997, the US Committee for Refugees (USCR) reported that there were 250,000 internally displaced people in Guatemala. As of end 1998, however, these IDPs were no longer included in the organization's listing of figures. The USCR explained that these populations were not

---

Box 5.1 *Guatemala: the unrecognized displaced*

The problem of internal displacement in Guatemala remains relevant because the majority of those displaced during the war have yet to attain recognition of their property restitution rights. According to a census sponsored by the UN Population Fund in May 1997, dispersed internally displaced people (IDPs) were calculated to total 242,386 persons.[1] Although the number is significant, the government chose not to recognize restitution rights for dispersed IDPs, and instead focused on the restitution right of refugees and 'collective' IDPs (Communities of People in Resistance – CPRs), who formed part of numerically smaller groups. The National Council of the Displaced in Guatemala (CONDEG) has accused the government of deliberately attempting to reduce the number of IDPs in order to avoid assuming responsibility for restitution. The land agencies in Guatemala state that many of the claims they receive are, indeed, from dispersed IDPs. Rather than being recognized as IDPs with a right to restitution, they are treated as part of the poor in general with no entitlement to property. In short, this group may be substantial in number but it has been deemed politically irrelevant in Guatemala by the state and international parties.[2]

Despite the fact that the peace accords in Guatemala have not been fully realized, particularly in relation to the reintegration of IDPs, Guatemala is now characterized as a protracted conflict situation. However, a devastating food crisis linked to drought, floods, soil erosion, inequitable land distribution and the fall of coffee prices on world markets have put the country's post-1996 stability under considerable strain. The complete absence of the rule of law has shaken society's faith in the government, as well as the democratic system itself. At the same time, the military and powerful non-state actors continue to occupy land taken during the war and appropriate additional property by way of forced evictions. There is a need for international efforts to assist IDPs in recovering their properties, thereby addressing the structural inequalities that are at the root of violence and displacement cycles.

Notes

1 Dispersed IDPs were also excluded from the International Conference on Central American Refugees (CIREFCA) and UN Development Programme for Displaced Persons, Refugees and Returnees in Central America (PRODERE) reintegration programmes, in part due to political reasons. See UNDP/UNHCR, May 1995, p11.
2 One exception is the Inter-American Commission on Human Rights (IACHR), which highlighted its concern for restitution needs of IDPs. See IACHR, 6 April 2001, pp238–240.

Author: C Bailliet

---

considered internally displaced for the purposes of its annual report because conflict or fear of persecution no longer impeded Guatemalans from returning home (USCR, 1999, p266). UN agencies also consider there to be no more internally displaced people in Guatemala. Other experts disagree, however, arguing that the 250,000 displaced people in Guatemala in 1997 remain so, since they have not regained their lands and have not resettled durably elsewhere in the country.

Several factors complicate an accurate assessment of the number of displaced in Guatemala. For one, no comprehensive surveys were conducted during the years of conflict, resulting in the use of widely varying figures for years. Secondly, many displaced in urban centres – fearing persecution – have preferred anonymity to seeking assistance. Thirdly, many displaced persons have either not felt comfortable with identifying themselves as 'displaced', or have simply not thought of themselves as such.

Protection and Living Conditions

As late as mid 2002, the Inter-American Commission on Human Rights (IACHR) reported that thousands of displaced persons still required access to basic services such as education and health care. In many cases, these people had not been incorporated within formal resettlement efforts, were marginalized from resident populations, and were living in extreme poverty. In the cities, displaced people lacked adequate housing and were squatting in abandoned buildings. The creation of durable housing solutions and a long-term rural development plan benefiting those uprooted during the conflict remained priority challenges for the government (IACHR, 6 April 2001).

The loss or destruction of personal identification documents during the conflict has also caused grave problems for thousands of displaced. Without documents, people are unable to carry out basic transactions, vote or access social services (IACHR, 6 April 2001). In 1997, a special law easing documentation procedures for the displaced and other vulnerable people was enacted for a three-year period. It was later extended to the end of 2001. In June 2001, however, the UN Human Rights Verification Mission in Guatemala (MINUGUA) still deplored the lack of progress in providing documentation to those in need (MINUGUA, June 2001).

Return and Resettlement

By the end of the 1980s, the signing of a Central American peace plan (Esquipulas II) and a return to civilian rule in Guatemala put the country on the path to peace. In June 1994, even prior to the final peace agreements of 1996, an accord was formulated by the government and by representatives of the insurgency movements to return and resettle uprooted populations. This accord provided guarantees for returning refugees and IDPs, most significantly with respect to land rights and economic reintegration. A technical commission was subsequently created to supervise the implementation of resettlement projects. In addition, a 'consultative assembly' has been established for displaced communities to express their needs and opinions to the technical commission.

The reintegration of the displaced as stipulated in the accords has been significantly delayed, and a new timetable for this element of the peace agreements was established at the end of 2000. While IDPs were specifically mentioned in the 1994 Resettlement Accord, many displaced have not been recognized as such and do not receive sufficient support from the state (IACHR, 6 April 2001). Furthermore, financial resources required to implement the 1994 accord have been minimal, and over time the government has shifted its strategy towards targeting poor populations as a whole, rather than focusing specifically on the displaced.

Six years after the end of the civil war, thousands of IDPs still lacked access to their land or security of tenure. Competition for scarce land resources intensified divisions in some regions, and many returnees were turned away on the pretext that communities were 'full'. The Guatemalan government blamed slow progress on resettlement on lack of land documentation, widespread squatting, high land prices, outstanding mortgages and disagreement among leadership groups (IACHR, 6 April 2001; MINUGUA, 26 July 2000).

Returning refugees in Guatemala also reported serious difficulties in reintegrating. According to the US State Department, 40 former refugee families decided to return to Mexico in August 2001, where they had previously found refuge, citing a lack of support from the Guatemalan government towards meeting their needs. Another 1500 former refugees have also expressed their wish to return to Mexico, should they be unable to regain their lands in Guatemala (USDOS, 2002, Guatemala, sect1d).

Response

Local human rights organizations working on behalf of the displaced have often been harassed. In 1998, the Roman Catholic Archbishop's Human Rights Office in Guatemala published *Never Again*, a report that reviewed, among other themes, the human rights violations suffered by displaced people. The leader of this project was murdered two days after the release of the report. Despite the risks, a handful of grassroots organizations continue to advocate for the displaced, the largest being the National Council of the Displaced in Guatemala (CONDEG), formed in 1989 to assist families in obtaining land and housing.

Only a couple of international organizations work with the displaced in Guatemala. The UN Development Programme (UNDP) has worked to ensure the implementation of the Resettlement Agreement. The UN High Commissioner for Refugees (UNHCR) has assisted some of the displaced in the context of refugee return. The UN General Assembly has mandated MINUGUA to verify the Global Agreement on Human Rights, signed in Mexico on 21 March 1994, and to monitor the various other peace agreements.

Mexico

Violent land disputes have been the cause of small-scale displacements in the southern Mexican states of Oaxaca, Guerrero and Chiapas for decades. More large-scale internal displacement occurred following the 1994 insurgency of the Zapatista Army of National Liberation (EZLN). Fighting broke out when government security forces attempted to stop EZLN's territorial expansion in Chiapas by deploying military as well as paramilitary troops in the region. At its height, the conflict forced up to 40,000 people – most of them indigenous peasants from Chiapas – to flee their homes. By the end of 2001, between 7000 and 10,000 people remained displaced in the mountainous region of the tropical Lacandon Forest (USDOS, 2002, Mexico, sect5; SIPAZ, 4 December 2001).

Background

The San Andres accords, signed by the then Mexican President Ernesto Zedillo and the EZLN in 1996, recognized indigenous rights and culture. The accord was, however, never ratified and a series of amendments rendered it ineffective. Hopes were raised by the election of Vicente Fox as president in 2000 and the subsequent reinvigoration of the stalled peace process in Chiapas. An indigenous rights and culture bill – a package of constitutional reforms building on the San Andres accords – was submitted to congress. But the bill was significantly amended and ultimately fell short of the indigenous people's demands for certain civic, cultural and land rights. President Fox hailed it as some proof of the resolution of the conflict in Chiapas; but the bill was rejected by the EZLN as well as by indigenous rights advocates.

Causes of Displacement

There are widely differing interpretations of the causes of displacement in Chiapas. NGOs and the displaced themselves say the government is waging 'low-intensity' warfare to remove indigenous communities from their ancestral lands. They say the government is protecting the political and economic interests of the ruling elite and wealthy landowners, specifically through the opening of the resource-rich mountains of Chiapas to foreign and private investment (CIEPAC, 28 August 1999; Schwartz and Saliba, 28 February 2002).

In contrast, Mexican authorities identify inter-community, inter-ethnic and religious conflicts as the root causes of displacement in the country.

The Mexican government has been criticized for polarizing civil society in Chiapas into pro-government and Zapatista groups by giving access to land and preferential treatment to the former. Proxy-war tactics such as these have functioned to fuel intra-community violence in Chiapas for decades. Since 2001, political and land disputes have even emerged between formerly allied indigenous organizations.

The military has repeatedly been accused of human rights abuses and excessive use of force against likely sympathizers of rebel groups in Chiapas (USDOS, 2002, Mexico, sect1). Despite regular reports of extra-judicial killings, torture and disappearances, the military continue to enjoy impunity, while civilians and human right advocates who have denounced abuses have suffered reprisals, threats and death (HRW, 5 December 2001).

Other perpetrators of violence in Chiapas include paramilitary groups, the most powerful of which is the Peace and Justice group. Paramilitaries have committed acts of violence with the tacit acquiescence of local authorities against anyone perceived to be sympathetic to the EZLN.

Human Rights and Humanitarian Needs

Internal displacement has mainly affected the indigenous rural poor in Chiapas. Most displaced have been treated as second-class citizens, marginalized from national political and economic spheres. They have been the targets of abuse, discrimination and acts of intimidation, including death threats (Cohen and Sanchez-Garzoli, May 2001, p5). The fact that many displaced people lack personal documentation and do not speak Spanish has excluded them from government-support programmes, credit facilities and public education. They have also been discriminated against in the job market.

Although security concerns and paramilitary harassments have remained a threat to indigenous communities, some gradual return movements took place in 2000, following government assurances of safety and assistance. A further 1336 people from the civil society group Las Abejas (the Bees) in Chenhaló returned to their communities between August and October 2001. This movement was prompted by a lack of access to drinking water and firewood, as well as an International Committee of the Red Cross (ICRC) decision to reduce food rations by 50 per cent (SIPAZ, 4 December 2001; USDOS, 2002, Mexico, sect5).

In Chiapas, displaced people have fled higher into the mountainous tropical forest. There, few are able to adapt to the cold climate with ease, and malnutrition has claimed the lives of the most vulnerable. IDPs have had difficulty in providing for themselves in the rugged environment and are inaccessible to humanitarian agencies. In 1999, 80 per cent of the inhabitants of the highland jungle were reported to be malnourished (CDHFBC, 1999, sectV).

National and International Response

In an effort to improve the human rights situation in Mexico, President Fox and UN High Commissioner for Refugees Sadako Ogata signed an agreement on technical assistance in this area in December 2000. The president also appointed a special ambassador for human rights with a mandate to ensure that the government complies with its human rights commitments.

The situation on the ground still gives cause for concern. People in Chiapas are systematically subjected to interrogations at military checkpoints. Humanitarian access to pro-EZLN areas and places where IDPs congregate has been tightly restricted (USDOS, 2001, Mexico, sect4). Furthermore, human rights workers, NGOs and clergy working with the displaced have commonly faced harassment, death threats or expulsion from the country, or even murder.

As of 2001, the EZLN had entered a new 'resistance' phase where it now seeks to put autonomy into practice and has rejected any form of government support. For this reason, only a few international organizations, such as the Mexican Red Cross and the ICRC, are working directly with the internally displaced populations in Chiapas. By the end of 2001, ICRC was providing food to over 7000 IDPs in Los Altos. Non-governmental organizations and church associations have also actively helped the displaced, albeit with limited resources.

Peru

Displacement in Peru is the result of a 20-year struggle between the Peruvian armed forces and two left-wing revolutionary groups. Sendero Luminoso (Shining Path) and the Túpac Amaru Revolutionary Movement launched separate guerrilla wars in 1980 and 1984, respectively. The total number of persons displaced by the violence during the 1980s and the early 1990s was between 430,000 and 600,000 persons. By the end of 2000, all but 60,000 displaced people had either returned or settled permanently in their current locations (USCR, 2001, p291). Since 2000, Peruvian NGOs have reported new waves of small-scale displacement in isolated rural areas following political violence and the government's forcible eradication of coca fields (CNDDHH, June 2002, p94).

Protection Concerns

Despite general improvements in the overall security environment in Peru since 1992, human rights abuses since then have persisted. At the same time, individuals who have sought to speak out against injustices or to help vulnerable populations, including IDPs, have been persecuted. Leaders of IDP organizations and local NGOs have regularly been threatened and, in some cases, killed. Church organizations helping the internally displaced have also been subject to attack. Leaders of displaced communities and human rights activists were often arrested for suspected 'terrorist' ties.

As of 2002, restrictions on freedom of movement instituted at the height of the armed conflict in Peru remained in effect. Though the government finally eliminated 'emergency zones' (areas in which access was prohibited to travellers, including human rights monitors) in 2001, public transport and private vehicles continued to be stopped and searched at checkpoints throughout the country.

Photo 5.2   Breakfast distribution to displaced children, Ayacucho, Peru (1990)

Source: Cristina Fedele/ICRC

Documentation Needs

Many displaced persons lack basic documentation, such as birth certificates and voter registration cards, which makes it difficult for them to secure social assistance. The government's Project in Support of Repopulation (PAR) has provided documentation that IDPs can use both to request PAR assistance to return to their communities of origin and to apply for national identity cards. In 1999, the government provided provisional identity documents to more than 356,000 people, many of them displaced. However, only 21,000 of those people then applied for and received permanent documents (Cohen and Sanchez-Garzoli, May 2001, p6).

Return Programmes

There are no agreed figures of how many displaced people have returned to their places of origin since 1995. While PAR estimates that almost half have returned, NGOs estimate less than 100,000 have gone home (CNDDHH, June 2002, p93; USDOS, 2000, Peru, sect2d). However, the government concedes that the majority of the displaced persons have not returned permanently to their original communities. This is due to a variety of factors, including lack of assistance and economic opportunities as well as pockets of insecurity. Indeed, there is no consensus about how many displaced people who returned were assisted through PAR, and estimates vary between 20,900 and 600,000 (CNDDHH, June 2002, p93; USDOS, 2001, Peru, sect2d).

In addition, PAR did not provide any assistance to the displaced people who wished to settle in the cities and other areas of refuge. In 1999, the Mesa Nacional sobre Desplazamiento y Afectados por Violencia Política (MENADES) reported that 80 per cent of the 350,000 persons who had by then not returned home, preferred to settle permanently in their current locations (USCR, 2001, p291). The Mesa also said that, although many no longer wanted to be called displaced, they were still being counted as such since they required special attention and assistance from the government (USCR, 2001, p291).

Response

In Peru, displaced women have formed their own organizations to raise awareness of their rights and needs (Cohen and Sanchez-Garzoli, May 2001, p12). UN agencies such as the UN Development Programme (UNDP), the World Food Programme (WFP) and the UN Children's Fund (UNICEF) have, in various ways, supported poverty-stricken populations in Peru. The International Committee of the Red Cross (ICRC) has also been involved in work with internally displaced people. NGOs have disseminated the UN Guiding Principles on Internal Displacement in the country and used its provisions as standards in monitoring and evaluating national policies and laws.

6

Asia and the Pacific

Regional Overview

As of early 2002, over 4.6 million people were internally displaced because of armed conflict in Asia and the Pacific, with another 3.4 million exiled across borders as refugees. These figures do not include displacement due to man-made or natural disasters, both of which are major causes of displacement in the region.

Indonesia has been one of the worst hit countries, with a displaced population of 1.3 million. Afghanistan and Sri Lanka both have close to 1 million internally displaced people (IDPs), and there are several hundred thousand in Bangladesh, Burma, India and The Philippines. Internal displacement is less acute, but still unresolved, in the Solomon Islands, Pakistan and Uzbekistan. Lack of information has excluded China from this survey, but it is commonly understood that forced resettlement and other violations of human rights have caused internal displacement in that country, too.

The launch of the global 'war on terrorism' since 11 September 2001 has had an impact on the situation of internally displaced people in Asia. Asylum regulations have been tightened and refugee barriers have been erected in many Western countries, including Australia, meaning that people fleeing conflict may be left with no other option than to seek protection within the borders of their native countries. Furthermore, the escalated counter-terrorist operations initiated by some Asian countries have raised concerns among human rights observers that personal and civil liberties may be infringed and the protection of vulnerable groups such as the internally displaced ultimately undermined.

Conflict Patterns and Main Causes of Displacement

Although the conflicts causing internal displacement are not directly interrelated in Asia, there are common patterns of shared colonial experiences, incomplete state-building, and regional, cultural and religious factors. Although seemingly ethnic or religious in nature, many conflicts in Asia are rooted in poverty and the exclusion of certain regions or social groups from the economic development process. These socio-economic divisions have been translated into political tensions and the stigmatization of certain ethnic or religious groups – often manipulated by local elites. The inter-religious conflict in the Maluku province of Indonesia, which has since 1999 resulted in the displacement of over 250,000 people, is a good illustration of how economic disparities and their exploitation by politicians and the military can fuel religious polarization and conflict.

Transmigration policies have often been at the root of conflicts in the region, especially in Indonesia and the Solomon Islands where violence has been linked to growing ethnic or

Map 6.1   Asia and the Pacific

Map by András Bereznay

religious differences and land disputes. The economic success and political predominance of migrant groups in the context of depressed national economies has created deep resentment among local populations. Major population movements in Indonesia prompted by President Suharto during the 1960s planted the seeds of contemporary conflicts in that country. Recurrent clashes between Madurese migrants and indigenous Dayak in West and Central Kalimantan have, since 1997, forced large numbers of Madurese to flee their homes, and in North Maluku, tensions between Muslim Makianese migrants and local Christians escalated into conflict and the mass displacement of people during 1999. Likewise, in the Solomon Islands, migrant Malaitans who dominated the capital Honiara were ultimately forced from their homes in June 1999 by local Guadalcanalese militias who, among other grievances, were frustrated by the lack of economic opportunities for indigenous people.

Fighting between secessionist movements and the ruling state has been a main cause for displacement in Burma, Sri Lanka, The Philippines (southern island of Mindanao) and in western Indonesia (Aceh). In many cases, it has been a strategy of government troops to forcibly displace civilians as a means of weakening the resource base of the insurgents. Displacement in north-east India reflects a situation where ethnic tensions arising from migrant influxes, land disputes and limited access to political or economic power have led to the emergence of secessionist movements, which often use violence to force immigrants out.

Other causes of displacement in Asia include the conflict between India and Pakistan for the disputed Kashmir region, civil and international war in Afghanistan and the assimilation policies and disputed land issues in the Chittagong Hill Tracts (CHT) in eastern Bangladesh. Displacement in Uzbekistan is the result of conflict between the government and Islamic groups.

Human Rights and Humanitarian Needs

IDPs throughout Asia are exposed to a number of violations of humanitarian and human rights law, including indiscriminate bombing of civilian areas, forced labour, forced recruitment, land mines and restrictions on freedom of movement.

In Afghanistan, the security of displaced people and other civilians was undermined during the US-led bombing campaign. Thousands of civilians were killed, including IDPs, in part as a result of the location of military garrisons near heavily populated areas (Conetta, January 2002; Herold, December 2001). In Burma, large numbers of people have been forcibly relocated and exposed to forced labour, while others hide in the jungle where they are at risk of malnutrition and lack access to health services. In Sri Lanka's government-run welfare centres, home to some 185,000 IDPs, men could be reportedly at risk of 'disappearance' after being taken into custody by the military, while women could be exposed to physical abuse and exploitation.

The needs and overall conditions of displacement in Asia are far from homogenous and reflect a wide range of circumstances. The difficult situation facing many internally displaced people is compounded by the fact that authorities in most Asian countries lack the political will or the national capacity to respond efficiently to their needs. People fleeing the civil and international war in Afghanistan were particularly at risk as the population as a whole was already facing poverty and destitution, and the authorities lacked the resources and willingness to provide assistance. Some Afghans reportedly walked for weeks in search of assistance, only to end up in overcrowded camps where assistance was limited or non-existent.

The psychological impact of war and displacement has been reported as a need that must be addressed urgently in most countries. Prolonged stay in Sri Lankan welfare centres has resulted in suicide rates three times those of the rest of the country. In central Sulawesi,

Indonesia, a government study of IDPs conducted in 2001 showed that between 55 and 60 per cent suffered from psychological troubles associated with violence, loss of property and forced displacement. In Afghanistan, the overwhelming majority of the IDPs have known nothing other than war and violence over the last 25 years, making the psychological rehabilitation of the country as urgent as its physical reconstruction.

In many conflict areas, displaced and host communities have been equally affected by war. This is especially the case for civilians displaced by the fighting on Mindanao Island in The Philippines, who were forced to seek shelter in urban centres or in neighbouring villages where the host population was already suffering the hardships of war. Similarly, in Sri Lanka, any distinction in terms of needs between IDPs and the local population living in the Vanni region makes little sense, as an embargo on food and non-food items, initiated in 1991, has left the whole population in the area without electricity, running water or access to basic health or educational services.

Return and Resettlement

During 2001 and early 2002, some positive developments emerged with regard to the return of displaced populations. In The Philippines, the vast majority of the more than 1 million people displaced by intense fighting on the southern Island of Mindanao during 2000 have been able to go home. Since the fall of the Taliban in Afghanistan in 2001, large numbers of IDPs have been able to return even though many had to temporarily resettle outside their home areas because of continued conflict. Also in Sri Lanka, the newly elected government and the Liberation Tigers of Tamil Eelam (LTTE) agreed in December 2001 – after 19 years of conflict – to engage in peace negotiations. Meanwhile, the easing of the embargo on the Vanni region in the north and the lifting of travel restrictions for Tamils allowed for some limited return by early 2002.

The Role of Regional Organizations

There are no regional mechanisms in Asia to deal with problems of internal displacement. The reluctance of inter-governmental regional organizations such as the Association of South-East Asian Nations (ASEAN) or the South Asian Association for Regional Cooperation (SAARC) to discuss this issue at the regional level is linked to their strong adherence to the concept of state sovereignty and non-interference in each other's affairs. Most regional efforts to coordinate and improve the response to internal displacement in Asia stem from non-governmental efforts. As Roberta Cohen of the Brookings–City University of New York (CUNY) Project on Internal Displacement has remarked, there is a 'sharp disconnect between the concerns of the civil society and those of their governments when it comes to the issue of forced displacement' (Cohen, 2000).

Afghanistan

Even before the events of 2001, Afghanistan was a country devastated by decades of foreign interference, civil war and the breakdown of central government. During the nine-year Soviet occupation, it was the source of the world's biggest refugee problem, with no fewer than 5 million people seeking shelter across the borders in Pakistan and Iran. At the beginning of 2001, with the fundamentalist Taliban regime in power, some 600,000 Afghans were estimated to be displaced within the country, victims of intermittent clashes between factional warlords and natural disasters such as drought.

Following the US-led intervention against the Taliban later that year, that figure rose to 900,000. By 2002, many had returned to their homes. But other civilians – mostly ethnic Pashtuns fleeing persecution in the north – were being newly displaced. As of mid 2002, the total IDP figure in Afghanistan stood at 1.2 million.[1]

Political Situation

In 1996, some seven years after the Soviet withdrawal from Afghanistan, the Taliban threw out the feuding and ineffective government of former anti-Soviet guerrilla leaders. Made up primarily of ethnic Pashtuns, the Taliban had strong support from elements in the Pakistani government, particularly the intelligence services. Though fighting against rebel forces of the Northern Alliance continued throughout their five years in power, by September 2001 the Taliban controlled close to 95 per cent of Afghan territory. Only small pockets in the mountainous north and central areas of the country remained in the hands of the insurgents.

The regime quickly collapsed with the US-led intervention in October 2001, and an Afghan Interim Authority was established with wide international support in December 2001. Hundreds of thousands of refugees and IDPs soon returned to their communities of origin, the majority of them spontaneously without any outside assistance. By April 2002, scarcely five months later, an estimated 250,000 IDPs and 465,000 refugees were said to have returned home (USAID/USDCHA/USOFDA, 12 April 2002).

Despite a relative calming of the situation in 2002, fighting and insecurity persisted in many parts of Afghanistan. The US, UK and France retained significant levels of troops in the country in their hunt for Al Qa'ida, the extremist Islamic organization blamed for the 11 September suicide attacks on New York and Washington, and its leader Osama bin Laden. Revenge attacks against Pashtun communities in the north were on the rise and many were forced to flee.[2] Kuchi nomads were also targeted. Foreign peacekeeping forces had no mandate outside Kabul and no effective international protection could be provided outside of the capital.[3] In early 2002, only 10 per cent of the displaced population in the Pashtun heartlands in the south expressed a willingness to return to their home communities, citing security concerns as a major reason for their decision to stay away (Marshall, 25 February 2002).

Figures and Patterns of Flight

According to the UN, the distribution of IDPs as of mid 2002 was:

- 600,000 in the northern and north-eastern provinces;
- 275,000 in the south;
- 250,000–300,000 in the west;
- 100,000 in Kabul; and
- 60,000 in the central region.

It should be noted that these figures are only rough estimates and do not distinguish between populations fleeing conflict and those escaping drought. Also included in these figures are a number of urban migrants seeking the humanitarian aid provided in IDP camps.[4]

People forced from their homes have often moved to neighbouring provinces; others have flocked to urban centres. In some cases, people have been forced to travel for weeks to reach IDP camps, only to arrive at overcrowded sites without enough supplies. The vulnerability

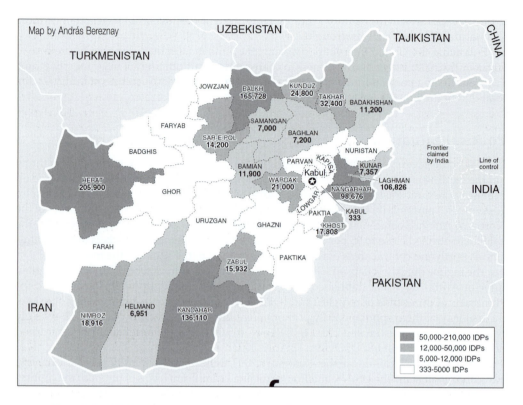

Map by András Bereznay

UZBEKISTAN

TAJIKISTAN

CHINA

TURKMENISTAN

JOWZJAN

BALKH
165,728

KUNDUZ
24,800

TAKHAR
32,400

BADAKHSHAN
11,200

FARYAB

SAMANGAN
7,000

SAR-E POL
14,200

BAGHLAN
7,200

BADGHIS

NURISTAN

Frontier
claimed
by India

Line of
control

BAMIAN
11,900

PARVAN

KAPISA

Kabul

KUNAR
7,357

HERAT
205,900

GHOR

WARDAK
21,000

LAGHMAN
106,826

NANGARHAR
98,676

INDIA

LOWGAR

URUZGAN

GHAZNI

PAKTIA

KHOST
17,808

KABUL
333

FARAH

ZABUL
15,932

PAKTIKA

PAKISTAN

IRAN

NIMROZ
18,916

HELMAND
6,951

KANDAHAR
136,110

50,000-210,000 IDPs

12,000-50,000 IDPs

5,000-12,000 IDPs

333-5000 IDPs

Map 6.2   Afghanistan: concentrations of IDPs by province (February 2002)

Note: This map does not include estimated positions and numbers of IDPs. As a result, this map is accurate but incomplete.

Source: AIMS, 20 February 2002

of host communities is itself a cause of serious concern. The Afghan population on the whole has to struggle to survive in an unforgiving terrain with few natural resources. Out of the total population of 24 million, some 9 million persons are expected to require assistance in 2002 (UN, January 2002, p6).

Protection

Due to failed state structures and the limited international presence, the displaced continue to have serious protection concerns. In the past, civilians were only able to secure physical protection by siding with either the Taliban or commanders of the armed opposition. In general, ethnic Pashtuns sought protection from the Taliban while other ethnic minorities, such as Tajiks, Uzbeks and Hazaras, kept ties with groups in the opposition.

During the US-led bombing campaign in Afghanistan, IDPs and civilians alike were vulnerable to attack due to the conduct of military operations in close proximity to civilian populations. Independent reports published since the campaign indicate that thousands of civilians were killed as a result of bombing near heavily populated areas.[5] During this period, IDPs were also vulnerable to forced recruitment by Taliban forces in the camps. Since the end of the bombing campaign and the defeat of the Taliban, protection of IDPs continues to be of concern. A Médecins Sans Frontières (MSF) survey of the Maslakh camp near the western city of Heart showed IDPs at risk from persistent crime, ethnic tensions and intimidation, as well as unequal distribution of food aid.

Land mines also pose a major threat to populations fleeing to the countryside or towards national borders. One quarter of last year's land-mine victims were people who were either fleeing or following traditional nomadic lifestyles (ICRC, 4 October 2001). The use of cluster bombs by the US military is another danger. These bombs fragment into 'bomblets', of which an average 20 per cent fail to explode on impact, leaving lethal anti-personnel devices scattered on the ground (MSF, 18 January 2002).

The Taliban imposed a strict version of Islamic Sharia, and numerous laws limited women's freedom and excluded them from political and economic participation in society. Displaced women were particularly affected by these restrictions, especially those women whose husbands had stayed behind or had been arrested or killed. Displaced widows often married a close male relative in order to secure some measure of protection (Farr, 2001, p134)

Food and Health Needs

The problem of conflict-induced displacement has been aggravated by a drought that has, for the past four years, severely hampered the already limited capacity of IDPs and the host populations to feed and accommodate themselves. In the most drought-stricken areas, the local population is sometimes more vulnerable than the newly displaced. In fact, it is often the people with the most resources who manage to flee areas hard hit by conflict or drought, while those without resources are forced to remain behind.

Food security is also a problem for people accommodated in camps. An MSF nutrition survey conducted in early 2002 in Maslakh camp found malnutrition rates of 26.4 per cent and severe acute malnutrition of 6.6 per cent among the IDP children. Lower malnutrition rates (of around 10 per cent) were recorded for children new to the camps, suggesting that children were actually at greater risk of malnutrition the longer they stayed in the camp.[6] MSF has concluded that unequal access to food aid and a lack of coordination among agencies in the camp were the underlying causes (MSF, 6 February 2002). In the IDP camp of Mazar-i-Sharif, media reports say food insecurity levels are so bad that many families have sold their children in exchange for a monthly food ration (AP, 8 February 2002).

The health picture is grim. 20 years of upheaval have resulted in a dysfunctional health infrastructure and caused many of the best doctors and nurses to flee the country. As of early 2002, an estimated 70 per cent of the population were dependent upon health services provided by the international community (UNOCHA, 29 January 2002). Though detailed health data on IDPs was not readily available in early 2002, some conclusions can be drawn from refugee information. A World Health Organization (WHO) fact-finding mission in Pakistan in late 2001 found that 30 per cent of Afghan refugees seeking medical assistance at local health care facilities were demonstrating psychosomatic problems resulting from psychological stress. Indeed, WHO has indicated that the greatest problem facing Afghans is psychosocial distress (RI, 8 January 2002).

National and International Response

Prior to the fall of the Taliban regime, its relations with aid agencies were strained due to a high level of government interference with United Nations (UN) and non-governmental organization (NGO) operations. UN economic sanctions imposed on Afghanistan in November

1999, and again in December 2000, to force the Taliban to close down the Al Qa'ida camps and hand over Bin Laden, did nothing to improve the ability of UN agencies and NGOs to help the displaced.

Following the defeat of the Taliban, the UN reviewed its assistance programme in order to adapt to the rapidly changing environment and to strengthen the link between humanitarian assistance and longer-term development. The Immediate and Transitional Assistance Programme for the Afghan People (ITAP), launched in Kabul in late February, outlined a comprehensive approach to relief, recovery, reconstruction and reintegration throughout 2002 (UN, January 2002, p6).

Under the overall leadership of Special Representative of the UN Secretary-General Lakhdar Brahimi, the UN agencies are now integrated within the UN Assistance Mission to Afghanistan (UNAMA) structure, which is responsible for all UN humanitarian and development activities, as well as political and security issues. The new coordination framework is a continuation of the Principled Common Programming (PCP) and the Strategic Framework adopted by the international community in 1998 to reconcile political and humanitarian action in the country. Some NGOs have voiced caution that within the new framework (and given the close ties between the UN and the Interim Authority) political considerations might prevail over humanitarian concerns. Furthermore, they have criticized the mixing of relief and development into one coordination structure, arguing that adopting a development-oriented approach at this stage did not address the humanitarian realities on the ground, particularly outside of Kabul.

Photo 6.1   Civilians fleeing by foot, near Konduz, Afghanistan (November 2001)

Source: Martin Adler/Panos Pictures

Endnotes

1 As of March 2002, a total of 921,000 IDPs had been registered by the Afghanistan Information Management Service (AIMS) database. The database only includes known point locations of IDPs verified in the field and geo-coded, and excludes estimated positions and numbers of IDPs. Real estimates stand at 1.2 million.

2 Human Rights Watch (HRW) issued a report in April 2002 documenting the campaign of violence and intimidation against Pashtuns in the north.

3 In late March 2002, the US and France reported to the UN Security Council that they refused to extend the mandate of the International Security Assistance Force (ISAF) beyond Kabul.

4 The International Organization for Migration (IOM) conducted a survey of IDP camps near Mazar-I-Sharif in early 2002 and found that out of the 45,000 families living in the 19 camps, only 15,000 were IDPs; the remaining 30,000 families were neighbouring urban poor trying to get food assistance.

5 According to a report published by Carl Conetta of Project on Defence Alternatives in January 2002, the estimate of civilian bombing casualties in Afghanistan is between 1000 and 1300 civilians. According to a report published by Marc Herold in December 2001, as many as 3400 civilians were killed as a result of the US-led bombing campaign. See Conetta, January 2002, and Herold, December 2001.

6 The results of the survey have drawn criticism from UN agencies who claim that the method used by MSF (the mid-upper arm circumference test, or MUAC) cannot accurately determine the level of malnutrition in the camp and that the weight/height test should have been used.

Bangladesh

Internal displacement in Bangladesh is most often associated with devastating cyclones, the inundation of floodplains, erosion and the shifting course of the country's major river systems. In the most difficult years, these natural disasters have displaced millions of people, at least temporarily. The fate of people displaced by conflict in the eastern part of Bangladesh – specifically the Chittagong Hill Tracts (CHT) – has received less international attention. A government task force reported in 2000 that some 128,000 families were internally displaced in this area. This equals approximately 500,000 individuals (CHTC, 2000, p48).

Background to the Conflict

Before the creation of Bangladesh as a state in 1971, the population in the CHT was dominated by some 13 different indigenous ethnic groups. These groups differed from the rest of the Bangladesh population with regard to religion, culture and social customs, and up to the 1960s experienced little interference from the central rulers. From the mid 1960s, however, the government began to encourage the settling of non-indigenous people in the CHT – a policy that was motivated, in part, by demands for autonomy by the indigenous people. This agenda led to the deployment in the CHT of a large number of troops who evicted indigenous populations and permitted landless Muslim Bengalis from the overcrowded delta region to settle.

A 25-year civil war ensued between government forces and the Shanti Bahini, an armed insurgency group formed to fight for the rights of the indigenous community in the CHT. At the same time, Bengali settlers mobilized against them. Families were not only forced from their lands, but were subjected to other human rights abuses by military forces. Affected populations sought refuge in neighbouring villages and urban areas, after hiding and trekking through dense forests.

The civil war in Bangladesh officially ended in 1997 with the signing of a peace accord between the government and leaders of the indigenous populations. The accord called for a higher degree of CHT self-governance, as well as a reduction of troops in the region. By the end of 2001, however, only a small number of the more than 500 military camps in CHT had been dismantled (Feeny, October 2001, p27). There were continuing reports of human rights violations against the indigenous people; and Bengali settlers continued to express reservations about the peace process (CHTC, 2000, p13).

Figures

During the period of conflict, the demography of the CHT has changed dramatically. While the presence of non-indigenous people in CHT was insignificant before the conflict, the eviction of indigenous communities and the influx of new settlers resulted in the growth of non-indigenous populations to constitute one half of the CHT (estimated at 1 million) by 1997 (USDOS, 2002, Bangladesh, sect5). The exact number of persons displaced during the conflict varies. On the one hand, the US Committee for Refugees (USCR) has carefully estimated that 'more than 60,000' people from CHT were internally displaced by the conflict and another 64,000 made refugees in India (USCR, 2001, p156). On the other hand, the government task force created to supervise the rehabilitation process compiled, in 2000, a list of 90,000 indigenous families and 38,000 settler families who could be considered internally displaced (CHTC, 2000, p48).

The peace accord paved the way for the return of indigenous people who had sought refuge in India; but it did not solve the problem of internal displacement in the CHT. The inability of IDPs to regain their lands continues to block the return of the dispossessed. One major obstacle to the repossession of properties is the lack of official land titles for indigenous populations. Unlike Bengali settlers who have been granted official documents certifying ownership of land in the CHT, the registration of property by indigenous owners is through local traditional structures, making it difficult for them to make land claims.

Many Bengali settlers – backed by the military and the main opposition party in Bangladesh – have refused to give up land to the returning indigenous people. Some 30,000 returning refugees have been unable to regain their lands, placing them in a situation of internal displacement upon return to the country. In accordance with the 1997 peace accord, some Bengali settlers lost the right to use or occupy land and have had to relocate several times over the last years.

Limited International Presence

The presence of international actors on the ground is limited, and updated information about IDPs is scarce. Anecdotal information indicates that many of the internally displaced remain scattered in the remote and inhospitable hill and forest areas, with poor access to social services and few options for earning a living. The civil war has resulted in significant stockpiles of small arms in the CHT. Subsequent crime and social disintegration – including drug abuse – is an increasing problem among indigenous youth (Feeny, October 2001). In recent years, the government has initiated a number of development programmes in areas of return.

Burma/Myanmar

The Burmese military campaign to control areas populated by ethnic minority groups has caused significant internal displacement of civilians since the late 1980s. This campaign has particularly affected the eastern border areas where Karen, Karenni, Mon and Shan ethnic groups live. The Muslim Rohingya people, as well as other minority groups in areas bordering Bangladesh and India, have also suffered as a result of military operations (MSF, March 2002).

The precise number of internally displaced persons in Burma is uncertain because the government does not allow outside observers to visit them. But available figures in early 2002 suggest that between 600,000 and 1 million persons had been displaced from the eastern areas of the country (see Table 6.1). Inhabitants of urban areas in central Burma have also been victims of internal displacement (BERG, September 2000).

Table 6.1   Burma: major areas of internal displacement (January 2002)

State	Estimated figure
North-eastern Shan	300,000
Kayin/Karen	100,000–200,000
Kayah/Karenni	70,000–80,000
Mon	60,000–70,000
Northern Rakhine	100,000

Source: UNCHR, 10 January 2002, para100

Background and Causes of Displacement

Before the crushing of the democratic movement in 1988, Burma's regional ethnic minorities had maintained a fair amount of autonomy, protected by inaccessible jungle and their own military strength. After 1988, the military regime (known as the State Peace and Development Council, or SPDC) more than doubled the strength of the forces deployed to control these populations. Troops are now deployed throughout the ethnic minority regions. Some IDPs have been forced to relocate by the army; others have fled when abuses and threats by the military became intolerable.

Although 17 ceasefires were agreed between the SPDC and insurgency groups between 1989 and 2001, hostilities continued unabated in various pockets of the country, mostly in areas near the Thai border where armed insurgents retained some territorial control. During 2001, there were continued armed activities by the Karen National Liberation Army (KNLA) in Karen State, Mon State, Tenasserim Division and Pegu Division. The Shan State Army (SSA) and a Karenni insurgent group also remained active (USDOS, 2002, Burma, para1g).

The widespread use of forced labour in Burma has been both a cause of displacement and a threat to people after becoming displaced. In 1998, the International Labour Organization (ILO) documented the scale of this problem, describing how forced labour was both directly linked to military operations – for activities such as portering and the construction of military camps – and to public infrastructure projects (ILO, 2 July 1998). In March 2002, the ILO expressed concern about the limited impact of new legislation introduced by the military regime to combat this practice (ILO, March 2002).

Patterns of Displacement

Hundreds of thousands of villagers have been forcibly relocated by government troops for the officially declared purposes of combating insurgency movements. An Amnesty International (AI) report of 2001 indicated that a total of 1400 villages in the Shan State alone had been evacuated and their inhabitants moved elsewhere (AI, 13 June 2001). A significant number of Karen and Karenni villages have been emptied, as well. In the Tenasserim Division, people were forced to leave their villages in order to create a 'security corridor' on either side of a new gas pipeline. The government maintained that this measure was necessary to reduce the threat to the pipeline from armed insurgents. Human rights organizations have linked the mass relocation of populations to the widespread use of forced labour in the area.

A common pattern appears to be that villagers are given up to one week's notice to leave their village. Later, government troops reportedly enter the abandoned hamlets to destroy housing structures and food crops and to loot remaining belongings – thus discouraging the people from returning. The civilians are offered no support for the journey to designated relocation sites.

A large number of civilians escape moving to the resettlement sites by seeking refuge in the jungle or with host communities outside the reach of SPDC troops. In the jungles, people encounter extremely difficult conditions because hunting and foraging are constrained by the constant presence of government troops in the area. In some cases, they hide out near their villages so that they can continue some cultivation of food crops. As many as 120,000 Karen were in hiding or on the move away from SPDC troops during 2001 (Burmese Border Consortium, June 2001, p8).

Some relocation victims have sought refuge across the border in Thailand. But the vast majority of these refugees have been internally displaced for several years before crossing the frontier. Seeking refuge in Thailand is most often considered a final option, chosen only when all possible protection mechanisms inside Burma have been exhausted. The Thai government implements a strict asylum policy and offers asylum only to civilians fleeing direct fighting (Burmese Border Consortium, 2002).

Protection and Subsistence Needs

The human rights situation in the border areas of Burma is considered one of the worst in the world, characterized by counter-insurgency operations directly targeting civilians, forced labour, restrictions on farming, and land confiscation. There are regular reports of torture, arbitrary executions, sexual violence, forced recruitment by both government and armed opposition forces, and the indiscriminate use of land mines with the purpose of making areas uninhabitable.

Chronic insecurity is a major problem for displaced populations in hiding and in relocation sites. The absence of independent observers in conflict areas means that the displaced are extremely vulnerable. Some reports have indicated that people scavenging for food outside of their relocation areas have been killed. Others describe the widespread use of people in relocation sites by the SPDC for carrying military supplies and building and maintaining army camps. The security of IDPs is also threatened by intense military operations conducted to hunt down people hiding outside of relocation sites. Ethnic minority women are said to be at particular risk of human rights abuses during counter-insurgency operations.

The relocation sites in Burma do not have the appearance of a 'normal' refugee or IDP camp. Instead, they are often just empty stretches of land where families are expected to erect their own makeshift shelters. Once in relocation sites, the displaced are offered little means of survival with minimal health and sanitation facilities and limited food supplies. Tight

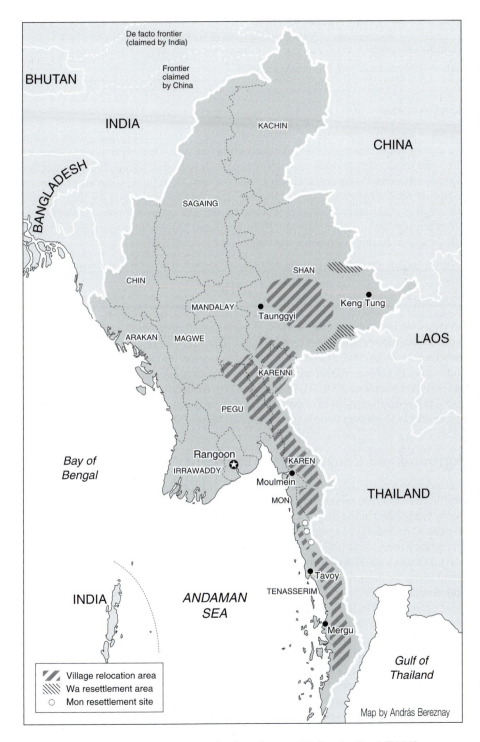

Map 6.3   *Burma: areas of relocation and 'villagization' (2001)*

Source: Burmese Border Consortium, 2001

restrictions on the freedom of movement of IDPs in the sites only worsen the already poor living conditions. In some cases, SPDC troops have closed down sites due to a lack of supplies, but without allowing civilians to return to their former villages or providing them with alternative settlement (CSW, November 2000).

Lack of Access

International organizations are not permitted access to displaced populations. As a result, there is a near total absence of official humanitarian aid. Operational assistance by UN organizations inside Burma consists mainly of social development projects that target the poor in government-controlled areas, including the southern Shan State, Chin and Kachin states. International NGOs operating inside Burma face severe restrictions on their freedom of movement. It is commonly known that some 'unofficial' international support is reaching displaced populations across the border from Thailand. This enables local support groups to provide people in hiding with some medicines and food assistance.

India

Ethnic-based or inter-communal strife in Kashmir, the north-east and Gujarat has led to widespread population displacement in India. The number of conflict-induced IDPs was estimated at 500,000 in 2001. But new waves of displacement in Kashmir at the end of the year and in Gujarat in February 2002 raised the estimate to more than 650,000 by the following spring (AFP, 30 December 2001; AI, 28 March 2002). In addition, development initiatives are at the root of the displacement of untold millions more throughout the country, with estimates ranging from 21–33 million people (SAHRDC, 16 March 2001; Lama, August 2000, pp24–29)

Background and Causes of Displacement

Since its independence in 1947, India has continuously experienced outbreaks of armed conflict and problems of internal security. The largest population displacements have been related to the protracted conflict in the disputed state of Jammu and Kashmir. Since 1989, approximately 34,000 people, including thousands of civilians, have died as a result of the conflict between Indian military forces and police, on the one hand, and separatist Muslim militants, on the other (AI, 3 October 2001). In addition, some 350,000 Kashmiris have been internally displaced as a result of the fighting. Most are living in Jammu (240,000) or Delhi (100,000), many of them with relatives (SAHRDC, 16 March 2001). In the Muslim-dominated Kashmir Valley, 90 per cent of the minority Hindu Pandits fled the valley during 1990 (USCR, 2000, p166).

The security situation in Kashmir worsened after September 2001, with more frequent attacks by Muslim separatist groups in Kashmir and renewed clashes between the Indian and Pakistani armies along the Line of Control (dividing the region into Indian- and Pakistani-controlled sectors). Towards the end of 2001, another wave of displacement took place, with some 60,000 Kashmiris fleeing heavy shelling and a massive build-up of troops on both sides of the border (AFP, 30 December 2001).

Another region that has seen significant displacement is the geographically isolated and economically underdeveloped north-east. The seven states there are home to 200 of the 430 tribal groups in India. The influx of migrants from neighbouring areas has led to land conflicts and struggles for political autonomy or secession.

Box 6.1 Development-induced displacement in India

Development projects generally contribute to fulfilling human rights, but sometimes lead to the displacement of large populations. Such development-induced displacement falls within the definition of the UN Guiding Principles when the project causing it cannot be considered of 'compelling and overriding public interest'.

The definition of overriding public interest will always be a matter of opinion. But it determines whether forced displacement of a population as a consequence of, for example, the construction of a dam is a human rights violation or a legitimate development project. In search of an objective definition, it is important, first, to determine who is the 'public'. If international human rights are universal in scope, it follows that the public is the whole population in a given area and not only the economic and political elite. In India, 250 million people do not have access to clean drinking water and more than 80 per cent of rural households have no electricity. It might therefore be argued that expanding the electricity supply network in rural areas should be a higher priority than increased electricity production for a mostly urban elite.

In addition to the eviction itself, victims of development-induced displacement often have their rights violated afterwards. Many are left landless and destitute. If the displaced are not properly resettled and rehabilitated, it is irrelevant whether the project forcing them off their land is of an 'overriding public interest' or not. Their rights have still been violated. In 1994, the Indian government reported that 10 million displaced were still 'awaiting rehabilitation'. Most researchers would argue that this figure is far too low. Some would suggest that very few of the 21–33 million development-induced IDPs in India have had their livelihoods fully restored.

Governments and international organizations alike are hesitant to address the sensitive issue of development-induced displacement, deferring to national sovereignty – a concept that many people today find old fashioned. Misguided 'development projects' that displace millions should be an issue of legitimate international concern when addressed for what they are: international violations of human rights.

Author: B Pettersson

Sources: Roy, 1999, pp94–95; Pettersson, January 2002, pp16–18

One way in which people have been displaced in the north-east has been through the 'ethnic cleansing' of certain areas. Often, communities or ethnic groups who have been unable to access political and economic power via elections or other democratic means have sought to gain a voting majority through the forced displacement of certain ethnic groups. Ethnic cleansing of this kind and resulting violence has taken place in the states of Assam, Manipur, and Tripura, among others, and has involved as many as eight different ethnic groups.

In June 2001, an agreement on a ceasefire extension without territorial limits was concluded between the National Socialist Council of Nagaland–Isak–Muivah (NSCN–IM) and the central government, receiving widespread approval in Nagaland. However, the agreement was seen to intrude upon the territorial integrity of the neighbouring states of Manipur, Assam and Arunachal Pradesh and led to widespread protests and large-scale violence there, especially in Manipur. The central government was consequently forced to review the decision regarding the extension of the ceasefire. The Nagas, fearing attacks from the protesters, left the Imphal Valley in Manipur for remote villages in Naga-dominated districts in Manipur and in Nagaland. A Naga support centre stated in January 2002 that some 50,000 Nagas were internally displaced (NPMHR, 5 January 2002).

Violence also broke out in the western province of Gujarat in February 2002. More than 600 people, most of them Muslims, were killed and 90,000 displaced (AI, 28 March 2002). The violence began after a Muslim mob in the town of Godhra, apparently angered by the provocative behaviour of Hindu activists, set fire to a train on which the latter were riding, killing more than 60 passengers. Human rights organizations have expressed serious concern about the conditions of the internally displaced in makeshift camps in Ahmedabad, Gujarat, and in other areas. At least 50,000 people have been sheltered in 20 relief camps in Ahmedabad, while over 40,000 are living in camps in other cities (AI, 28 March 2002). According to the Citizen's Initiative for Justice and Peace, local authorities have been preventing riot victims from leaving the camps (HRW, 13 March 2002).

Return and Resettlement

Most Kashmiri IDPs have expressed the will to return, but so far the security situation in the areas has not allowed this. The state government abandoned a proposal designed to facilitate the return and rehabilitation of Hindu Pandits in the Kashmir Valley at the end of 2000 (USDOS, 2001, India, sect5).

In the north-east, security threats have also been an important obstacle to return. The immediate return of some 30,000 Reangs from Mizoram, currently in camps in Tripura State, has been ordered by the central government and the Indian National Human Rights Commission. However, the state government of Mizoram has refused to take back the displaced and has argued that only half of them could be defined as original residents of Mizoram.

Subsistence Needs

Most internally displaced persons from the north-east have been living in temporary camps. Assistance, primarily provided by state governments and NGOs, has been insufficient and sporadic. In March 2001, over 200,000 internally displaced persons in the district of Assam were living in relief camps, where conditions were abominable; shelter was insufficient, people were sleeping on the ground, clean drinking water was in short supply, and diseases were a major threat (SAHRDC, 16 March 2001). The Reangs in the camp in Kanchan (Tripura) were reportedly living under life-threatening conditions, leading to a number of deaths from curable diseases.

As of early 2002, the camps for the nearly 90,000 displaced from the Gujarat violence lacked the most basic necessities, including food and medical supplies. Scorching heat, lack of sanitation and overcrowding threatened to turn them into health disasters, according to doctors and relief workers. Little was being done by the Gujarat government to ensure the safety, well-being and rehabilitation of the displaced. There were attacks on the camps, as well as on survivors attempting to return to their homes. Systematic and discriminatory violence against Muslims and a discriminatory approach to providing relief were also reported. Besides this, the internally displaced were not able to exercise their right to vote in the absence of identity documents.

National and International Response

India has no national policy or institutional legal framework concerning internally displaced persons. The Draft National Policy for Rehabilitation of Persons Displaced as a Consequence of Acquisition of Land proposed by the Ministry of Rural Development applies only to displacement arising from land acquisition. It therefore disregards displacement caused by human rights violations, physical violence and communal or ethnic violence. Due to the low priority given to displacement issues by both central and state governments and the absence of a clear-cut government policy on pre-and post-displacement situations, an immediate solution to internal displacement and the plight of the internally displaced appears unlikely in the foreseeable future (Lama, August 2000). Moreover, neither national nor state governments have taken preventive measures to avoid the outbreak of ethnic violence, nor have they implemented programmes to provide opportunities for sustainable return.

At the same time, India shuns international scrutiny and often denies international humanitarian access to the internally displaced populations. Most of the north-east of India, host to more than 150,000 internally displaced, has been inaccessible for foreigners. Médecins Sans Frontières (MSF–Holland) has been denied state government permission to provide health care in the Reang camps in Tripura. Similar obstacles have been reported with regard to assistance to the IDP camps in Kashmir. Meanwhile, in international forums, the Indian government has argued that local state governments are currently meeting the subsistence needs of the internally displaced persons, and foreign observers have to respect Indian national sovereignty (Permanent Mission of India to the UN–NY, April 2000).

Between 1990 and 2000, the government reportedly spent US$63 million on food and financial aid for the internally displaced who fled the Jammu and Kashmir conflict. Another US$4.6 million has been spent on compensation for destroyed houses. Schools for the displaced children have been constructed and medical care provided, although the displaced populations have claimed that this has been insufficient to cover their needs. While their situation has been far from ideal, the government response to the internally displaced from Kashmir has been much more generous than the response to the plight of the displaced in the north-eastern states.

Indonesia

In the aftermath of the financial crisis that hit Indonesia in 1998, religious and ethnic violence and renewed separatist aspirations surfaced across the vast nation of 13,000 islands. Conflict and the displacement of more than half a million people in 1999 culminated in the collapse of the 32-year rule of President Suharto. By late March 2002, that number had more than doubled to an estimated 1.3 million.[1] More than half of these were displaced by clashes in the Maluku (Moluccas) Archipelago, the remainder by violence associated with the independence struggle in Aceh, by ethnic conflict in West and Central Kalimantan (Borneo), and by inter-religious violence in Central Sulawesi.

Background of Conflict and Location of IDPs

The root causes of displacement are related to the transmigration programmes undertaken by the Suharto regime, aimed at reducing demographic disparities between different regions of the country. The relocation of large groups of people – most notably from the relatively metropolitan and overcrowded island of Java to low-population areas on other islands – led to ethnic imbalances, land disputes and eventually to inter-communal tensions. The roots of the separatist struggles that emerged in Aceh and in West Papua were somewhat different in nature in that they stemmed from economic inequalities between the elite and working classes of the islands. However, transmigration programmes have also played a role in the conflict in Aceh, with tensions between the indigenous population and non-Acehnese (mainly ethnic Javanese) resulting in the displacement of the latter to North Sumatra.

The main areas of displacement are in the provinces of Maluku and North Maluku (538,000 IDPs), on Sulawesi Island (389,000), on Java Island (216,000), in North Sumatra (94,000), in West Kalimantan (37,700) and in Aceh (13,000). Other areas of displacement include West Papua (16,800), Riau (7900) and Bali (2900) (WFP VAM Unit, 24 April 2002). Around half the displaced live in camps or temporary shelters; the other half have found refuge with relatives or in private accommodation.

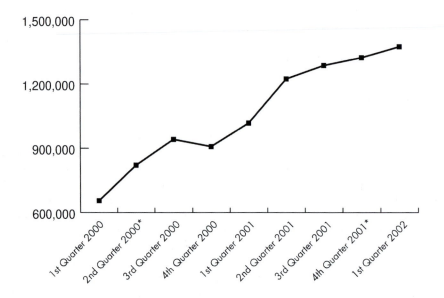

* Figures include one monthy estimate each based on the average of the two contiguous monthly figures.

Figure 6.1   Number of internally displaced in Indonesia, 2000–2002

Source: WFP VAM Unit, *IDP Source and Recipient Regions* reports, 2000–2002

Needs

Most of the conflicts in Indonesia over the past three years have left serious destruction in their wake. Housing facilities and infrastructure have been severely damaged. Medical and teaching staff have fled, especially from Aceh and the Malukus. According to UNICEF, the teacher-student ratio in areas with high concentrations of IDPs at the end of 2001 had shot up from 1 teacher to 40 students, to 1 teacher to 70 (UNICEF, 11 February 2002). Psychological assistance to cope with the traumas experienced during the different conflicts has been identified as an urgent need.

The UN estimates that the vast majority of the displaced are women and children, with children under 18 years old numbered as many as 750,000 (UN, November 2001, p18). According to a World Food Programme (WFP) survey conducted at the end of 2001, more than half of IDPs are unemployed and 55 per cent of IDP households are living below the poverty line. The most important common denominator among the IDPs surveyed was extremely poor sanitation – 80 per cent of interviewees indicated that they had no access to latrines. Lack of sanitation was reflected in widespread disease among IDP households (WFP, 7 May 2002).

In October 2001, the government formulated a national policy to address the problem of internal displacement in the country, indicating that the problem could be solved by the end of 2002.[2] The international community has been sceptical about government plans, pointing out that most of the conflicts that have generated displacement have still not ended. Furthermore, aid agencies have voiced concern about the speed at which the government would like to 'solve' the problem, underlining the importance of safe and voluntary return movements.

Faced with emergency needs beyond its capacity, the Indonesian government has requested assistance from the UN. In November 2001, the UN launched an appeal requesting US$40 million to implement support programmes for IDPs.

The Maluku Provinces[3]

In January 1999, a dispute between a Christian bus driver and a Muslim youth on Ambon Island prompted an outbreak of sectarian violence that rapidly spread to other areas of the province. Scores of churches, mosques and houses were burned down, and rioting caused a large number of casualties as well as massive displacement within and outside of the province.[4] Most people were displaced within Ambon and to south-east Sulawesi. In late 1999, violence also erupted in North Maluku (although with no apparent direct connection to the Ambon conflict) when Muslim Makianese clashed with Christians in the town of Kao in the north-east of the province. Some 30,000 Makianese were displaced. In the following months, the conflict spread to other areas of North Maluku.

In the course of 2000, violence and destruction continued unabated in both provinces, displacing half a million persons by the end of the year. The situation remained insecure throughout 2001; but the number of new displacements was small and there was no significant increase in emergency needs. Despite the signing of a peace agreement between Muslim and Christian leaders, insecurity and violence, particularly in Ambon, continued to hinder the return of IDPs in 2002. An estimated 250,000 persons remained displaced within the province, most of them in Ambon city.

As of mid 2002, the emergency phase of the conflict was over and the immediate needs of the IDPs were being met. A survey conducted by Action Contre la Faim (ACF) in Ambon in May 2001 indicated that IDPs were no longer dependent upon external food assistance, and most had found ways in which to cope in their new environments. Only 25 per cent of the displaced were experiencing economic difficulties (ACF, May 2001).

In North Maluku, the improved security situation has been more conducive to return. In April 2001, approximately 40,000 IDPs returned to Halmahera, Morotai and Bacan (*Indonesian Observer*, 20 April 2001). As of early 2002, over 200,000 persons were still considered displaced in North Maluku.[5]

Aceh

Displacement in Aceh, on the north-western tip of the island of Sumatra, has occurred as a result of a conflict between Indonesian security forces and the separatist GAM (Free Aceh Movement). Since the lifting of Aceh's 'special military operations area' status in 1998 and the resignation of Suharto in 1999, renewed aspirations for independence have been aired in the province. The government response has mainly taken the form of an increased crackdown on GAM and its sympathizers. Peace talks were initiated in late 2000 between GAM and the

Indonesian government; but frequent clashes and an increase in human rights violations during 2001 have led to a suspension of the negotiations. In early 2002, the two warring parties were reportedly trying to restore confidence for future peace talks.

Displacement in Aceh tends to be short term and localized. There are large waves of IDPs when clashes occur and sudden decreases when fighting subsides. In 1999, the conflict gained in intensity and by mid year an estimated 200,000 persons had been forced to seek refuge in mosques, public buildings and IDP camps. Fighting has often been accompanied by human rights abuses and the harassment of civilian populations, for which both sides are responsible (HRW, August 2001, p39). By the end of the year, most IDPs had returned, and only a few hundred remained displaced.

During 2000, however, fighting, human rights abuses, and the virtual collapse of civilian authority, again gave rise to displacement. Over 60,000 persons were displaced, most of whom were able to return by the year's end. As of April 2002, some 13,000 persons remained displaced within Aceh and over 90,000 non-Acehnese were living in dire conditions in North Sumatra. Living conditions are poor for the IDPs, particularly in East Aceh, where the authorities stopped providing logistical support for the delivery of aid to IDPs (ACRA, 2001).

Humanitarian access is seriously impeded anywhere outside Banda Aceh, the provincial capital, by the harassment and killing of aid workers. Some NGOs continue emergency operations despite the security constraints. In 2002, these included Médecins Sans Frontières (MSF), the Consortium for Assistance to Refugees and Displaced Persons in Indonesia (CARDI), Save the Children–US and Jesuit Refugee Service (JRS), as well as the International Committee of the Red Cross (ICRC). UN operational agencies pulled out, and at the end of 2001, the only UN presence in Aceh was a UN resource centre.

Central Sulawesi

Displacement in Central Sulawesi is the result of communal violence between Christians and Muslims since late 1998. The generalized violence has caused the death of hundreds of people and displaced over 70,000, most of them Muslims (WFP, 22 August 2000, p1).

In April 2001, renewed violence caused thousands to flee their homes, with the Muslims seeking refuge in Palu, and the Christians heading for Tentena and Manado. The displaced were accommodated in camps where living and security conditions were difficult (ACT, 6 August 2001, pp3–4). By June 2001, an estimated 78,000 persons were displaced in Central Sulawesi (WFP VAM Unit, 17 July 2001). At the end of 2001, fresh clashes sparked new displacements, significantly increasing the number of IDPs in Tentena and its surroundings.

In December 2001, the Malino peace agreement was signed, and the security situation improved. The agreement provides for the creation of working groups to facilitate the return or resettlement of IDPs. Some return has occurred, although this is limited due to the still fragile security situation. For the most part, Muslim IDPs have returned to Muslim-dominated areas, and Christians have returned to Christian-majority areas. Christians have returned in fewer numbers due to their fear of attacks from Laskar Jihad, a Muslim paramilitary group.[6] As of April 2002, an estimated 39,000 persons were waiting to return or resettle in central Sulawesi.

A mental health assessment conducted by the government in 2001 concluded that 55 per cent of IDPs in Central Sulawesi were suffering from psychological trauma (UNOCHA, February 2002, p7)

The government has been slow to respond to the needs of the displaced. In February 2002, it had built only 169 temporary houses out of 8000 planned. CARE had built some 2000 temporary shelters and was planning to construct another 2000. Poor coordination between government agencies and international NGOs was reported.

West and Central Kalimantan

A peace agreement signed in February 1997 between indigenous Dayaks and Madurese migrants in the province of West Kalimantan on the Indonesian part of Borneo ended two months of clashes that had forced at least 7000 people to flee their homes. Two years later, violence erupted once again in West Kalimantan. This time, more than 35,000 people (35 per cent of the Madurese population in West Kalimantan) fled the town of Sambas and headed to Pontianak, the provincial capital, while others fled to Java. Further violence and displacement occurring during 2000 raised the number of displaced in Sambas and Pontianak to 60,000, with thousands more still displaced in East and West Java. As of April 2002, some 37,000 people were still displaced in Sambas and Pontianak.

In February and March 2001, yet another outburst of ethnic violence between Dayaks and Madurese in Sampit, Central Kalimantan, forced an estimated 100,000 Madurese to flee to East Java and Madura Island (WFP, March 2001). The strong opposition of the Dayak and Malay populations to the return of the Madurese in Central Kalimantan, and the high level of psychological trauma endured by the Madurese IDPs, makes it difficult to envisage a large-scale return in the foreseeable future. In fact, the People's Congress of Central Kalimantan has advised Madurese populations to wait between 5 and 25 years before returning. This being the case, the resettlement of Madurese in other provinces or areas of Central and West Kalimantan would appear to be a more likely outcome.

Endnotes

1 These are estimations based on the UN World Food Programme's (WFP's) register of beneficiaries of its food assistance programmes, estimated to be 1,375,735 as of 24 April 2002. The estimation of 1.3 million used in this survey excludes some IDPs displaced by natural disasters. Furthermore, the 30,000–50,000 East Timorese refugees in West Timor are not included since they benefit from the refugee status.
2 The policy paper addresses the problems of both refugees and IDPs (in Indonesian there is only one word – *pengungsi* – to designate refugees as well as IDPs), and proposes three options to solve the problem:

   • return to the area of origin with government assistance;
   • government assistance to integrate in area of displacement; and
   • resettlement to a new area.

3 North Maluku separated from Maluku in October 1999 and became a new province.
4 Estimated by Indonesian media to range from 5000 to 9000.
5 Approximately 40 per cent of the 200,000 IDPs have returned to their areas of origin, only to find their homes and villages destroyed. They live in barracks and public buildings.
6 The Laskar Jihad first arrived in the Maluku in May 2000 to wage a holy war against Christians. In July 2001, they came to Central Sulawesi and made repeated attacks on Christians, exacerbating the conflict there.

Pakistan

Fighting over the long-disputed territory of Kashmir has led to waves of displacement in Pakistan since 1947. The majority of the 3000 people estimated to be internally displaced in the country in 2002 fled clashes during the late 1990s.

Background

During the period of colonial rule in India, the area of Kashmir was a quasi-independent state with a majority Muslim population. In 1947, the partition plan provided for by the Indian Independence Act stipulated that regions could opt for accession to India or Pakistan. All other Muslim-majority areas opted for Pakistan. But the Maharaja of Kashmir, a Hindu, chose India. The decision has never been accepted by Pakistan and was the cause of two of the three wars fought between the two countries during 1947–48 and 1965.

Since July 1972, Kashmir has been separated by a Line of Control (LOC) – or ceasefire line – passing through a high mountainous region. India controls two-thirds of the territory and Pakistan one third. The LOC is monitored by 45 military observers from the UN Military Observer Group in India and Pakistan (UNMOGIP). On the Pakistani side, one part of Kashmir is under direct Pakistani rule while the other has a semi-autonomous status.

A Kashmiri Muslim separatist movement has been waging an armed struggle there since 1989.

Displacement

Over the years since 1947, thousands of Kashmiris have fled to Pakistan or to the Pakistani-controlled sector of Kashmir. Fighting broke out again in 1999, and tens of thousands of Kashmiris – on both sides of the LOC – were displaced. The majority of these people were able to return home by late 1999.

By the end of 2000, some 2000 Kashmiris were internally displaced in Pakistan. The majority found shelter in camps, while the remainder were accommodated with relatives and friends (USCR, 2001, p163). Approximately 3000 persons were reported to be internally displaced in Pakistan-controlled Kashmir as of August 2001 (ICRC, 31 August 2001).

National and International Response

The government of Pakistani Kashmir has provided housing, drinking water, education and medical facilities to refugees living in 14 camps located throughout Pakistani Kashmir (IMTD, 2001). According to the US Committee for Refugees (USCR), authorities in Pakistan itself have not provided the same level of assistance to IDPs since they want the displaced to return to their villages along the frontier in order to reinforce Pakistan's claim to that area (USCR, 2001, p163).

The International Committee of the Red Cross (ICRC) is the only international humanitarian organization with access to internally displaced persons in Kashmir, and it visited or assisted about 1750 internally displaced in the Pakistani-controlled sector between 1999 and 2001 (ICRC, August 2001). In 2000, relief supplies were distributed to internally displaced people fleeing unsafe areas along the LOC in the Neelum Valley. The ICRC also continued to negotiate with the authorities on more permanent solutions for displaced people sheltered in two camps in the Neelum Valley (ICRC, 1 June 2001, pp103–104).

The Philippines

The main area of fighting and displacement in The Philippines is Mindanao, the second largest island in the archipelago, where Islamist groups have been struggling for either autonomy or independence for the past 30 years. The Moro Islamic Liberation Front (MILF), a 15,000-

member insurgency group, is today the main armed opposition group in the country. Other armed opposition groups include the communist New People's Army (NPA) and the Abu Sayyaf Group (ASG), notorious for kidnapping for ransom and beheading its hostages.

A ceasefire was signed in June 2001 between the MILF and the government and was reinforced in August by the establishment of guidelines explicitly providing for the return and rehabilitation of the internally displaced (or 'evacuees').[1] But armed clashes between the MILF and The Philippines armed forces continued to trigger new displacements throughout the second half of 2001, undermining the possibility of return for the 130,000 to 150,000 persons still displaced in the country. Military operations against the ASG in south-western Mindanao were also resulting in new displacements in early 2002. At this time, the US government was deploying troops to the country in support of the government battle against the insurgency.

Background

The conflict in Mindanao is attributed to a general under-development of the region, an unequal distribution of wealth, and a lack of serious efforts by the central government to integrate the Muslim population of Mindanao within the political and institutional fabric of the country. The rich reserves of untapped natural resources and raw materials of Mindanao, in particular in the Moro areas, have also provided a strong incentive for the government to fight the Muslim secessionist movements there since the 1970s (Oxfam, November 2000, pp4–5).[2]

In 1996 the Moro National Liberation Front (MNLF), the main insurgent group for nearly three decades, signed a ceasefire agreement with the government. This provided for the creation of a priority development zone (SZOPAD) that comprised 14 provinces and ten cities considered the poorest in the country. There were high hopes at the time that this agreement would put an end to the military activities of the Muslim groups; but by 2000 hopes for peace had considerably diminished. Instead, an increasing number of militants were leaving the MNLF to join the more radical MILF. The MILF was not party to the 1996 agreement. It had, however, signed an agreement with the government on the general cessation of hostilities in 1997. This ceasefire was repeatedly violated.

The main wave of displacement in The Philippines did not occur until 2000, when intense clashes between the MILF and the armed forces started in the western Maguindanao Province and rapidly spilled over into other regions of Mindanao. By August 2000, an estimated 800,000 to 1 million persons had been forced to flee their homes (USCR, 2001, p146).

Figures

Internally displaced people have sought refuge in neighbouring villages and in the principal metropolitan centres of the region. They have been sheltered in schoolrooms, mosques, chapels and other public buildings. At the height of the crisis, over half a million displaced persons were seeking refuge in evacuation centres. An estimated 300,000–500,000 were accommodated by friends or relatives.

Most of the people displaced during the 2000 clashes were able to return home over the following two years. But periodic skirmishes impeded return movements and sometimes provoked new displacements. In 2001, for example, as many as 161,000 persons were displaced by conflict and only 50,000 were able to return by the year's end (ECDFC, 10 December 2001). As of early 2002, the total number of internally displaced persons stood at between 130,000 and 150,000, mostly in western Mindanao (Maguindanao and North Cotabato provinces) and in the south of the island (Basilan and Sulu provinces).

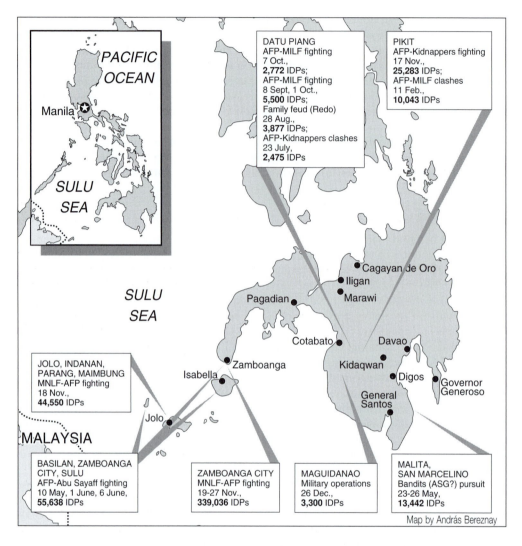

Map 6.4   Clashes and displacement in The Philippines during 2001 (December 2001)

Source: ECDFC, 10 December 2001

Protection

The Philippines government's Commission on Human Rights visited Mindanao in May 2000 and reported human rights violations by both government and rebel forces. Violations have consisted of forced recruitment of children, the use of civilians as human shields, torture and indiscriminate bombings of civilian areas (Balay Research, Documentation and Information Programme, 23 November 2000). In addition, access to evacuation centres has sometimes been blocked by government soldiers, who have set up roadblocks and raised road tolls. Relief workers also accuse soldiers of delaying the delivery of goods by checking rice bags for guns and ammunition, as well as harassing them (Human Rights Now, 9 May 2000).

Land mines represent both a risk for civilians fleeing armed clashes and an obstacle to return. Land mines are used by at least three rebel groups, the Moro Islamic Liberation Front (MILF), the New People's Army (NPA) and the Abu Sayyaf Group (ASG). In 2000 President Joseph Estrada's 'all-out war' campaign against the MILF led to an increase in mine use by the rebel group in the provinces of Lanao del Sur and Maguindanao. Areas particularly affected are Barira and Matanog towns where Camp Abubakar, the main stronghold of the MILF, is located. It has also been reported that the ASG planted at least 3000 land mines around its camps on the island of Jolo, south-west of Mindanao (ICBL, August 2001, p475).

Food Security and Health Conditions

War and displacement have greatly disrupted the lives of the people in Mindanao. Before the eruption of the most intense violence in 2000, Mindanao, and in particular the Autonomous Regions of Muslim Mindanao (ARMM) region, already ranked among the poorest regions of the country.[3]

Conditions in the overcrowded evacuation centres have been described as inadequate, with poor medical facilities and sanitation resulting in health risks for the most vulnerable. Prolonged stay in the evacuation centres has exposed IDP children – reported to constitute 60–70 per cent of the displaced – to ailments such as measles and cholera. Other causes of death in the centres have included stomach disorders and upper respiratory problems. In the aftermath of the 2000 fighting, it was estimated that 30–40 per cent of preschool children in the five provinces of the ARMM, where most of the fighting took place, suffered from moderate to severe malnutrition (USDOS, 2002, Philippines, sect5). As of November 2001, over 500 civilians had died as a result of the armed conflict, most of them IDP children in evacuation centres (USDOS, 2001, Philippines, sectg).

Return and Rehabilitation

The August 2001 guidelines established for the cessation of hostilities provide for the safe return of IDPs to their villages of origin. In some areas, where fighting has subsided, local governments have encouraged the return of the displaced by providing transportation and food.

The government estimates that the fighting in Mindanao in 2000 destroyed over 6000 houses and damaged another 2000 (Oxfam, January 2001, p2). The government's strategy is to construct temporary 'halfway' evacuation centres situated near places of origin and to encourage returnees to use these sites as a base from where they can go to their farms on a more regular basis. The main obstacles for the return of displaced populations are limited reconstruction of housing, the continued presence of MILF and government security forces in villages of origin and, in some areas, the presence of land mines.

National and International Response

The Philippines government has not issued any international appeal during the conflict and has rejected several offers from donors to provide direct aid, preferring resources to be channelled through its governmental institutions (UNRC, 6 June 2000). During 2000, it responded to displacement mainly through the National Disaster Coordinating Council, which coordinated the actions of the Department of Social Welfare and Development, the Office of Civil Defence, the Philippine National Red Cross and local governments. However, the scale of displacement has resulted in relief needs beyond the capacity of these national institutions (UNRC, 8 May 2000).

In order to strengthen coordination and rehabilitation efforts, the government established the Mindanao Coordinating Council and, within it, the Presidential Task Force for Relief and Rehabilitation, placing under the president all agencies and bodies charged with relief and rehabilitation (UNRC, 7 August 2000). Towards the end of 2001, local NGOs were asking for clarification on coordination arrangements as some government reshuffling during 2001 led to confusion about which government entity was responsible for the coordination of relief and rehabilitation of the displaced (CFSI, October 2001).

Immediately following the massive displacement of 2000, the United Nations responded to the humanitarian needs of the displaced population through its Multi-Donor Programme, providing over 12,000 displaced families with 2.5 million Philippine pesos worth of relief goods, mainly food (UNRC, 31 May 2000). Other UN activity on behalf of the war-affected people of Mindanao has included support to the 1996 peace agreement, through peace-building efforts and improvements of their living conditions (UNDP, 6 September 2001). The UN has also supported the government's actions on behalf of internally displaced, through such projects as food-for-work programmes.

Endnotes

1 Internally displaced people in The Philippines are often called 'evacuees'.
2 The 'Moro' is the collective term for people belonging to the 13 ethno-linguistic groupings in Mindanao. The Moro People's religion is Islam, except for some non-Muslim Moro tribes who possess a culture distinct from the rest of the people of The Philippines.
3 Created on 6 November 1990 and considered the 15th region of The Philippines, the Autonomous Regions of Muslim Mindanao (ARMM) is an administrative area located in the southern portion of Mindanao and includes the provinces of Lanao del Sur, Maguindanao, Sulu and Tawi-Tawi. In August 2001, following a plebiscite, Basilan Province and Marawi City chose to join the ARMM.

Solomon Islands

An outbreak of ethnic violence during 1998–1999 forced nearly one in ten of the Solomon Islands population from their homes. Few have returned since then, despite a peace agreement signed in October 2000. While it is hard to estimate the precise number of IDPs, given the lack of comprehensive data, most observers estimate that some 30,000 people were still displaced in the West Pacific archipelago in early 2002.

Background

Fighting between Malaitan and Guadalcanal communities on the main island of Guadalcanal during 1998–1999 forced 35,000 persons (9 per cent of the national population) from their homes.[1] An estimated 24,000 Malaitans fled to the capital, Honiara, while some 11,000 Guadalcanalese fled the capital and the coast for the interior of the island (Schoorl and Friesen, 2002). By the end of 1999, the majority of displaced Malaitans had returned to their original home island of Malaita, while others had settled in Honiara.[2] Some of these joined the Malaita Eagle Force (MEF), a militant group formed to counter attacks by the Guadalcanalese Isatabu Freedom Movement against Malaitan populations (Roughan, October 2000, p7).[3] Few displaced Guadalcanalese were able to return to their homes and remained displaced on Guadalcanal Island.

With a worsening of the conflict and the overthrow of the Solomon Islands government by the MEF in June 2000, an additional 3000 persons in rural Guadalcanal were displaced. In October 2000, the Townsville Peace Agreement was signed to end the conflict but it has proved ineffective at securing peace. Generalized violence and lawlessness continue in some areas. Incomplete data makes it difficult to estimate the exact number and location of IDPs. Most observers estimate, however, that some 30,000 persons were still displaced in early 2002, most of them in Malaita, Guadalcanal and the Western Province. The main obstacles to return have been slow progress on disarmament and an extremely depressed national economy.

Protection

With the June 2000 coup, police forces on the islands of Malaita and Guadalcanal were disarmed, and many of the police – 75 per cent of whom were of Malaitan origin – moved over to the MEF. No national police force has functioned since, meaning that inhabitants of the Solomon Islands are without civilian protection. Local armed militias have replaced the police on both islands, using extortion to extract financial support from IDP and resident populations (AI, 7 September 2000, ASA 43/05/00, p16).

Food Security and Health

The situation of IDPs is little documented in the Solomon Islands. Nevertheless, there are some indicators of how these populations are living. Food and other basic needs are required in all affected provinces – in particular, in Guadalcanal and Malaita where the influx of IDPs has placed considerable strain on the limited resources of a predominantly traditional subsistence economy. The prolonged civil conflict has led to a severe deterioration of the economy. The formal sector workforce has diminished by 15 per cent (Rarawa, October 2000).

As of 2000, severe food shortages affected more than half of the displaced in Malaita – three-quarters indicating that they were dependent upon assistance for their survival (Kudu, October 2000). Persistent insecurity on Guadalcanal Island has hampered access to the Guadalcanalese IDP populations, and aid workers have faced difficulties in providing the needed assistance. Although some IDPs have been able to gain access to land and to re-establish some form of livelihood, the lack of agricultural tools and seeds continues to undermine their attempt at self-reliance.

The health and education networks throughout the country have been seriously damaged. Half of the medical clinics and schools in the country remained closed as of early 2002 (EU, 19 March 2002, p6). Unpaid staff salaries and the shortage of medical supplies have undermined the operational capacity of those health care centres that are up and running. At the height of the crisis, nearly all clinics in the hard-hit areas of Guadalcanal were closed due to security reasons and thus unable to provide health care to the displaced. A health study conducted after the initial displacement movement of 1999 indicated that 40 per cent of displaced families were suffering from malaria, 12 per cent complained of acute respiratory infection and 7 per cent were affected by diarrhoea- and abdominal-related illnesses (UNICEF, 21 December 2001).

National and International Assistance

The main provisions of the Townsville Peace Agreement were a restoration of peace and order, increased autonomy for Malaita and Guadalcanal provinces, assistance to those who suffered lost or damaged property, and an amnesty to militants of both sides for abuses committed during the ethnic strife in exchange for a surrender of arms. The amnesty clause has been criticized by human rights advocates, who maintain that a general amnesty may create a climate of impunity not conducive to reconciliation (AI, 19 December 2000, ASA 43/013/2000).

Since no government organization existed to cope with a disaster of such magnitude at the outbreak of the violence, a Repatriation and Rehabilitation Committee was established and charged with providing housing and agricultural tools to IDPs in 1999. Government assistance has been provided mostly through small financial compensation grants. As government funding has dwindled, these grants have fallen from US$1000 to $500 (Saemane, October 2000, p3). That said, most assistance to the displaced has been provided by way of the traditional social safety net of the 'wantok', church organizations, and local and international aid agencies.[4]

Under the UN Resident Coordinator's Office, the UN Development Programme (UNDP) coordinated humanitarian assistance during the emergency phase, and since that time has remained engaged in post-conflict peace-building and rehabilitation. Other UN agencies involved in IDP support include the UN Population Fund UNFPA, the UN Children's Fund (UNICEF) and the World Health Organization (WHO). The UN High Commissioner for Human Rights set up an Office of the Human Rights Adviser in the country, and in early 2002 was conducting human rights training.

Endnotes

1 Following the end of World War II, Malaitans migrated in large numbers to Honiara, where most employment opportunities were. They have since come to dominate Honiara as a political and economic force, resulting in strong resentment by local Guadalcanalese.
2 Since most Malaitans living in Guadalcanal were descendants of settlers who had migrated from Malaita decades before, the majority of IDPs resettling to Malaita Island had never resided there previously.
3 The Malaita Eagle Force (MEF), through its armed struggle, has sought to obtain compensation for land and properties lost during the Isatabu Freedom Movement (IFM) attacks of June 1999.
4 The wantok system is a traditional social security system of care and share based upon the notion of reciprocity within the extended family. During the crisis, it offered a safety net to the displaced for the provision of land and food.

Sri Lanka

For the first time in nearly 20 years of civil war – one that has caused the deaths of more than 60,000 people and the displacement of over 1 million – there was some hope in early 2002 that the conflict might finally end. In December 2001, after a particularly violent pre-election period, Ranil Wickremesinghe's United National Party won the general election on a campaign pledge to end the ethnic strife between the minority Tamils and majority Sinhalese, and to start peace talks with Tamil rebels.

Almost immediately upon taking office, the new government opened the way for peace talks with the Liberation Tigers of Tamil Eelam (LTTE), reciprocating a call for a truce from the LTTE in late 2001.[1] Further steps towards peace since that time have been an easing of the government embargo on rebel-held areas in the north and a lifting of travel restrictions on Tamil civilians. By February 2002, an open-ended ceasefire between the warring parties was already in effect, with full negotiations between the government and the rebels due to follow.

With the cessation of military activities in early 2002, the government began focusing on the estimated 800,000 persons displaced by the conflict. It was envisaged that 200,000 IDPs would be returned or resettled by the end of 2002 and the remaining 600,000 by the end of 2004. By early 2002, displaced persons had already started returning to their homes – at least temporarily – in order to check on security, as well as the state of their lands and other belongings. The presence of land mines and the need for major reconstruction in communities of origin posed serious stumbling blocks to the return process.

Figures

Since the armed campaign for an independent Tamil state began in 1983, there have been repeated and massive displacements of civilians. Estimates of the total number of IDPs at the beginning of March 2002 were in the area of 800,000 (RI, 4 March 2002). The main areas of displacement included the Jaffna Peninsula; the 'Vanni'; and the government-controlled or 'cleared' areas of Mannar and Vavuniya districts.[2] As of March 2002, an estimated 185,000 of the 800,000 displaced persons continued to reside in 346 welfare centres, mainly in the north.

Protection Needs

During the course of 2000, the previous Sri Lankan government stepped up its military response to the Tamil insurgency, declaring new emergency regulations in the country.[3] In the same year, Amnesty International (AI) expressed concern about the linkage between these new regulations and increasing reports of alleged torture by military forces (AI, 1 July 2000). Since 2000, there have been regular reports of IDPs 'disappearing' after being taken into custody from the welfare centres.

Other security concerns affecting the displaced have included extra-judicial killings, arbitrary detentions and harassment by soldiers at checkpoints. A report issued by Amnesty International in January 2002 warned of a rise in rape incidents allegedly perpetuated by police, army and navy personnel. Many IDPs were among the victims (AI, 28 January 2002). Populations living in the war-affected areas in the Vanni and in the east have apparently been at the greatest risk of human rights abuse.

One of the main features of Sri Lanka's war has been a pattern of repeated displacement of populations. Many families have been displaced several times, making them increasingly vulnerable and dependent. Generally, displaced persons have avoided taking refuge in welfare centres as their freedom of movement there is severely restricted by a daily pass system.[4] This restriction has hampered their ability to cope independently with their displacement and so deepened their reliance on food aid.

Sri Lanka has an estimated 25,000 land mines, most of them located in the northern and eastern regions (ICBL, August 2001, p579). The UN reported in April 2001 that land mines were a major concern to the internally displaced returning to the Jaffna and Vanni areas (UNMAS, 4 June 2001).

Living Conditions in the North

Throughout the war, the government has maintained a civilian administrative structure in the LTTE-controlled areas in the north (Vanni). However, staff shortages, strict control of supplies and inadequate infrastructure have severely limited the functioning of local services, including health, education, roads and agriculture.

Although the government-imposed embargo on 'war-related material' – in force since 1992 in the rebel-held areas in the north – was eased in early 2002, the humanitarian situation in the Vanni remained alarming. The embargo meant that the flow of food and non-food items into the area, including essential drugs and medical equipment, fuel and cement, was seriously restricted. These restrictions contributed to a general deterioration in medical care and the provision of food and shelter in the region. Further to the problem of supplies, many medical professionals and health care workers have fled the area, resulting in a severe shortage of doctors, nurses and other medical specialists (MSF, 9 February 2002).

The situation in the state-run welfare centres is also a matter of concern. As of early 2002, over 80 per cent of 185,000 IDPs were living in 215 welfare centres across five districts: Puttalam, Mullativue, Killinochchi, Vavuniya and Mannar (CGES, January 2002). Historically, the centres were seen as a practical answer to the needs of the displaced, who were unable to find accommodation with friends or relatives. However, as the conflict dragged on, the temporary solution became a semi-permanent one, with some IDPs living in the centres for as long as ten years.

Scores of problems stem from long-term stays in the centres, including a culture of dependence, loss of self-esteem, alcoholism, depression and a consequently high level of suicide (UNHCR, September 2000, p5). Suicide rates were three times higher in the welfare centres than in the rest of the country. A Médecins Sans Frontières (MSF) survey conducted among residents of the Vavuniya welfare centre in 2001 indicated high levels of traumatic stress due to past experiences or present living conditions. Stress was often associated with physical complaints, such as chest or heart problems or generalized body pains (MSF, 31 May 2001, p25).

Food security has also been a serious problem in the welfare centres. In early 2002, the World Food Programme (WFP) identified some 77,000 IDPs living in welfare centres who had received very little food assistance in the last three months and who – without alternative sources of food – were going hungry. The main cause of this shortage was a lack of resource mobilization on the part of the international community (WFP, 28 February 2002).

National and International Response

The government's assistance to IDPs is channelled through the Ministry of Rehabilitation, Resettlement and Refugees (MRRR), which was established in December 2001 by the new government. All coordination arrangements for IDP support are regulated through the MRRR, and the Resettlement and Rehabilitation Authority of the North (RRAN) is now incorporated within the MRRR.

According to the Centre for Policy Alternatives (CPA) – a Sri Lankan-based think-tank that issued a comprehensive analysis of the situation of the internally displaced in October 2001 – various departments, ministries and aid agencies were responsible for relief, protection and assistance to war-affected populations under the previous government, but none had an overall responsibility for IDPs (CPA, October 2001, p7).

The UN High Commissioner for Refugees (UNHCR) is the international lead agency for the internally displaced in Sri Lanka. In 2002, it was working with the government to develop a framework for assistance, relief and rehabilitation of war-affected communities, including the collection of data on the needs and expectations of IDPs. UNHCR was also involved in assistance activities, such as the delivery of non-food items and education. Other activities included water and sanitation improvements and IDP protection schemes in collaboration with the International Committee of the Red Cross (ICRC) (UNHCR, November 2000, pp11–12).

Photo 6.2   Sri Lankans displaced by the conflict, Madhu (July 1999): UNHCR provides emergency relief, which includes plastic sheets for building temporary shelters

Source: M Kobayashi/UNHCR

Endnotes

1 Norway acts as an intermediary between the two sides.
2 The 'Vanni' is the LTTE-controlled or 'uncleared' area south of the Jaffna Peninsula and north of Mannar and Vavuniya.
3 On 3 May 2000, following a series of military setbacks, President Chandrika Kumaratunga announced that the government would assume new extended national security powers, including increased power to detain suspected terrorists, wider powers of censorship and a temporary suspension of all non-essential development activities. For more information, see AI, 1 July 2000.
4 The pass system was relaxed in June 2000, allowing IDPs to apply for a three-month restricted pass enabling them to exit the centres in search of work, provided they returned at night (JRS, December 2000). In February 2002, the pass system for Tamil civilians living in the northern district of Vavuniya was simplified from 24 different types to just 3. For more information, see JRS, December 2000.

Uzbekistan

Internal displacement in Uzbekistan is the result of a government campaign since the 1990s to stamp out militant Islamists. Following the outbreak of violent clashes in August 2000 between government forces and armed units of the Islamic Movement of Uzbekistan (IMU), the government forcibly resettled about 3500 civilians from mountain villages in an area on the border with Tajikistan (HRW, 2002, p374).

Background

Uzbekistan has a population of 24.5 million people, 90 per cent of them Sunni Muslims. The government pursues a strict policy of suppressing religious activity outside state-sponsored mosques and has, since the early 1990s, conducted a number of campaigns against certain ethnic groups and organizations associated with Islamic extremism. This policy has created tensions and several underground Islamic groups have emerged (ICG, 21 August 2001, pp13–15).

The IMU is generally perceived as the most militant opposition group in Uzbekistan, operating partly from bases in neighbouring countries. IMU fighters have taken hostages during the fighting. Several were taken to Kyrgyzstan in August 1999 (AI, June 2001). One year later, fighting escalated between government troops and the IMU in south-eastern Uzbekistan.

Forced Displacement

During this conflict, government troops forcibly evacuated at least five villages in the Surkhandarya region near the border with Tajikistan. It has been argued that this forced displacement was not only a strategic move to control rebel activity in border areas, but also a way of punishing civilians suspected of supporting the IMU (IHF, 18 July 2001, p12).

Displaced civilians from these villages were reportedly not given time to prepare for their departure or allowed to take any belongings with them. When the villages were emptied, the armed forces destroyed properties. After a transit period in tented camps, the government resettled the displaced on a more permanent basis in areas as far as 250km away from their homes of origin (IHF, May 2001, p352).

It has been reported that the displaced suffered mistreatment by Uzbek security forces and that most male members were temporarily detained and beaten in custody (US Mission to the OSCE, 22 February 2001). Living conditions in the resettlement sites are reportedly poor, with a shortage of food and houses not prepared for winter conditions.

The plight of the displaced civilians in Uzbekistan has, to some extent, been monitored by the Organization for Security and Cooperation in Europe (OSCE). Overall, however, there has been a near total absence of international initiatives to provide humanitarian assistance.

7

Europe

Regional Overview

As of early 2002, Europe had a population of at least 3.3 million internally displaced people (IDPs). The crisis of internal displacement affected 11 of the 45 countries of the Council of Europe (including the Federal Republic of Yugoslavia, which has only a Special Guest status). The internally displaced population remains larger than the continent's refugee population, which, according to the UN High Commissioner for Refugees (UNHCR), comprised 2.7 million persons in January 2002.

The level of internal displacement has fallen gradually since the mid 1990s, when the total number of IDPs in Europe reached a peak of nearly 4 million. The cessation of armed hostilities and violence has paved the way for return in only a limited number of countries, mainly in the Balkans, where agreements providing for the right of refugees and internally displaced persons to return home have been concluded (see Box 7.1). In the rest of the continent, protracted displacement is the rule, with almost no prospects for durable return or resettlement in the near future.

Background and Causes of Displacement

The break up of two multi-ethnic states, the Soviet Union and the Socialist Federal Republic of Yugoslavia, in the early 1990s triggered the most serious crisis of internal displacement in Europe since World War II. The collapse of these authoritarian regimes opened the door to aspirations of self-determination among ethnic groups and led to the creation of 20 new independent states (15 in Europe alone). It also launched a decade of massive population movements both between and within the newly independent states.

The vast majority of the displacement crises during the 1990s sprang from the uncertain status of ethnic minorities within the redrawn boundaries and the conflicts that followed between groups, or between minorities, and the central authorities. Interference from third countries, based on ethnic ties or other political interests, often aggravated the violence and prolonged the conflicts. The pan-Serb policy of the government in the Federal Republic of Yugoslavia (FRoY) until the end of 2000 lay behind the ethnic violence in Croatia and in Bosnia and Herzegovina. The support given by Turkey and Armenia to kindred ethnic groups in Cyprus and Azerbaijan was decisive in the displacement crises in these two countries. In Georgia, the intervention of the Russian Federation in Abkhazia, in the form of peacekeeping troops posted between Georgia proper and the secessionist province, is seen as an obstacle to the settlement of the Abkhaz conflict.

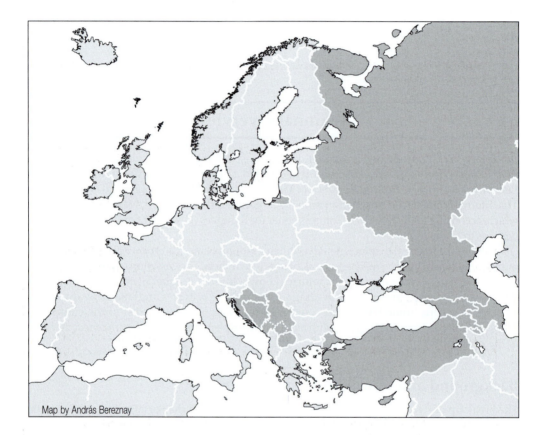

Map 7.1   Europe

Box 7.1 *The right to return home: a growing recognition*

Organization for Security and Cooperation in Europe (OSCE) Charter for European Security, Istanbul (November 1999)

22. We reaffirm our commitment …to facilitate the voluntary return of refugees and internally displaced persons in dignity and safety. We will pursue without discrimination the reintegration of refugees and internally displaced persons in their places of origin.

Stability Pact for south-eastern Europe – Sarajevo Summit Declaration (10 June 1999)

9. We also reaffirm the right of all refugees and displaced persons to return freely and safely to their homes.

Bosnia: Dayton Agreement – The General Framework Agreement for Peace in Bosnia and Herzegovina; Annex 7: Agreement on Refugees and Displaced Persons (signed 14 December 1995)

Article 1.1: All refugees and displaced persons have the right freely to return to their homes of origin.

Croatia: Erdut Agreement – Basic Agreement on the Region of Eastern Slavonia, Baranja, and Western Sirmium (signed 12 November 1995)

Para 7: All persons have the right to return freely to their place of residence in the region and to live there in conditions of security.

Federal Republic of Yugoslavia: UN Security Council Resolution 1244 (1999), 10 June 1999 on the situation relating to Kosovo, 1199 (1998)

The Security Council [r]eaffirm[s] the *right* of all refugees and displaced persons to return to their homes in safety.

Macedonia: Ohrid Agreement – Framework Agreement; Annex C: Implementation and Confidence-Building Measures (signed 13 August 2001)

3. Refugee Return, Rehabilitation and Reconstruction
3.1. All parties will work to ensure the return of refugees who are citizens or legal residents of Macedonia and displaced persons to their homes within the shortest possible timeframe, and invite the international community and in particular UNHCR to assist in these efforts.

Georgia: UN Security Council Resolution 1393 (2002) 31 January 2002 on the situation in Georgia

11. The Security Council…*reaffirms* also the inalienable right of all refugees and internally displaced persons affected by the conflict to return to their homes in secure and dignified conditions, in accordance with international law and as set out in the Quadripartite Agreement of 4 April 1994 (S/1994/397, annex II).

In all situations of displacement in the continent, forced displacement was not a mere side-effect of fighting and violence, but the result of a deliberate policy. The process of 'ethnic cleansing', aimed at creating ethnically homogenous areas, was a distinctive feature of the conflicts in Croatia and Bosnia and Herzegovina, but also took place in the South Caucasus and in Kosovo. Armed forces and groups also used forced displacement as a means of regaining control of an area by depriving the enemy of the support allegedly provided by the local population. Displacement from, and within, Chechnya and in south-eastern Turkey has followed this pattern.

Conditions of Displacement

As of early 2002, there were few situations where the displaced remained exposed to direct threats to their physical security. The main exception is North Caucasus (Russian Federation). Since the resumption of the conflict in August 1999, the civilian population has been the victim of violence from both federal forces and Chechen rebel groups. Although the intensity of the conflict has decreased significantly since April 2000, the large-scale presence of federal security forces and guerrillas continues to create a high level of insecurity for the civilians. In neighbouring Ingushetia, more than 150,000 displaced have been under pressure from the federal authorities to return to Chechnya as soon as possible, raising fears among human rights observers that return movements may be premature. The other place where the physical safety of the displaced population is under threat is Kosovo. Since August 1999, human rights organizations have reported serious threats to the lives and personal security of ethnic minorities, mainly Serbs and Roma, who are compelled to live in enclaves with limited access to essential services or sources of income.

Elsewhere in Europe, the majority of the internally displaced population lives in relative safety but remains in need of external assistance to meet basic needs. In Serbia and Montenegro, displaced households have generally found shelter among the host population; but a growing number of them have become unable to pay rents and have been forced to move to collective centres (public buildings, such as schools or sports halls). There, the poor state of sanitation and water facilities, the lack of privacy, and the deprivation of occupation and sources of income have kept the displaced in extreme poverty. This scenario is common in other situations of displacement, such as Georgia or North Caucasus. The lack of prospects of early return or integration in areas of displacement have also pushed large segments of the displaced population in the region to urban centres in search of employment opportunities. In Turkey, but also in the Balkans and in the South Caucasus, internally displaced persons have moved in numbers to the main cities, often concentrating in poor peri-urban settlements, where they continue to suffer from insufficient access to assistance and social services.

Return versus Resettlement

Since the end of the armed hostilities in the Balkans, security and freedom of movement have been gradually restored, allowing for the return home of refugees and internally displaced persons in large numbers. However, displaced persons returning to areas controlled by a different ethnic group (minority return) remain exposed to a hostile environment. Returnees have been subjected to persistent violence perpetrated by members of the dominant ethnic group. They have also been subject to discriminatory practices affecting access to pre-war properties, health care, education, reconstruction assistance or the labour market. In numerous instances, only some members of displaced households have returned to their original home, mostly in rural areas where tensions are more diffuse, and have lived in very precarious conditions.

Elsewhere in Europe, IDPs have so far been unable to return home. In many cases, the displaced persons have not even been given the option of resettling permanently in areas of displacement or elsewhere in the country. In Turkey, the resettlement policy conducted by the state has been far from effective and has benefited only a few thousand households. Despite the protracted nature of the displacement crises in Georgia and Azerbaijan, national authorities have kept the displaced communities in a social and legal limbo. Preventing the integration of the displaced persons within mainstream society has been used as a way of maintaining sovereignty claims on secessionist or occupied territories.

National and International Response

Internal displacement has hit countries that have gone through a painful transition towards a market economy, depriving state authorities of the means of responding adequately to the needs of the displaced population. In Georgia, the state has adopted generous laws and regulations; but the monthly stipend to which the internally displaced persons are entitled is insufficient to meet their food needs and is not paid regularly. A decade of isolation and economic sanctions has also left the authorities in Yugoslavia unable to respond to the needs of the displaced persons without the strong support of the international community.

But the lack of financial resources is not the only explanation for the insufficient assistance provided by national authorities. In the Russian Federation, federal authorities have kept the level of assistance to the displaced in Ingushetia to a minimum, in a deliberate policy of inducing their return to Chechnya. Despite its oil resources, the government of Azerbaijan has long been reluctant to devote adequate public funds to providing decent living conditions for the displaced, in order to keep international attention on the unsolved conflict over Nagorno–Karabakh.

The international community has demonstrated its readiness to fill the gaps in the national responses to the plight of internally displaced persons where possible. As of early 2002, lack of humanitarian access was hampering the work of humanitarian organizations in only two situations: Chechnya, as a result of insecurity and bureaucratic obstruction, and Turkey, where authorities denied international agencies the authorization to work with displaced Kurds. Elsewhere, the international response to the plight of the internally displaced populations has been substantial. For instance, UN agencies have launched consolidated inter-agency appeals for south-eastern Europe without interruption since 1994.

The donor community has, however, shown signs of 'fatigue' in the face of the protracted nature of displacement in the Balkans or the South Caucasus. Decreasing donor support has obliged national authorities and international agencies to accelerate the transition from humanitarian operations to the rehabilitation and development phase. Poverty reduction programmes, community mobilization and support for the IDPs' self-reliance capacity have become favoured by the agencies on the ground. This transition involves a risk for the most vulnerable members of displaced communities who depend upon direct humanitarian assistance.

The regional dimension of internal displacement has been increasingly acknowledged by all relevant actors in Europe, including regional organizations such as the Organization for Security and Cooperation in Europe (OSCE) and the Council of Europe. In 1996, the UN High Commissioner for Refugees (UNHCR), the OSCE and the International Organization for Migration (IOM) cosponsored a regional conference on the issue of forced displacement in the Commonwealth of Independent States (the CIS conference). The latest regional initiative has been the Stability Pact for south-eastern Europe, adopted in June 1999 by 40 countries and international organizations to coordinate their efforts in the Balkans. The Agenda for Regional Action, launched within the framework of the Stability Pact in June 2001, provides for a comprehensive framework and timetable for resolving issues still hindering the durable return of refugees and IDPs. It has proved a relatively efficient mechanism for monitoring the commitments of the Balkan states and coordinating global assistance.

Armenia

Since 1992, the government of Armenia has used a figure of 72,000 to describe persons displaced from villages bordering Azerbaijan as a result of the armed conflict over the disputed territory of Nagorno–Karabakh (1992–1994). The government's figure, however, includes an undetermined number of refugees from Azerbaijan who were initially settled in the border areas inside Armenia and became internally displaced at a later stage. The US Committee for Refugees (USCR) estimates that 60,000 people have been displaced as a result of the conflict, but considers that they have integrated locally. In 2000, the government indicated that 28,000 displaced persons returned spontaneously to their villages since the ceasefire in May 1994. Nevertheless, a clear picture of the current situation of internal displacement is lacking in the country. In the report following his visit to Armenia in May 2000, the Representative of the UN Secretary-General on Internally Displaced Persons noted the lack of information on conflict-induced displacement in Armenia and issued as a recommendation that 'as a first step, detailed data must be collected on the situation of internal displacement' (UNCHR, 6 November 2000, paras11, 51).

Lack of Visibility

Unlike Georgia and Azerbaijan, Armenia has not adopted any specific legislation to address the protection and assistance needs of the population displaced as a result of the conflict with Azerbaijan. The low visibility of this population explains the lack of attention given to their problems. The displaced have not congregated in large camps but live in small temporary settlements, or have found accommodation with relatives or friends. Furthermore, the vast majority of the displaced population originates from areas where Armenian sovereignty has never been contested, and thus have remained marginal to the dispute with Azerbaijan. Finally, the scale of conflict-induced displacement is modest compared to other groups of displaced in the country: the 1988 earthquake in north-western Armenia left 500,000 persons homeless, of which 100,000 were still displaced as of 1999, while the conflict in Azerbaijan resulted in an influx of 300,000 ethnic Armenian refugees between 1991 and 1994.

National authorities have long assumed that the displaced in Armenia have progressively been absorbed into the general population. However, the process of integration of the displaced in return or resettlement areas has been constrained by unfavourable socio-economic conditions. The transition to a market economy, the disruption of traditional trade and financial links with the rest of the former Soviet Union, as well as the blockade imposed by Azerbaijan and Turkey, have further degraded the living conditions of the whole population – displaced and residents alike. World Bank surveys have indicated persistent poverty in the country, with 55 per cent of the population living below the poverty line. Severe droughts in 2000 and 2001 have also seriously affected subsistence farmers in the northern and southern parts of the country. The country has lost about 20 per cent of its population during the 1990s as a result of emigration, which further constrains its development capacity.

During his visit to Armenia, the UN Representative on Internally Displaced Persons stressed that the population displaced because of the conflict still had particular vulnerabilities that had not been addressed (UNCHR, 6 November 2000, para48). Regions of Armenia bordering Azerbaijan, where the government indicates about 30,000 persons have returned, have been hardest hit by the conflict with Azerbaijan. These areas suffered a high level of destruction, especially with regard to housing and infrastructure. Reconstruction and rehabilitation efforts have been largely insufficient to address the damage. It is estimated that 75 per cent of the displaced in the border areas live in temporary dwellings and 18 per cent with relatives (Government of Armenia Department of Migration and Refugees, 2000). Insecurity resulting from occasional clashes between Azerbaijani and Armenian forces and the presence of land mines continue to hamper a durable return of the displaced, access to cultivable lands and implementation of reconstruction projects (IOM, January 1999, Chapter 2).

Poverty Alleviation and Development

Primary responsibility for the displaced lies with the Department for Refugees and Migration, an independent body within the Armenian government since 1999. In 2000, the department prepared a project proposal to support the return and integration of some 67,000 internally displaced in border areas. Although not specifically targeting internally displaced persons, the general poverty alleviation programmes initiated by the government since 1992 have benefited destitute displaced families. The unified Family Benefit System, created in January 1999, uses a vulnerability index (the PAROS index), based upon the family composition, income level and place and conditions of residence. However, internal displacement itself does not receive any specific consideration in the index. Because of financial constraints, the system covered only 230,000 of the most vulnerable households out of 430,000 households considered eligible for welfare assistance in 1999.

The closure of the UN Office for the Coordination of Humanitarian Affairs (UNOCHA) field office at the beginning of 2000 signalled that the displacement situation in Armenia was no longer considered a humanitarian emergency by the international community. Although humanitarian assistance requirements remain high, international humanitarian aid has decreased since 1995, replaced progressively with support for development programmes. Since 1998, the UN Development Programme (UNDP) has implemented a sustainable development programme in four of the poorest provinces, including Tavush and Sunik, areas of return along the conflict zone with Azerbaijan. The programme includes the rehabilitation of social infrastructure, capacity-building of local communities, and agricultural and environmental rehabilitation. The World Food Programme (WFP) remains the largest inter-governmental agency implementing relief activities through food distribution. In 2001, WFP relief distribution, food-for-work and food-for-training activities targeted 140,000 vulnerable persons, partly using the PAROS index (WFP, 5 April 2001). WFP has also implemented an emergency assistance programme in the drought-affected regions.

Azerbaijan

Statistics from the government of Azerbaijan show a population of 570,000 internally displaced persons in government-controlled territory as of January 2002. This population, the majority of whom are ethnic Azeris, fled the autonomous republic of Nagorno–Karabakh, a predominantly ethnic Armenian enclave in Azerbaijan, and neighbouring districts following ethnic violence and fighting between Armenian and Azeri forces during 1990–1994. Since the ceasefire of early 1994, only a small fraction of the displaced has returned home. The majority has remained unable to go back to their areas of origin, which are either under Armenian occupation or in war-affected areas along the ceasefire line.

The Nagorno–Karabakh Conflict

Ethnic tensions between Azeri and Armenian communities in the autonomous region of Nagorno–Karabakh in western Azerbaijan were already manifest before the independence of Armenia and Azerbaijan in 1991. Armenian communities were forced to leave Azerbaijan for Armenia between 1988 and 1991, while ethnic Azeris in Armenia took flight in the opposite direction during the same period. In 1991, the situation degenerated into an armed conflict between forces of the self-proclaimed 'Republic of Nagorno–Karabakh', supported by Armenia, on the one side, and Azeri armed forces, on the other. The biggest wave of displacement occurred in 1993 when Karabakh Armenian forces made significant military gains beyond Nagorno–Karabakh, displacing an estimated 450,000 to 500,000 ethnic Azeris. An offensive in April 1994 led to further territorial gains by Armenian forces in districts north and north-east of Nagorno–Karabakh. This led to the displacement of another 50,000 persons. When the fighting stopped as a result of the ceasefire agreement in May 1994, Azerbaijan had lost about 20 per cent of its territory to Armenian and Karabakh forces, including Nagorno–Karabakh and large portions of neighbouring districts (UNCHR, 25 January 1999, paras 20–28).

Negotiations held under the auspices of the Organization for Security and Cooperation in Europe's (OSCE's) Minsk Group have so far failed to bring significant concessions from the contending factions – in particular, regarding the status of Nagorno–Karabakh and the participation of the Armenian leadership in Stepanakert (Nagorno–Karabakh) in negotiations. The new attention given by the US to stability in the region since 11 September 2001 has raised hopes for a more productive conflict settlement process. In January 2002, the US lifted restrictions on its assistance to the government of Azerbaijan, which had been in force since 1992. However, three rounds of talks between the parties in Paris and Key West in 2001 did not result in significant progress (RFE/RL, 7 March 2002).

Humanitarian Concerns

Pending a solution to the conflict, the displaced in Azerbaijan have remained in a precarious position. Most of the displaced have settled in areas close to their region of origin along the ceasefire line, forming a so-called 'IDP belt' around the occupied area, while a quarter of the internally displaced population have moved further east to the capital Baku (see Map 7.2). In general, the shelter conditions of the displaced have been inadequate, with most households living in camps or public buildings with insufficient access to water or sanitation facilities. A US Agency for International Development (USAID)-funded survey conducted in southern Azerbaijan shows that prevalence rates for disability and chronic and acute diseases are higher among the displaced than the rest of the population. Displaced households consider lack of money to be the main obstacle to medical care (IMC, November 2000).

The displaced households typically depend upon subsidies and pensions from the government and direct assistance from humanitarian organizations for their survival. Only a small minority has access to land, which they can often not cultivate as a result of financial constraints. Displaced persons have been excluded from the land privatization process, which is open only to Azerbaijani citizens in their home districts (UNDP, 1999, p50). Lack of economic opportunities in the areas of internal displacement have obliged males to leave their families in camps and move to urban areas or third countries such as Russia. However, the freedom of movement of displaced persons is still constrained by the de facto *'propiska'* system inherited from the Soviet period: displaced persons can only reside in approved locations and humanitarian assistance will only be provided to them in camps or resettlement sites where they are registered.

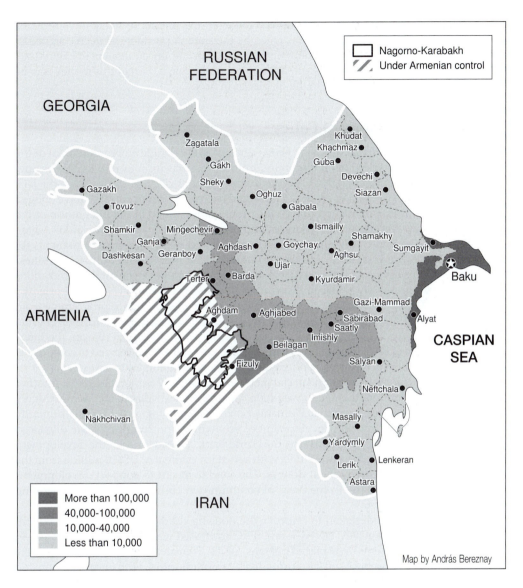

Map 7.2   Azerbaijan: concentrations of IDPs by district (January 2002)

Source: Azerbaijan State Committee of Statistics, 2002

The various measures taken by the state to respond to the needs of the displaced show what the Representative of the UN Secretary-General on IDPs called a 'sense of solidarity' with the affected population (UNCHR, 25 January 1999). The state provides most of the displaced with various subsidies, and they are exempt from all taxes and utility and public transportation costs. The Law on the Status of Refugees and Forcibly Displaced Persons (persons displaced within Azerbaijan as a result of 'military aggression, natural and technological disasters') and the Law on the Social Protection of Forcibly Displaced Persons, both adopted in May 1999, guarantee subsidies and other exemptions. However, the impact of these laws remains seriously limited by financial constraints faced by the state. A presidential decree signed in August 2001 compelled the state oil company to transfer an amount equivalent to US$190,000 to the State Committee for Refugees and IDPs on a monthly basis. Part of this money is to be used to fund food aid distribution to the displaced in need.

Return and Resettlement Policy

The government of Azerbaijan has long been reluctant to encourage any resettlement of the internally displaced, fearing that it might undermine prospects for return to territories now occupied by Armenian forces (UNCHR, 25 January 1999, paras109–113). However, the lack of any perspective for a return in the near future, and decreasing donor support, have obliged the government to show more acceptance for programmes aimed at the integration of the displaced into new communities. In August and September 2001, President Haidar Aliyev decreed the allocation of US$37 million to the building and rehabilitation of settlements for IDPs and refugees from Armenia, and the allocation of land plots for agricultural activities.

In line with this new policy, international agencies and non-governmental organizations (NGOs) have progressively replaced humanitarian assistance with development-oriented activities.[1] The World Food Programme (WFP) scaled down its assistance programme from 300,000 people in 1999 to some 160,000 in early 2002, and was planning a further gradual reduction (WFP, 3 April 2002). In charge of seven camps in southern Azerbaijan, the International Federation of Red Cross and Red Crescent Societies (IFRC) has decided to cease direct food assistance to most of the camp residents and to reduce dependency upon external assistance through agriculture projects and social mobilization (IFRC, 7 September 2001). Another major contribution to strengthening the self-help capacity of the displaced comes from Mercy Corps International, whose Azerbaijan Humanitarian Assistance Programme focuses primarily on community support and the development of economic opportunities for the displaced (MCI, May 2001). Following a proposal by the World Bank, a social fund for the development of IDPs was also created in December 1999 with a seed investment of US$10 million from the World Bank and other international donors. The fund is meant to support development-oriented projects, particularly in the areas of community mobilization, income-generating activities and micro-credit.

Efforts have been undertaken to improve the housing conditions of the displaced still residing in camps. During 2001, UNHCR and IFRC addressed water and sanitation needs in various selected settlements of displaced persons. UNHCR created new settlements for a few hundred displaced households on sites provided by the authorities, with improved housing and access to basic infrastructure and services. Reconstruction plans have also been designed for regions along the ceasefire line in western Azerbaijan, mainly the districts of Fizuli, Agdam and Terter, from which a significant portion of the displaced originate. A multiyear reconstruction programme benefiting some 36,000 returnees and 250,000 persons who remained in the war-damaged area was initiated by the government in 1998, with the support of UNDP, UNHCR, the World Bank and the European Union (EU) (UNDP, 1999, pp52–54). Through its Fizuli Repatriation Project, the IFRC supported the repatriation of 160 families during 2001 with the provision of building materials, while the government provided water, electricity and irrigation. IFRC is planning to facilitate the rehabilitation of an additional 160 houses in another village of the Fizuli district in 2002 (IFRC, 7 September 2001).

Although various organizations have received financial contributions from international oil companies based in Azerbaijan (such as IFRC and UNHCR), decreasing support from the donor community has obliged them to reduce their interventions. Donor interest is likely to increase only with the implementation of a peace agreement.

Photo 7.1   Azeri IDPs living in abandoned wagon trains, Saatli (December 2000)

Source: Andy Johnstone/Panos Pictures

Endnotes

1 For detailed and updated information on humanitarian and development activities in Azerbaijan, consult the website Azerweb, a comprehensive information system maintained by the Open Society Institute – Assistance Foundation Azerbaijan: www.azerweb.com.

Bosnia and Herzegovina

Years after the Dayton Peace Agreement of November 1995 ended the armed conflict in Bosnia and Herzegovina, the divisions between the main ethnic groups – the Bosnian Muslims or Bosniacs, the Bosnian Croats and the Bosnian Serbs – continue to plague the country. The tensions within and between the two entities that make up the country, the Bosniac and Croat-dominated 'Federation' and the Serb-controlled 'Republika Srpska', pose a serious obstacle to the return of refugees and displaced persons to their homes of origin, a right enshrined in the Dayton Agreement. The significant breakthrough in return movements since 2000 has been made possible only through strong pressure from the international community, resulting in a reduction of at least half of the internally displaced population since the end of the armed conflict. The return of the remaining 440,000 internally displaced persons (January 2002) will continue to require international support, particularly in areas where returnees do not belong to the ethnic majority ('minority return').

The conflict (1992–1995)

The conflict in Bosnia and Herzegovina followed the break-up of the Socialist Federal Republic of Yugoslavia (FRoY) in 1991 and 1992. Refusing to live with other ethnic groups in an independent Bosnia and Herzegovina, ethnic Serb extremists implemented a policy of ethnic cleansing, with the objective of creating a territorial continuity between Serb-dominated areas in Bosnia and Herzegovina and Serbia. Serious violations of humanitarian law were committed during the conflict, including large-scale expulsion of civilian populations, indiscriminate attacks and mass murder. Although officially united in an alliance against Bosnian Serbs, the two other ethnic groups in the country, the Bosnian Croats and, to a lesser extent, the Bosnian Muslims, also attempted to create homogenous ethnic areas through the forced displacement of civilians. At the end of the conflict in December 1995, more than 1 million persons were internally displaced, while 1.3 million had been forced to flee abroad.

The Challenge of Return

The right of refugees and displaced people to return to their places of origin was set down in Annex 7 of the Dayton Agreement. To facilitate the exercise of this right, the agreement provides for a strong international presence, comprising a civilian office headed by the High Representative as well as a North Atlantic Treaty Organization (NATO) peace implementation force, converted in December 1996 into a stabilization force (SFOR). The agreement also calls for the creation of a mechanism to ensure the enforcement of the property rights of the displaced – namely, the Commission for Real Property Claims of Displaced Persons and Refugees. However, this commission has encountered enormous obstacles in implementing its mandate. As the agreement also indirectly confirms the areas of influence of the various ethnic groups – particularly through the recognition of two entities whose border corresponds to the front line between the Croat–Muslim alliance and the Bosnian Serbs – the right to return has, in practice, been difficult to uphold. Croat extremist attempts to create their own entity distinct from the Federation during 2001, and the persisting influence of nationalist parties on the political scene, continue to demonstrate the reality of war-inherited ethnic divisions in the country.

The return of the displaced to areas where they would no longer be part of the ethnic majority ('minority return') has been the main challenge since the end of the conflict. Long an issue of concern to the international community, 'minority return' did make progress during 2000–2001. With 92,000 'minority returns' recorded in 2001 – out of which 74,000 were IDPs – return figures showed a significant improvement on the previous year.[1] This positive result is mainly attributed to the better implementation of property rights through the concerted approach of international agencies in the country (the Property Law Implementation Plan). It is also due, in part, to action by the High Representative, who made use of his power to remove obstructionist local officials and to impose legislation at the community and federal levels.

While approximately 40 per cent of the property cases have been solved countrywide, there remain considerable disparities among municipalities. Eastern Republika Srpska and Croat-dominated cantons in the Federation show the lowest rates of implementation. The main causes for the low level of return have been the failure of local authorities to provide alternative accommodation to persons due to be evicted, persisting bureaucratic obstruction, cancellation or postponement of scheduled evictions, and failure to address cases of double occupancy. International organizations estimate that at the current pace of implementation, it would take roughly four more years to solve all property claims (OHR, 5 March 2002, VI). Property rights of the Roma community have also raised concerns among international agencies. Before the war, people of this community usually lived on socially owned land, but without any recognition by the authorities. Therefore, Roma lack any legal entitlement to their pre-war residences and are unable to make claims for their losses.

The current return momentum is also endangered by security problems in areas where minorities are returning to their homes. This is especially the case in Republika Srpska, where incidents against minorities have included shooting, use of explosives, and other physical violence.[2] The lack of an independent justice system and the mono-ethnic composition of police forces ensure that most ethnically motivated crimes remain unpunished, especially in Republika Srpska.

The economic crisis faced by the country leaves returnees with few options for regaining their livelihoods. Many live in tents next to their destroyed houses, waiting for reconstruction assistance. The unemployment rate stands at 40 per cent in the Federation and is even higher in Republika Srpska, particularly in rural areas where most return movements have taken place. Elsewhere, limited employment opportunities are compounded by widespread discrimination based on ethnicity, political affiliation and gender, especially in the public sector. Ethnic discrimination regarding access to utilities, education and health care is present, as well. Furthermore, lack of cooperation between pension and health-insurance systems in the two entities continues to affect the sustainability of return movements to minority areas.

Perspectives for the Displaced Population

Although not, on the whole, exposed to any physical violence, people still displaced by the war continue to live in precarious conditions. Accommodation constitutes the main problem; the housing capacity of the country is insufficient to meet the needs created by the eviction of displaced people from contested properties and the return of refugees from abroad. A small proportion of the displaced – about 7000 persons as of August 2001 – continue to live in collective centres. Other displaced individuals illegally occupy houses or flats left behind by still other displaced families. Vulnerable households are dependent upon the social welfare system, which does not possess sufficient public resources to grant adequate allowances.[3]

The 2000 UNHCR re-registration of the displaced population in the country revealed that only 16 per cent of the displaced in Republika Srpska wish to return to their places of origin in the Federation, against 74 per cent of the displaced in the Federation who wish to return to Republika Srpska. As observed by international organizations on the ground, authorities in the Republika Srpska have preferred to support the durable resettlement of the displaced population on their territory, rather than encouraging them to return to areas controlled by other ethnic groups.

Strong International Involvement

The international community maintains a massive presence to ensure the implementation of the peace agreement by all parties under the supervision of the High Representative. UNHCR has been designated the lead agency for the return of both refugees and internally displaced persons. The UN, the Organization for Security and Cooperation in Europe (OSCE) and the Council of Europe focus their efforts on the restoration of the rule of law and democratic institutions in Bosnia and Herzegovina, in particular through the reform of the police and the judicial system. The World Bank coordinates assistance for reconstruction and private-sector development, with some emphasis on areas where refugees and displaced persons are returning. The cooperation between international agencies in charge of return and the

NATO-led stabilization force has proved essential to restoring freedom of movement within Bosnia and Herzegovina and the security of minority returnees.

Since the entry into force of the Dayton Agreement, humanitarian agencies have either pulled out of the country (as the WFP did in 1999), or have gradually reduced their activities (as has been the case with UNHCR, whose budget has shrunk from US$87 million in 1998 to US$22 million in 2002). However, a certain 'donor fatigue' has also affected the financial resources of both humanitarian and development agencies, who operate in the country. The inadequate level of international financial support, especially to housing programmes for returnees, undermines the search for durable solutions and endangers the sustainability of return movements.

Endnotes

1 In 2001, a total of 47,000 Bosniacs, 34,000 Serbs and 9500 Croats – refugees and displaced persons alike – returned to their municipalities of origin in areas controlled by another ethnic group, according to UNHCR. 2000 marked a breakthrough for minority return, with 67,500 movements recorded by UNHCR. Regularly updated return statistics are available on the website of the UNHCR Office of the Chief of Mission in Bosnia and Herzegovina: www.unhcr.ba.
2 The UN International Police Task Force documented 290 violent incidents against minorities across the country between August 2000 and August 2001, 193 of these occurring in Republika Srpska. For more information on security, refer to the website of the High Representative: www.ohr.int.
3 Laws on the rights of displaced persons and returnees have been adopted both at the central and entity levels: Bosnia and Herzegovina (BiH) – Law on Refugees from BiH and Displaced Persons in BiH (BiH Official Gazette, No 23/99, 23 December 1999); Republika Sprska – Law on Displaced Persons, Returnees and Refugees (RS Official Gazette, No. 33/99, 26 November 1999); Federation – Law on Displaced-Expelled Persons and Repatriates in the Federation of Bosnia and Herzegovina (FBiH Official Gazette, No 19/2000, 26 May 2000).

Croatia

The number of internally displaced people in Croatia has decreased radically since armed hostilities between the Croat majority and the Serb minority ended in 1995. As of April 2002, the Croatian government reported that only 22,000 persons remained internally displaced. This comprised 18,600 ethnic Croats still waiting to return to eastern Slavonia (the Danube region) and other areas restored in 1995, and 3400 ethnic Serbs in eastern Slavonia who wished to return to other areas in Croatia (Government of Croatia Ministry of Public Works, Reconstruction and Construction, April 2002).

Background

Croatia's declaration of independence from Yugoslavia in June 1991 was rapidly followed by armed conflict and large waves of population displacement – affecting up to 15 per cent of the country's population at the height of the crisis in 1992. The attempted secession by Serbs in eastern and western Slavonia and in the south-eastern Knin region (the so-called 'Republika Srpska Krajina') forced about 220,000 ethnic Croats to seek safety elsewhere in the country. During the same period, Croatia was facing an influx of some 350,000 ethnic Croat refugees fleeing ethnic cleansing in Bosnia and Herzegovina. The recapture of most of the lost territories by Croatia's armed forces during the Flash and Storm military operations in 1995 provoked an additional flight of persons – this time more than 200,000 ethnic Serbs from these areas. They fled mainly to the rump of Yugoslavia or to eastern Slavonia, which was still under Serb control.

The November 1995 Erdut Agreement provided for the hand-over of eastern Slavonia to Croatia in 1998, after an interim period of transitional administration by the United Nations. An agreement signed in 1997 between the UN administration, UNHCR and the Croatian government set standards and procedures to enable the displaced to return to and from eastern Slavonia.

Return

Return movements only partially explain the decrease in internal displacement in Croatia since 1995. Of at least 70,000 internally displaced Serbs by the end of the conflict, only 22,700 have returned. The majority have sought refuge outside the country, primarily in Yugoslavia. As a result, the Serb ethnic minority in Croatia decreased from 12.2 per cent of the population in 1991 to about 4.5 per cent in 2001.

Policy Shift

Up to 2000, the Croatian government supported the resettlement of ethnic Croat refugees from Bosnia and Herzegovina in Croatia. Croat refugees were given easy access to Croatian citizenship and encouraged to occupy properties left behind by the displaced Serb population. The election in early 2000 of a new parliamentary majority and a new president marked a change in government policy towards the Serb minority. New officials reaffirmed the right of the Serb minority to return. Several discriminatory constitutional or legislative provisions were amended or cancelled – in particular, in the Law on the Status of Displaced Persons and Refugees, the Return Programme, and the Law on Reconstruction. However, as of 2002, regulations and administrative practices continued to perpetuate the effects of the discriminatory and obstructionist policy implemented under former President Franjo Tudjman (NRC, 2002).

The Property Issue

As highlighted by the Croatian ombudsman in his annual report for 2000, the return of the internally displaced or refugee Serb minority has been, in particular, hampered by slow progress on property repossession. The failure of local authorities to provide temporary occupants with alternative accommodation – to which they are legally entitled – is one of the main obstacles to the repossession of Serb-owned properties. Since the lack of alternative accommodation is often used by courts and housing authorities as a reason to deny ethnic Serb property owners the right to recover homes occupied by ethnic Croats in central and southern Croatia, few Serbs have been able to regain their homes. Property claims lodged by ethnic Croat owners are handled in a different pattern. Here, evictions of ethnic Serb occupants – particularly in the Danube region – are ordered and speedily implemented even in the absence of housing alternatives. No measures have been taken to address the issue of lost tenancy rights in socially owned apartments, thought to affect up to 60,000 households, primarily those of ethnic Serbs.

The Croatian government announced in October 2000 that property repossession pro-cedures would be reformed. A survey of 'decisions of temporary use' of Serb properties allocated to Croat displaced persons or refugees up to 1998 was conducted. The objective of the survey was to identify cases of multiple occupancy and to speed up the repossession pro-cess during the second half of 2001. The survey, completed in May 2001, established that about 10,000 properties remained temporarily occupied, mainly by ethnic Croat households. In December 2001, the government adopted an action plan to implement the recovery of these properties by the end of 2002.

Discriminatory Practices

Reconstruction assistance has been another area where discrimination has had a negative impact upon minority return. Minority returnees who have been able to return to their pre-war properties have done so with little or no adequate reconstruction assistance. In instances where their homes have been damaged, ethnic Serb returnees have been compelled to live with relatives or in collective centres. Despite the amended Law on Reconstruction, regulations and practices of local authorities regarding construction assistance continue to discriminate against Serb-displaced households and to benefit Croat-owned properties.

Poor economic conditions in Croatia, particularly in areas of return where unemployment can be as high as 90 per cent, pose serious problems to returning Serbs. Because of discrim-inatory practices blocking Serb access to social benefits and employment, the depressed economy has made it nearly impossible for Serb returnees to reintegrate. In many cases, ethnic Serb returnees have been held responsible for phone and power bills accumulated by departed Croat occupants of their property. Sometimes, disputes between ethnic groups have led to the harassment and intimidation of ethnic Serbs.

International Response

The return of the ethnic Serb minority to Croatia has been encouraged and carefully monitored by the international community. In order to facilitate Croatia's admission into international structures, such as NATO or the EU, the new government has responded constructively, at least at the legislative level, to recommendations from the international community regarding human rights and cooperation with the International Tribunal for the Former Yugoslavia. In response to positive steps made by the Croatian government in 2000, various inter-govern-mental institutions, such as the UN Commission for Human Rights and the Council of Europe, decided to terminate monitoring procedures for Croatia. OSCE and UNHCR continue to monitor the situation of minorities and the return process in the country (OSCE, 2002).

Cyprus

The invasion of northern Cyprus by Turkey in 1974 triggered the displacement of more than 200,000 Greek and Turkish Cypriots from the north and south of the island. The resulting partition of the island into two mono-ethnic areas, separated by a buffer zone under UN control, has remained effective until today. Continuous efforts by the Greek Cypriot displaced community to change the political status quo has kept the issues of return and property high on the agenda of the UN-sponsored negotiations between the Greek Cypriot government and the Turkish Cypriot authorities.

The Ethnic Partition

The independence of Cyprus in 1960 was rapidly followed by tensions between the Greek Cypriot majority (80 per cent of the island's population in 1960) and the Turkish Cypriot minority (20 per cent of the population). The debate over power-sharing by the two communities degenerated into intercommunal violence by the end of 1963, resulting in a decision by the UN to send a peacekeeping force to the island (UN Peacekeeping Mission in Cyprus, or UNFICYP). A coup d'état in July 1974, led by Greek Cypriot officers against the then Greek Cypriot President Makarios, was immediately followed by the Turkish invasion of the island – purportedly to protect Turkish Cypriots against extremist Greek nationalists. The military operation and the subsequent occupation of the northern part of the island by Turkey triggered the transfer of most of the Greek Cypriots living in the north to the southern part of the island, while the Turkish Cypriots in the south fled in the opposite direction. The northern part of the island was proclaimed the Turkish Federated State of Cyprus in 1975, and became the Turkish Republic of Northern Cyprus in 1983. It is recognized only by Turkey.

There are no agreed estimates of the internally displaced population in Cyprus. The UN High Commissioner for Refugees (UNHCR) figures, as of December 1999, put the number at 200,000 in the south and 65,000 in the north.[1] These figures are considered inflated by the UN Peacekeeping Force in Cyprus, which estimates that there are only 165,000 in the south and 45,000 in the north.

Property Issues and Right to Return

A quarter century after the Turkish invasion of northern Cyprus, the UN no longer sees the humanitarian situation of the displaced population on the island as a problem. The displaced in both parts of the island are considered to have been integrated by the respective authorities. Displaced in the south have received strong support from the Greek Cypriot government in the form of a comprehensive programme of housing and relief. A special status (called 'refugee' status) giving access to social and tax benefits has been granted to the displaced and their children. The integration of the displaced in the Greek-controlled area has also been greatly facilitated by successful economic growth since the end of the conflict. In the north, the assistance provided by the Turkish Cypriot administration to the displaced has consisted mainly of the allocation of properties left behind by their Greek Cypriot owners.

Despite their successful integration, the Greek Cypriots displaced in the south continue to protest at their eviction by Turkish forces and publicly defend their right to return and to repossess their properties. The Greek Cypriot government has also strongly supported the claim of the displaced by actively campaigning in international and regional forums to raise awareness of their rights and to compel authorities in the north to grant them (see Box 7.2).

For their part, the Turkish Cypriot authorities consider the resettlement of the Turkish Cypriots displaced in the north as an irreversible process, as evidenced by the absence of any formal status granted to the displaced population. The ethnic partition of the island seems to have always been the objective of the Turkish Cypriot leaders. The Greek Cypriot and Maronite minorities who remained in the north after 1974 have progressively left for the south as a result of severe limitations imposed upon their movements. The considerable migration of settlers from Turkey has also contributed to the ethnic consolidation of northern Cyprus. There is no information on what the displaced Turkish Cypriots think of the situation.

Box 7.2 *Cyprus: the European Convention on Human Rights*

Since 1976, the government of Cyprus has lodged four complaints against Turkey with the European Commission of Human Rights in relation to human rights abuses resulting from the Turkish occupation of the northern part of the island. In all cases, the commission has refused to acknowledge the Turkish Republic of Northern Cyprus (TRNC) as an independent state and has held Turkey responsible for the violation of the rights of displaced Greek Cypriots to return to their homes and enjoy their properties (as stipulated in Article 8 of the 1954 European Convention on Human Rights and Article 1 of Protocol No 1). In a separate decision handed down in May 2001, the Grand Chamber of the European Court asserted that 'the official policy of the TRNC authorities to deny the right of displaced persons to return to their homes is reinforced by the very tight restrictions operated by the same authorities on visits to the north by Greek Cypriots living in the south'.

In the case of *Loizidou versus Turkey* issued on 18 December 1996, the European Court of Human Rights established that the government of Turkey was responsible for the violation of the right to property of a Cypriot national resident in Nicosia, reaffirming the validity of property titles issued prior to 1974. Turkey has, so far, refused to pay damages and costs ordered by the court in relation to this case. Approximately 150 similar cases filed by Greek Cypriots against Turkey were declared admissible, but no judgement was passed as of early 2002.

Sources: Cyprus versus Turkey, European Court of Human Rights, 10 May 2001; Case of *Loizidou versus Turkey*, European Court of Human Rights, 18 December 1996; USDOS, 2002, Cyprus, sect2d.

International Response

Since 1974, successive UN secretaries-general have conducted missions of 'good offices' to facilitate a settlement between the two parties without success. Property, security and constitutional matters are among the topics that have been proposed for discussion between the two parties by Secretary-General Kofi Annan and his Special Adviser Alvaro de Soto during 'proximity talks', reopened in December 1999. The talks were interrupted in November 2000 and then, with the proposed accession of Cyprus to the EU in 2004 looming, restarted at the end of 2001 (UNCHR, 4 March 2002, para1).

The United Nations Peacekeeping Force in Cyprus has been charged with supervising the ceasefire and military status quo along the buffer zone since 1974. Part of its mandate also includes humanitarian and protection support for the Greek Cypriot and Maronite communities remaining in the north, as well as the Turkish Cypriots in the south.

Endnotes

1 From 1999, UNHCR has ceased to include statistics on internally displaced persons in Cyprus in the 'populations of concern to the organization'. See UNHCR 1998 Statistical Overview, July 1999, p9.
2 The issue of missing persons (more than 2000 cases) was among the matters discussed by the Greek and Turkish Cypriot leaders in December 2001 and January 2002. They agreed to pursue the matter further during the course of 2002. See UNCHR, 4 March 2002, para6.

Federal Republic of Yugoslavia

Until 1996, Yugoslavia had experienced only external displacements, with Serb refugees from neighbouring republics flooding in. Since then, it has also suffered several waves of internal displacement in the regions of Kosovo (1998–1999) and Southern Serbia (2000–2001), followed by yet another refugee influx from Macedonia (2001). As a result, by January 2002, Yugoslavia found itself playing host to more than 400,000 refugees and about 330,000 internally displaced persons.

The election of Vojislav Kostunica as president in October 2000 and the victory of a democratic alliance in the Serbian parliamentary election three months later put an end to a decade of isolation. The defeat of the former Yugoslav president, Slobodan Milosevic, and his transfer to the International Criminal Tribunal for the Former Yugoslavia in June 2001 finally allowed for international support to the country's economic and social restoration. But the transition from a mainly humanitarian agenda to a long-term development strategy has risked creating gaps in meeting the needs of destitute IDP populations. Furthermore, the strong antagonism between the ethnic communities in the southern province of Kosovo has scarcely improved, and conditions remain far from conducive for a return of the Serb population.

Displacement in Kosovo

Citizens of Yugoslavia were first displaced in 1998, following the launch of an armed rebellion by the Kosovo Liberation Army in 1996, largely supported by the Albanian community.[1] In response, the Serb nationalist regime in Belgrade implemented a deliberate policy of ethnic cleansing in Kosovo in 1998, and again in 1999, spreading terror among the Albanian majority and forcing many of them to leave. The North Atlantic Treaty Organization (NATO) air campaign of March–June 1999 compelled the Yugoslav authorities to hand over civilian and military control of the province to a NATO-led military force (Kosovo Force, or KFOR) and a UN Interim Administration Mission in Kosovo (UNMIK), and enabled Albanian refugees and internally displaced persons to return to their villages. During the course of this mass return, another 230,000 Kosovars, most of them ethnic Serbs and Roma, fled to Serbia proper and to Montenegro in fear of retaliation from the Albanian majority.

The Crisis in Southern Serbia

In 2000, ethnic Albanian armed groups attacked Serb security forces in an area of southern Serbia next to Kosovo, triggering the displacement of up to 15,000 civilians from Presevo, Bujanovac and Medvedja municipalities. Most of these people moved to Kosovo. The international community supported the Yugoslav authorities in restoring order in the area – in particular, by allowing Yugoslav security forces access to the demilitarized Ground Safety Zone between Serbia and Kosovo, where the rebels were operating. A peace agreement was signed between the Yugoslav authorities and the Albanian armed groups in May 2001. By the end of 2001, only 10,000 persons displaced by this conflict remained so.

Humanitarian and Human Rights Concerns

Since their departure from Kosovo in 1999, Serb and Roma displaced persons have had to face a severe economic crisis in Serbia and Montenegro, the two remaining states in Yugoslavia. High unemployment rates, low salaries and the collapse of essential social services have undermined their social integration in nearly every way. The most preoccupying conditions exist for the displaced living in collective centres (about 7 per cent of the total internally displaced population). Numerous NGOs have reported on the extremely poor living conditions in these centres, where rates of suicide are high among the elderly (HelpAge, November 2001).

The situation for the displaced within Kosovo, and more generally for the ethnic minorities in the province, is extremely fragile. Persistent tensions between the Kosovar Albanian population and other ethnic groups – most notably, the Serbs and Roma – have forced ethnic minorities to move to enclaves where their safety can be better ensured. However, life in the enclaves is barely sustainable, with no access to income-generating activities or public services. Security risks for ethnic minorities outside their settlements continue to be high. Non-Albanian communities, especially the Serbs, have continued to suffer disproportionately from major crimes and have remained the targets of threats, intimidation and harassment.

Apart from insecurity, unsolved property disputes continue to hamper the return and reintegration process. The Housing and Property Directorate and the Housing and Property Claims Commission, created in 1999 to solve property disputes in Kosovo, have been far from effective (OSCE/UNMIK, January 2002). Ethnic minorities have been pressured to sell their properties as a means of accelerating their departure from the province (so-called 'strategic sales'). In response to this trend and in order to protect minorities, the Special Representative of the UN Secretary-General for Kosovo issued a regulation in 2001 creating a procedure of registration for property sales in certain designated areas. However, the regulation has raised fears among minorities that they might be prevented from selling their main assets and from using the money to resettle elsewhere (UNHCR/OSCE, October 2001).

Return Perspectives

Since the election of a new government in Yugoslavia, relations between the authorities in Belgrade and Kosovo have improved significantly, contributing to an enhanced dialogue between communities in Kosovo.

A Joint Committee on Returns of Kosovo Serbs, set up in May 2000, adopted a Framework on Serb Return and Return Principles in 2001. An action plan for return to some ten initial locations was presented to donors in June of that year. Similar steps have been taken regarding the return of the Roma communities, with the adoption of a 'Platform for Action' and a 'Statement of Principles' by the leaders of the Roma and the Albanian communities. Despite these encouraging developments, the return of the displaced to their homes of origin in Kosovo has been slow, with hardly 2000 return movements recorded for the whole of 2000 and 2001. In fact, some returnees have again left Kosovo to settle permanently elsewhere in Serbia (UNSC, 23 October 2001, para21).

National and International Response

After two years of large-scale humanitarian assistance to the internally displaced populations, a transitional phase has begun focusing primarily on long-term development needs (UN, November 2001, pp21–26). As an example, the International Committee of the Red Cross (ICRC), which has been the main provider of food aid to IDPs in Serbia since 1999, tightened its criteria for assistance. In parallel, the agency has developed income-generating projects mainly in the agricultural sector to promote self-sustainability among the displaced communities. NGO watchdogs, such as Refugees International (RI), have warned against any premature reduction of humanitarian aid in Yugoslavia, arguing that IDPs will remain in need of assistance during the whole of the reconstruction process.

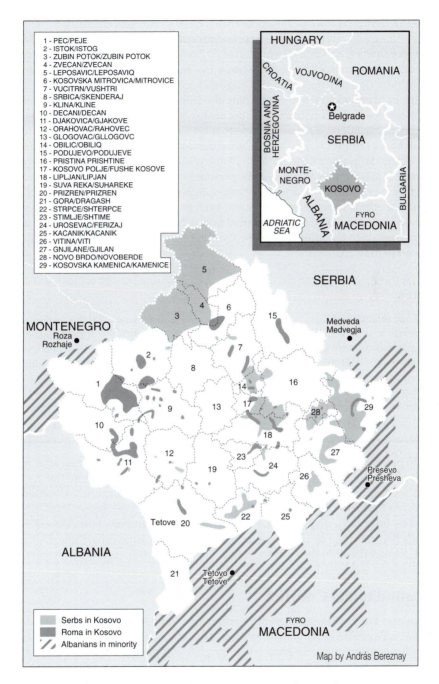

1 - PEC/PEJE
2 - ISTOK/ISTOG
3 - ZUBIN POTOK/ZUBIN POTOK
4 - ZVECAN/ZVECAN
5 - LEPOSAVIC/LEPOSAVIQ
6 - KOSOVSKA MITROVICA/MITROVICE
7 - VUCITRN/VUSHTRI
8 - SRBICA/SKENDERAJ
9 - KLINA/KLINE
10 - DECANI/DECAN
11 - DJAKOVICA/GJAKOVE
12 - ORAHOVAC/RAHOVEC
13 - GLOGOVAC/GLLOGOVC
14 - OBILIC/OBILIQ
15 - PODUJEVO/PODUJEVE
16 - PRISTINA PRISHTINE
17 - KOSOVO POLJE/FUSHE KOSOVE
18 - LIPLJAN/LIPJAN
19 - SUVA REKA/SUHAREKE
20 - PRIZREN/PRIZREN
21 - GORA/DRAGASH
22 - STRPCE/SHTERPCE
23 - STIMLJE/SHTIME
24 - UROSEVAC/FERIZAJ
25 - KACANIK/KACANIK
26 - VITINA/VITI
27 - GNJILANE/GJILAN
28 - NOVO BRDO/NOVOBERDE
29 - KOSOVSKA KAMENICA/KAMENICE

Serbs in Kosovo
Roma in Kosovo
Albanians in minority

Map by András Bereznay

Map 7.3   Federal Republic of Yugoslavia: geographic distribution of ethnic minorities in and outside Kosovo (March 2000)

Note: Only those geographic areas outside of Kosovo with an Albanian minority have been noted here. Albanian communities may also be in minority in areas of Serb and Roma concentration in Kosovo.

Source: HCIC, 2000

While international humanitarian agencies have progressively shifted their focus to capacity-building and advocacy, the Yugoslav government has played an increasingly large role in the coordination and implementation of IDP policy in the country. In the Presevo Valley, the international community has established a UN Inter-Agency Support Office to back the peace plan negotiated directly by the Yugoslav government with the ethnic Albanian community in May 2001, and to coordinate the international contribution to confidence-building measures and reconstruction in the area (UNOCHA, 29 January 2002).

Since June 1999, efforts have been made to meet all emergency housing needs in Kosovo. Nearly half of the families whose houses were damaged or destroyed in 1999 were living in decent accommodation as of October 2001. Housing authorities in the province estimated that an additional 12,000 families (60,000–72,000 persons) were in need of reconstruction assistance in 2002 before they could go back to their homes. Measures have been introduced to improve the security of ethnic minorities in Kosovo, such as the creation of escorted bus services and legal advice centres. The involvement of non-Albanian communities in local affairs has also progressed since the adoption of the Constitutional Framework for Provisional Self-Government in May 2001.

Endnotes

1 Inter-ethnic relations in Kosovo sharply deteriorated in 1989 when the autonomous status of the province was abolished by authorities in Belgrade. The initial response of the Albanian community was mainly in the form of a non-violent resistance, until 1996 when the failure of the Dayton peace talks to address the Kosovo crisis resulted in growing popular support for an armed movement.

Former Yugoslav Republic of Macedonia

Internal displacement in the Former Yugoslav Republic of Macedonia (hereafter referred to as Macedonia) began only in January 2001. The National Liberation Army (NLA), an ethnic Albanian rebel group, took up arms to fight for the rights of ethnic Albanians within Macedonia. At the height of the conflict in August/September 2001, some 70,000 people were registered as internally displaced. By March 2002, the situation had calmed and many individuals had returned to their homes of origin. At this time only some 17,000 persons remained displaced within the country (MCIC, 11 March 2002).

Background to the Conflict

Some 23 per cent of the Macedonian population are ethnic Albanians. Despite new political cooperation between the Albanian minority and the Macedonian majority, relations between the two ethnic groups have been marked by growing geographic, economic and social segregation. They belong to different cultures and religions, they use different languages and they live in geographically separate areas, even within cities. Within the civil service, the trend has been an under-representation of ethnic Albanians; with regard to employment, it can be noted that the two ethnic groups generally operate in different economic spheres (IHF, 8 June 2001).

The first ethnic Albanian demand related to the taking up of arms by the NLA concerned their complaint that the constitution was discriminatory. The primary issue centred on whether Macedonia should become a 'civic state' disregarding the ethnic background of its citizens, or a 'national state' dominated by ethnic Macedonians (IHF, 8 June 2001). The ethnic Albanians felt that the constitution divided the population into first- and second-class citizens, forming the basis for discrimination against them. A second issue was the Albanian demand to have their language recognized as a second official language, to be used in public administration, courts, parliament, and in education. Finally, Albanians criticized the Citizenship Act adopted in 1992 and its new draft, labelling it restrictive and discriminatory. For example, the rule that ethnic Macedonians might be given citizenship regardless of which country they resided in has been described as unjustly favouring this ethnic group over the ethnic Albanians.

In August 2001, a peace agreement was reached between the Macedonian government and the NLA. It concluded that the constitution would be changed to recognize all of the country's ethnic groups. Furthermore, it declared that Albanian would become the second official language in communities with an ethnic Albanian population of more than 20 per cent. It was also agreed that there would be proportional representation for ethnic Albanians in the constitutional court, in government administration and within the police forces. It also created the 'double majority' voting system in parliament, enabling parliamentarians from ethnic minority groups to block legislation that is only supported by ethnic Macedonian legislators. The agreement left the question of amnesty for former NLA combatants open; but this was resolved in March 2002 when the Macedonian parliament passed an amnesty law for former ethnic Albanian fighters.

Patterns of Displacement

The conflict in Macedonia can be characterized by several waves of violence, each resulting in the displacement of people. The first phase of the conflict began in March 2001, when fighting broke out in the Skopska Crna Gora region, causing the displacement of some 22,000 people. Most of these people were able to return home by April 2001, in large part due to the conclusion of a ceasefire. The situation worsened again at the beginning of May 2001 when fighting broke out in the Kumanovo, Aracinovo and Lipkovo regions, causing the main wave of displacement in Macedonia that continued until August 2001. The peak in the number of displaced occurred in August/September 2001, when some 70,000 persons were registered as internally displaced, 60 per cent of them ethnic Macedonians (UNHCR, 25 September 2001). A final wave of displacement, involving only hundreds of people, occurred in November 2001, caused by fighting around Tetovo.

An important characteristic of displacement has been the forced evacuation of villages by police forces, as well as the humanitarian evacuation of civilians and displaced, trapped in villages in close proximity to the fighting. Another pattern of displacement in Macedonia has been the frequent movement of displaced people to and from their homes of origin during the course of the fighting, and the large movement of people fleeing to Kosovo and back to Macedonia, but not always to their original homes. This last characteristic has complicated the counting of the number of displaced.

Protection and Assistance

Protection was a major concern for the whole of the Macedonian population during the sometimes intense fighting that took place in 2001. Over the course of the year, many civilians, including displaced persons, were trapped in villages affected by the fighting. At the same time, other individuals were targeted by armed units from both sides. Human Rights Watch (HRW) reported that ethnic Albanian males fleeing fighting were separated systematically from the rest of the population and were, in some instances, beaten at police stations. HRW

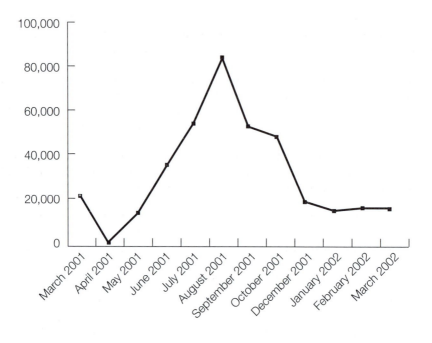

Note: Data unavailable for November 2001

Figure 7.1   IDP figures in the Former Yugoslav Republic of Macedonia in 2001

Source: MCIC, 2001, various situation reports

has documented various cases of this kind, stating that this conduct by police forces violates international human rights law and, in the most severe cases, amounts to torture (HRW, 31 May 2001).

With regard to assistance to IDPs, it is necessary to distinguish between the different kinds of accommodation for displaced persons in the Macedonian context. The majority of the displaced have settled with host families (in most cases, relatives), while a minority have been accommodated in collective centres. During the month of August 2001, when the number of displaced was at its highest, 60,660 displaced were residing with host families, while 3857 persons were accommodated in 21 different collective centres (IFRC, 7 December 2001). Displaced persons living in collective centres have been in a less favourable position than those with host families. Most families have provided generous support to the internally displaced, although host family fatigue was noticed. In a worse position were the people who moved in with their relatives in remote rural areas and people still inside the affected areas.

Return of the Displaced

Despite the political breakthrough in August 2001, full-scale return has been inhibited by prevailing instability in many rural regions, as well as damaged infrastructure and houses in communities of origin. The presence of rebels (during the conflict phase), checkpoints and land mines has further impeded the safe return of displaced populations. Overall, ethnic Albanians, who made up 40 per cent of the displaced, have been far more likely to return to their villages after a short period of displacement than ethnic Macedonians (USCR, September 2001).

The international community has been quick to respond to the needs of the displaced and is still well represented in Macedonia. The main humanitarian actor during the conflict has been the International Committee of the Red Cross (ICRC), which has provided relief to displaced, evacuated the most vulnerable people and reunited separated families. Another significant response came from UN agencies such as the UN High Commissioner for Refugees (UNHCR), the UN Development Programme (UNDP), the World Health Organization (WHO) and the UN Children's Fund (UNICEF), as well as numerous NGOs, who distributed food and non-food items, offered health care and have repaired homes.

Georgia

The overwhelming majority of internally displaced people in Georgia originate from the secessionist territory of Abkhazia. They were forced to flee from this western area into Georgia proper during 1992–1993. According to government estimates, as many as 252,000 of these persons remained internally displaced at the end of 2001.[1] In addition to these IDPs from Abkhazia, several thousand persons were still displaced in Georgia during 2002 as a result of ethnic conflict in South Ossetia (1989–1991).[2] In both cases, the number of internally displaced has remained stable for most of the past decade, with only a low level of return movements registered in the Gali district of Abkhazia and in South Ossetia. There are no prospects for a large-scale return to Abkhazia in the near future as tensions remain high.

Background to the Displacement from Abkhazia

According to the 1989 Soviet census, ethnic Georgians made up 45 per cent of the pre-war population of the autonomous republic of Abkhazia in the north-west of Georgia. Ethnic Abkhaz represented 17 per cent of the population, hardly more than Armenians and Russians (14 per cent each). A declaration of sovereignty in 1992 triggered the confrontation between Abkhaz and Georgian forces. 13 months of war and ethnic violence followed. Instances of murder, destruction, looting and evictions forced the entire ethnic Georgian population to leave Abkhazia and settle in neighbouring districts under Georgian control (Dale, 1997, sects2–4).

In 1994, the Georgian and Abkhaz sides signed an agreement in Moscow on the separation of forces to be monitored by a Russian-dominated peacekeeping force and the UN Military Observer Mission in Georgia (UNOMIG). A Quadripartite Agreement on Voluntary Return of Refugees and Displaced Persons was also signed by the two sides, the Russian Federation and the UN High Commissioner for Refugees (UNOCHA, 15 March 2001, Abkhazia). Following the adoption of this agreement, about 30,000 persons returned to the Gali district (eastern Abkhazia), where the pre-war population was 90 per cent ethnic Georgian.

Renewed violence in 1998 once again displaced the returnees from Gali into Georgia proper, where they have remained without any prospects for return in the near future. Political dialogue under the auspices of the Special Representative of the UN Secretary-General in Georgia has failed to produce agreement. The Abkhazian side has refused to even discuss returning to Georgian sovereignty (UNOCHA, 15 March 2001, Abkhazia; UNSC, 18 January 2002, paras3–7).

Limited Return to the Gali District

Since 1999, many ethnic Georgians have regularly commuted across the ceasefire line between the Gali and Samegrelo districts in order to cultivate their lands or orchards, while a small number have returned full time, with very little assistance and protection (ICRC, May 2001, pp6–7). Persistent insecurity, mainly related to banditry, land mines and confrontations between Abkhaz forces and irregular Georgian armed groups, prevents a larger return or assistance from humanitarian agencies and the UN peacekeeping forces. Recommendations issued by a UN-led mission in November 2000 for a safe and dignified return of the displaced to the Gali district remained largely unfulfilled as of early 2002 (UNSC, 2001, Annex II; UNSC, 2002, para26)

Protracted Displacement in Georgia Proper

The vast majority of the displaced population has remained unable to return to homes of origin elsewhere in Abkhazia and has been dependent upon state assistance. The 1996 Displaced Persons Act and additional government decrees entitle them to social aid, especially in the form of a monthly stipend which, while far below the minimum-survival food basket cost, is not paid regularly. While differences between the local population and the displaced are apparently negligible with respect to health and education, unemployment rates among the displaced are two to three times higher than among the local population. The displacement experience has modified gender roles within displaced households, with many women becoming the main breadwinners and often showing more initiative in their new environment than men.

About half of the displaced live in private accommodation with host families. There have been signs of 'hospitality fatigue', perhaps because of Georgia's economic difficulties and the length of the displacement. Evictions of displaced households have been reported. The remaining displaced live in collective centres, mainly former hotels, sanatoriums and hospitals, with often only one room per family. In rural areas, the displaced rely partly on land plots provided by the state for temporary use. But the land provided is often of poor quality and too distant from their accommodation.

The Georgian government has been reluctant to facilitate the durable resettlement and socio-economic integration of the displaced in order to keep up political pressure on the Abkhazian authorities for their return. (UNCHR, 25 January 2001, paras59–69).[3]

Little Progress on Return in South Ossetia

Although of a smaller scale than the displacement from Abkhazia, internal displacement from and within South Ossetia (also referred as the Tskhinvali region) has not proved easier to solve. The war during 1989–1991 displaced up to 12,000 persons, mostly ethnic Georgians, from the area and 50,000 ethnic Ossetians from the rest of Georgia or within South Ossetia. Some 40,000 of these latter sought refuge in North Ossetia, across what is now an international border in the Russian Federation. With the help of the Organization for Security and Cooperation in Europe (OSCE) and the UN High Commissioner for Refugees (UNHCR), an agreement was reached regarding the return of refugees and internally displaced persons in 1997. Since then, the authorities on both sides have done little to facilitate any return. The poor economy in South Ossetia and a lack of will to enforce property rights there or elsewhere in Georgia also impede any return (UNOCHA, 15 March 2001, South Ossetia; USDOS, 2002, Georgia, sect2d).

The International Response

In the absence of an effective settlement to the political disputes over Abkhazia and South Ossetia, support from the international donor community has dwindled, obliging the Georgian authorities to move away from direct assistance to enhancing the self-reliance capacity of the displaced. A self-reliance fund launched in 1999 to finance innovative self-sufficiency projects brought in only US$1 million in preliminary pledges, limiting its impact to merely pilot project development.

Insecurity in Abkhazia has prevented the UN observer mission from undertaking more regular patrolling in areas of return, while the peacekeeping forces have been accused of passivity in the face of violence against ethnic Georgian returnees (IHF, September 2001, p140). The work of international agencies such as the UNHCR, the UN Office for Human Rights, the International Committee of the Red Cross (ICRC) and other international NGOs has also been hampered by insecurity in the area (UNSC, 24 October 2001, para32). In South Ossetia, the absence of political commitment to return has discouraged donors from supporting development and transitional assistance programmes, while funding for humanitarian assistance has decreased over time (UNOCHA, 15 March 2001, South Ossetia).

International agencies have started switching from humanitarian assistance to integration and development elsewhere in the country. Activities include shelter rehabilitation, community capacity-building, training and support to income-generating activities among internally displaced communities and other vulnerable groups. Certain populations, however, still require sustained humanitarian support. The ICRC has decided to renew a large assistance programme covering food, water and habitat needs for 20,000 of the most vulnerable residents and IDPs in western Georgia during 2002.

Endnotes

1 According to a socio-economic survey of the International Federation of the Red Cross (IFRC) conducted in 2000, 20 per cent of the IDP addresses surveyed were non-existent or incorrect. See IFRC, November 2000, Annex A.
2 There are no reliable estimates for the population still displaced as a result of the conflict in South Ossetia. By early 2002, a few hundred IDPs still lived in collective centres in North Ossetia, while other displaced Ossetian families returned or moved back and forth between South Ossetia and the Russian Federation. The Georgian government still gave the figure of 12,000 IDPs from South Ossetia in Georgia proper in 2002; but UNHCR estimated, in 2000, that this population numbered only 6000 persons. See UN Commission for Human Rights (UNCHR), 25 January 2001, para21.
3 IDPs have been denied the right to vote for local candidates in parliamentary elections, or to vote at all in local elections unless they register as local residents and thereby renounce their status as internally displaced persons. Legislation on IDPs' voting rights in line with the UN Guiding Principles on Internal Displacement was due to have been introduced in 2001. The possession of land in Georgia proper makes IDPs lose their status and the benefits attached to it (GYLA, 1999).

Republic of Moldova

Civil war in the separatist Transdniestrian region in 1992 displaced up to 51,000 persons within the Republic of Moldova and pushed 56,000 refugees mainly to neighbouring Ukraine. The ceasefire that was declared in July 1992 between the Moldovan government and authorities in the Transdniestrian region has enabled most of the displaced population to return home.

However, several thousand displaced persons have preferred to resettle in the government-controlled area; but there has been no reliable information on the exact size of this group. The only data available concerning the population still internally displaced comes from the UN High Commissioner for Refugees (UNHCR), who gave the figure of 1000 internally displaced persons still seeking durable solutions as of December 2001 (UNHCR, 16 May 2002, table 15).

A UNHCR-sponsored survey reported that displaced persons who returned to Transdniestria were often exposed to harassment and mistreatment and that IDPs' properties were re-allocated by the authorities to other persons (Nantoi, 1999). In addition, human rights organizations have reported discrimination against Romanian/Moldovan speakers in schools, forced conscription into Transdniestrian armed forces and intimidation of political opponents. As a result, international organizations in Moldova have confirmed recurrent movements of individuals from Transdniestria to Moldova proper since the cessation of armed hostilities (UNHCR, 29 May 2002; OSCE, 30 May 2002).

The registration of persons newly displaced from Transdniestria has been suspended since 1992, while most public assistance programmes targeting IDPs (cash assistance or housing allocation) have ceased since the mid 1990s. The government of Moldova has shown little interest in the issue since then. As of 2002, UNHCR was the only international agency providing some assistance to the internally displaced persons, such as refurbishment of schools and health facilities in areas of return; but it lacked funds to expand its involvement to the scale needed.

Russian Federation

Up to 460,000 persons are currently displaced in the Russian Federation as a result of armed conflict and violence in the North Caucasus. The vast majority of displaced persons have been forced to leave their homes in Chechnya, a region devastated by two conflicts in less than a decade. The precise scale of internal displacement is difficult to determine because figures in the field diverge widely as a result of continuous population movements, insecurity and inconsistent registration practices.

Conflict in Chechnya

The first armed conflict between federal forces and secessionist armed groups in Chechnya (1994–1996) took the lives of 30,000 civilians and displaced as many as 600,000. Most ethnic Russians and other non-Chechen groups left Chechnya during this period and settled elsewhere in the Russian Federation. Federal authorities granted them the status of 'forced migrant', which entitles beneficiaries to social assistance in support of their resettlement.[1] As of 31 December 2001, about 87,000 persons maintained this status.

However, the majority of the displaced from the 1994–1996 conflict in Chechnya were ethnic Chechens and were not recognized as 'forced migrants'. Many of these people were still displaced in neighbouring republics when the second conflict in Chechnya broke out in September 1999.

The resumption of armed hostilities between federal military forces and the Chechen separatists in 1999 plunged the North Caucasus into a new humanitarian disaster. As during the first conflict, both sides conducted armed operations in disregard of humanitarian principles. By the end of 1999, disproportionate use of force, indiscriminate attacks, arbitrary arrest, torture and inhuman treatment – mainly attributed by human rights organizations to federal forces – had forced up to 600,000 persons from their homes. The majority remained displaced within Chechnya; but a significant number of them (up to 200,000 persons) fled during the winter of 1999–2000 to the neighbouring republic of Ingushetia – the only escape route left open by federal authorities.

The main military campaign of the second conflict was declared over in April 2000. Chechen fighters were reported to have withdrawn from the lowlands to consolidate in the mountains. Since then, some return movements have occurred, although low-level warfare has persisted. Civilians in the Chechen republic are still exposed to indiscriminate military action, extortion, disappearances and random violence by Russian soldiers and Chechen rebels. Armed clashes between federal forces and Chechen rebels, often followed by village sweep operations and raids carried out by federal forces, continued to be reported by human rights organizations throughout 2001 and early 2002 and belied the return to normalcy in Chechnya reported by the authorities.

As of early 2002, the registration system maintained by the Danish Refugee Council showed a population of 140,000 IDPs from Chechnya in Ingushetia and 135,000 IDPs in Chechnya. Local authorities claimed the internally displaced population to be larger, exceeding 200,000 persons in each republic as of the end of 2001. Since 2000, civilians have continued to leave Chechnya because of insecurity. Displaced persons from Chechnya in Ingushetia have returned only temporarily to Chechnya to check on properties and visit relatives. This constant to and fro movement and the suspension of the registration of newly arrived IDPs from Chechnya, ordered by the federal authorities in April 2001, are both factors that have made it difficult to estimate the exact number of IDPs in each republic.[2]

Humanitarian Concerns

In both Chechnya and Ingushetia, the majority of IDPs have found shelter with the local population; but significant groups in Ingushetia live in collective shelters (see Figure 7.2). The capacity of local communities to support displaced people is overstretched. In August 2001, UNHCR reported that evictions of displaced families from private accommodation in Ingushetia were taking place on a daily basis. The high level of evictions has prompted a Swiss humanitarian aid agency to provide support to host families in 2001 and 2002 through a cash payment programme targeting about 15,000 people.

According to the UN Consolidated Inter-Agency Appeal for 2002, international relief operations in the North Caucasus helped to stabilize the health situation among the displaced population in Ingushetia, while 'emergency conditions' continued to prevail in Chechnya. However, humanitarian organizations report serious health risks in both republics, linked to malnutrition, poor shelter conditions and psychological stress. Alarming rates of tuberculosis, Hepatitis A, HIV, mental disorders and injuries caused by land mines and unexploded ordnance are among the most serious problems for internally displaced populations. As of early 2002, nearly all internally displaced people in Ingushetia and Chechnya remained dependent upon food aid.

Freedom of Movement

Ethnic Chechen IDPs who have attempted to leave Chechnya or Ingushetia for more favourable conditions elsewhere in the Russian Federation have faced numerous difficulties. One problem has been their inability to register as residents. Although the system of residence permits inherited from the Soviet period (the 'propiska') has been legally abolished, de facto limitations on free choice of residence remain in place in numerous regions, including major urban centres, such as Moscow and St Petersburg. Furthermore, displaced persons from the

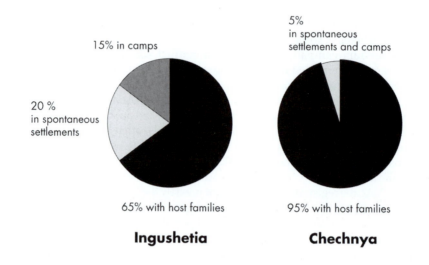

Figure 7.2   Chechnya and Ingushetia: IDPs by type of shelter (November 2001)

Source: UN, November 2001, p8

current conflict in Chechnya have not been granted the 'forced migrant' status, which federal authorities refuse to offer to persons exposed to war violence perpetrated by federal forces. Deprived of any legal status, most Chechen IDPs in urban centres have been unable to gain access to essential services and social benefits. Their precarious situation has been aggravated by continual harassment by police and local authorities. The Chechen conflict has exacerbated racist sentiments among the population at large and has even led to the marginalization of other minority groups. During 2001–2002, the Roma and Meskhetian Turk ethnic minorities in the south Russian region of Krasnodar, for example, were subject to eviction and threat of eviction by local authorities (USDOS, 2001, Russian Federation, sects1f & 2d).

Return Policy

Since 1999, Russian federal authorities have been keen to see the displaced in Ingushetia return to their homes as early as possible, raising concerns among the humanitarian community that movements to unsafe areas may be made prematurely. Although UNHCR reports that there has been no instance involving involuntary return since September 1999, when IDPs living in train wagons were forcibly transferred from Ingushetia to Chechnya, the agency has acknowledged that the principle of voluntary return has been compromised on various occasions (UNHCR, January 2002). Federal practices in Ingushetia, including the chronic disruption of federal food aid in camps, opposition to the provision of new tents, and the suspension of registration of newly arrived Chechen IDPs, have been denounced by human rights organizations as exerting undue pressure on displaced persons to return to Chechnya. Security operations in collective settlements and camps in Ingushetia have also functioned to intimidate IDPs.[3]

Despite pressure from federal authorities on populations to return to Chechnya, departures continuously outweighed return movements during 2000 and 2001. Security conditions in Chechnya are still inadequate for large-scale return. In January 2001, the federal government adopted a programme for the socio-economic reconstruction of Chechnya, with plans to allocate up to US$500 million from the federal budget and other sources. However, the transfer of funds to Chechnya has been painfully slow.

In the area of human rights, Russian President Vladimir Putin appointed Vladimir Kalamanov as his special representative for human rights in Chechnya in February 2000. The special representative's office has received several thousand complaints regarding cases of theft, property destruction, disappearances, rape and murder, which it then refers to military or civil prosecutors. As of March 2002, only 23 servicemen had been convicted of abuses against civilians.

Displacement from the Prigorodny District

In 1992, Ingushetia faced an influx of several thousand displaced persons from neighbouring North Ossetia. Between 34,000 and 64,000 ethnic Ingush were displaced by communal violence in the district of Prigorodny, an area in North Ossetia disputed between ethnic Ingush and Ossetians. By the end of 2001, only 20,000 ethnic Ingush displaced persons had been able to return. Another estimated 20,000 persons were still awaiting return to North Ossetia, some of whom were likely to settle in Ingushetia permanently. Most ethnic Ossetians displaced by the conflict – about 9000 persons – returned to their homes after the conflict.

Photo 7.2   A camp in the village of Uarabulak, Ingushetia (November 2001)

Source: Alexander Glyadelov/MSF

Humanitarian Access

Insecurity in the North Caucasus has seriously hampered the delivery of assistance and protection to the displaced. International humanitarian workers have been exposed to major threats, including kidnapping, land mines and other forms of danger. As a result, UN agencies have limited their presence in Ingushetia to the strict minimum and have entered Chechnya only for rapid assessment missions. Armed escort for international staff is the rule for all UN agencies and the vast majority of international NGOs working in the region.

Despite the Russian assertion that they wish to restore conditions for the early return of the displaced, civilian and military authorities have consistently obstructed the work of international NGOs in Chechnya through numerous bureaucratic impediments. UN special rapporteurs, including Representative of the UN Secretary-General on Internally Displaced Persons Francis Deng, have not been able to visit Chechnya.

Despite problems of access, assistance provided by the international community has proved essential in meeting the basic needs of the displaced in North Caucasus. This aid has been particularly critical as federal authorities have failed to provide humanitarian and reconstruction aid in sufficient quantities. Protection is also an area where several organizations, such as the UNHCR, the Council of Europe and the Organization for Security and Cooperation in Europe (OSCE), have been actively involved by providing support to governmental and non-governmental human rights structures in Chechnya and Ingushetia.

Endnotes

1 The 'forced migrant' status is defined in the Law of the Russian Federation on Forced Migrants, first adopted in February 1993 and revised in 1995. The status is granted for an initial period of five years and can be extended on an annual basis should the individual remain in need of assistance.
2 For planning purposes, UN agencies used the following estimates in 2001: 160,000 IDPs in Chechnya and 150,000 IDPs in Ingushetia. See UN, November 2001, p8.
3 In April 2002, the election of a new president in Ingushetia, who is reportedly closer to authorities in Moscow than his predecessor, also raised fear among the displaced population that Ingushetia may no longer remain a safe haven.

Turkey

Fighting between Turkish security forces and Kurdish armed groups has resulted in the internal displacement of thousands of ethnic Kurds over the last 20 years. Though the most intense fighting ceased in 1999, due to the arrest of the Kurdistan Workers' Party (PKK) leader Abdullah Ocalan during that year, clashes still continued.

Background

With a current population estimated at 12 million persons, Kurds constitute the largest ethnic minority in Turkey (26 per cent of the total population). Ethnic Kurds have been denied rights as an ethnic minority, and manifestations of Kurdish identity have often been prevented by Turkish authorities. Ethnicity was not a concept recognized by the Ottoman Empire or by the founders of the Turkish republic. The government still sees Turkey as a unitary state made up of a patchwork of many different races and believes that any concession to individual ethnic groups would threaten its future.

In 1984, the PKK launched a guerrilla war in south-eastern Turkey that was fought, initially, for Kurdish self-rule in the south-east. The Turkish government responded to this uprising with a counter-insurgency campaign. A state of emergency was declared in ten provinces during 1987, resulting in a heavy military presence, the imposition of martial law and other restrictions to civil and political rights enforced by a special governor.

The Turkish armed forces have reportedly relocated entire villages in their struggle against the PKK. State authorities say 350,000 people were evacuated from about 3500 different villages in south-eastern Turkey between 1984 and 1999. A rough estimate of the number of internally displaced people stands at between 2 and 3 million people, making Turkey the country with the highest number of IDPs in Europe. However, these figures tend to include migrants who left impoverished rural areas in south-eastern provinces for economic reasons.

According to the US Department of State, the figure of 1 million internally displaced persons is a good working estimate to describe the total number of persons who fled because of the violence prevailing in their home areas (USDOS, 2001, Turkey, sect1g). Since 1999, the level of violence has considerably decreased in south-eastern Turkey, but most of the displaced persons are still unable to return to their homes.

Another cause of displacement in Turkey has been the construction of dams in the south-eastern part of the country for the purposes of hydro-electric power generation. As a result of land expropriation related to these dam projects, some 200,000 people have been displaced (ECGD, 22 December 2000, sect3.5).

Protection

During the conflict, it has been reported that the Turkish security forces, as well as the PKK, have exposed the civilian population to violations of human rights and humanitarian law, including arbitrary arrest, torture, extra-judicial killings and indiscriminate attacks.

One of the major sources of insecurity for the civilian population in south-eastern Turkey has been the 'village guard' system. This system, set up by the Turkish authorities to fight the separatists, was designed to combat PKK infiltration through the surveillance of areas by local villagers.

However, village guards and their families have often been the target of deliberate and arbitrary killing by the PKK, while the refusal of villagers to join the village guard has often been followed by the evacuation of their villages by the Turkish security forces. Evacuations have been carried out, with reports of property destruction, rape, torture and extra-judicial executions by the security forces. Only rarely have emergency shelters been provided to the evacuated villagers.

The evacuation of villages and the violence of the armed conflict have left the civilians with no other choice than to move to the nearest provincial capitals, such as Diyarbakir and Batman, which have seen their populations double during the Kurdish conflict. While some of the displaced have found accommodation with family members, most have gathered in slums on the outskirts of major cities. Housing programmes have, so far, been insufficient to address the needs of the Kurdish population in south-eastern Turkey. Ethnic Kurds in urban areas remain under close police surveillance and have been exposed to the risk of arbitrary detention, torture and disappearance (USDOS, 2002, Turkey, sect1c).

Discrimination and Poor Economic Conditions

The situation of the displaced has been further aggravated by the poor economic conditions prevailing in south-eastern provinces. Reports say that displaced households cannot afford to send their children to school and that an increasing number of displaced children in urban areas are trying to make their living on the street (HRFT, May 2001; *Turkish Daily News*, 7 August 2001). The psychosocial status of displaced women is also an issue of grave concern. Coming from a traditional rural background, they often suffer from isolation and lack of hope in their new urban environment. High levels of suicide among displaced women have been reported in the region (*Turkish Daily News*, 5 April 2001).

A significant proportion of the displaced have left the south-eastern region altogether and have moved further to western Turkey in search of a safer environment and better economic conditions. They have been part of a larger migratory movement from south-eastern Turkey that has significantly modified the geographical distribution of the Kurdish population in Turkey, with a majority now living outside eastern and south-eastern provinces.

Displaced households have found some support from Kurdish migrants who settled in western cities such as Ankara, Istanbul or Izmir, particularly with regard to lodging and employment. However, many human rights NGOs consider that big cities outside of the conflict zone do not offer safe conditions for displaced Kurds. While some segments of the Kurdish population have successfully integrated within the general Turkish population, many displaced Kurds live in slums around the cities. Numerous displaced Kurds reportedly prefer not to register with the authorities in localities where they have resettled in order to avoid any contact with the police. Deprived of valid identification documents, the displaced have no access to social services. Discrimination against the Kurds on the labour market is also widespread (Atreya, McDowall, Ozbolat, February 2001, pp24–25).

Problems of Return

Although the level of violence has decreased since 1999, the conditions for the large-scale return of the displaced to their villages of origin do not yet exist. Local human rights NGOs call, in particular, for the abolition of the village guard system as a condition for restoring security in the villages. They also demand more reconstruction aid from the state. They appeal for more compensation for lost properties and for better access to social infrastructure and services (HRFT, 31 May 2001). Moreover, they also point to the problems of land mines, the occupation of land by village guards and the more general question of highly unequal land distribution. There have also been reports that households applying for return assistance have been pressured by local authorities to abandon their claims for compensation (HRFT, January 2001, pp6–9).

Return programmes developed by national authorities have been insufficient to respond to the needs of the displaced. Initiated in 1994, the resettlement of evacuated villages or hamlets into newly built 'central villages' has not had a significant impact upon return. Displaced populations have been reluctant to move to the new settlements. In 1995, the government launched the 'return to the villages' project, providing reconstruction help to returning households. However, since that time, only a few villagers have been given permission by the provincial governors to return to their homes, and 'authorized' returnees have often not been allowed by the local military to enter their villages (HRFT, February 2001, pp11–12). According to the Interior Ministry, between June 2000 and December 2001, a total of 35,513 persons returned to 470 villages or pastures under the auspices of this and other government return programmes (USDOS, 2002, Turkey, sect2d).

International Access

The Turkish government has long obstructed the international monitoring of the human rights situation in the country. Most international humanitarian organizations, including the

International Committee of the Red Cross (ICRC), have been refused access to south-eastern provinces, while human rights organizations can only operate under close police surveillance. That said, an important breakthrough was made in early 2002 when Amnesty International (AI) was invited to reopen its office after an initial rejection by the government during the previous year. Furthermore, though long reluctant to issue any invitation to UN rapporteurs, the Turkish government has invited many rapporteurs to visit Turkey, including the UN Representative on Internally Displaced Persons.

Box 7.3 *Turkey and the European Union*

Turkish membership of the European Union (EU) has been a major political ambition of the government. A serious obstacle, however, has been Turkey's poor human rights record and treatment of national minorities, which have prompted criticism from EU member states. In order to push for an improvement of the human rights situation in Turkey, the EU has linked Turkey's membership prospects with progress in this area, with particular attention to the cultural rights of ethnic Kurds.

In response to pressure from the EU, the Turkish authorities released an ambitious plan in 2000 for improving the protection of human rights. In the same year, an EU draft partnership agreement was concluded, specifying terms on which negotiations for membership could begin.

In 2001, Turkey adopted a package of 34 amendments to its 1982 Constitution. This package introduced new provisions on issues such as freedom of thought and expression, the prevention of torture, the strengthening of civilian authority, freedom of association, and gender equality. However, the *EU Progress Report* of 2001 stated that these reforms were not enough to guarantee the basic liberties required for membership. Turkey still restricted fundamental freedoms, including linguistic and cultural rights for the country's 12 million ethnic Kurds, it said. Incidents of torture and ill treatment continued to take place during police custody. The report echoed doubts on the efficacy of the government's policy for the return and resettlement of the displaced and recommended stronger action for the development of the conflict-affected south-east.

Source: Info-Türk, November 2001

8

Middle East

Regional Overview

With approximately 1.5 million internally displaced people (IDPs) as of early 2002, the Middle East is the region with the least IDPs. Approximately 80 per cent of them have been displaced for over ten years. The vast majority are in Iraq, although the estimate of IDPs in that country is a rough one at best, as few independent organizations have been granted access by the Iraqi government. The Middle East is one of the few regions in the world where the refugee population, at present over 6 million, including 3.9 million Palestinians, exceeds that of the internally displaced.

While prospects for the return of internally displaced people in Lebanon and in some parts of Iraq have improved over the last couple of years, other situations have stagnated or worsened. The withdrawal of Israel from the south of Lebanon in May 2000 and the demise of its ally, the South Lebanese Army (SLA), gave IDPs the possibility of returning home. In Iraq, the Kurdish parties controlling the north of the country finally agreed to allow the return of their respective IDP populations. At the same time, the regime of Saddam Hussein has continued to expel the non-Arab population from the oil-rich region of Kirkuk. Grave tensions between Israel and its neighbours and the renewal of the Israeli–Palestinian conflict since September 2000 have caused additional internal displacement of Palestinians in the Gaza Strip and the West Bank and dimmed the prospect of return for IDPs in Syria and within Israel.

Causes of Displacement

Internal displacement in the Middle East stems from religious and ethnic conflicts that have spanned several decades, as well as competition over land and resources. In many cases, conflicts and subsequent displacement have resulted in the resettlement of populations along ethnic or religious lines.

Religious and ethnic tensions have played a primary role in every situation of internal displacement in the region. The Arab, Sunni Muslim, government of Iraq has killed or displaced members of the ethnic Kurdish minority for decades, and its Anfal policy during the late 1980s has been qualified as genocide by Human Rights Watch (HRW). The government has also uprooted Shia Muslim Arabs in the southern marshlands. In the context of the Lebanese civil war between Christians and Muslims, fighting has led to the displacement of hundreds of thousands of people. Several wars have broken out between Israel and its neighbours since 1948. These wars have caused the expulsion of Arab populations within Israel and Syria, but also to neighbouring countries. The violence since September 2000 has resulted

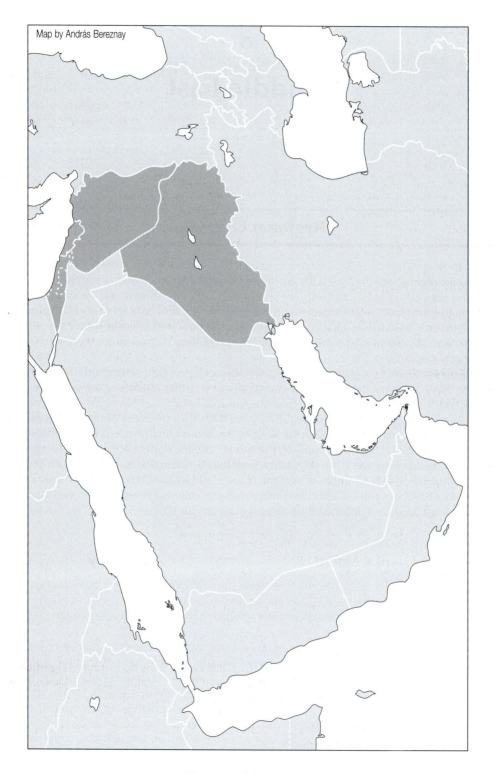

Map 8.1   Middle East

in the demolition of the homes of several thousand Palestinians in the Gaza Strip and West Bank.

The forced dislocation of populations has often been conducted in the Middle East to facilitate control over a territory and its natural resources. The most prominent example is the 'Arabization' policy of the Iraqi government, whereby Iraq has tried to change the ethnic character of the oil-rich region of Kirkuk. It has been expelling non-Arab inhabitants from this region – ethnic Kurds, Assyrians and Turkmen – and has offered land and employment to ethnic Arab citizens who have moved there from the south.

Internal conflicts in the region have been exacerbated by outside states, which have provided financial, political or military support to parties to the conflict. In Iraq, the governments of Turkey and Iran have supported the Kurdish armed groups fighting one another for control of the northern part of the country. In Lebanon, religious rivalries have been exacerbated by Syrian and Israeli intervention. Despite the withdrawal of the Israeli army from the south of the country in 2000, the Lebanese guerrilla group Hezbollah continued to clash with the Israeli army frequently in 2002, with support from Iran and Syria.

Patterns of Displacement

Over half of the internally displaced people in the Middle East have been so for at least 20 years. It is difficult to assess whether those who have been displaced for so long have, in fact, integrated within their new locations and even whether they should still be considered IDPs. This is particularly the case for many displaced villagers in Lebanon and in northern Iraq, who have been resettled in urban areas for decades and have little incentive to return to their areas of origin, where their villages were destroyed or, at best, still lack infrastructure and employment opportunities.

Another factor slowing or preventing return, particularly in Lebanon, is that children whose parents were displaced years ago generally lack strong childhood ties with their family's place of origin. In the case of Israel and Syria, however, where the absence of political solutions has prevented the return of IDPs for decades, children are still said to want to return to their parents' original homes. It remains to be seen if they will indeed go back when the political situation allows.

Human Rights and Humanitarian Situation

The human rights record in the Middle East remained poor in the first part of 2002. Violence against IDPs was particularly severe in Iraq and in the Palestinian Territories. In Iraq, extra-judicial killings, torture, forced evictions of minorities and political opponents are said to be widespread. In the Palestinian Territories, human rights organizations have reported violations committed by the Israeli Defence Forces (IDF), such as unlawful killings and the destruction of civilian property, since the beginning of the second Intifada in September 2000.

Internally displaced people are often among the poorest and most vulnerable, as is the case in Iraq and the Palestinian Territories. In other cases, IDPs do not have significant humanitarian needs over and above those of the rest of the population. The repossession of land and properties is generally their most pressing concern. In Israel, IDPs have been trying to return to their villages of origin for over 50 years; but so far the Israeli government has not allowed them to do so. People displaced within Syria still seek restitution of their lands in the Golan Heights, an area taken by Israel in 1967.

National and International Response

Governments in the region have provided little protection and assistance to the people displaced within their countries. In Lebanon, however, efforts have been made to assist IDPs, most notably through the establishment of a ministry for the displaced. Despite this measure, the return process in Lebanon has had mixed results.

In the Middle East, governments generally impose severe restrictions on freedom of speech and assembly, and the region lacks a strong civil society to draw attention to the plight of IDPs. The exception is Israel, where over 30 IDP associations have formed a coalition since the early 1990s to campaign for a return. In addition, several associations focus on the land rights of Palestinian Arab citizens of Israel.

The response to internal displacement at regional level has been weak. The Middle East does not have an organization that represents all the states in the region. The League of Arab States is the only body close to fulfilling a regional function, and it excludes Israel and Iran. Despite repeated declarations by Arab experts urging the league to work on behalf of IDPs and refugees, it has not followed these recommendations. The organization addresses the issue of displaced Palestinians, but not of other displaced peoples, such as the Kurds in Iraq (Cohen and Deng 1998, *Masses in Flight*, pp233–234).

Assistance to the region is moderate, and long-term IDPs are generally neglected. In Lebanon, however, IDPs receive some assistance in the context of poverty alleviation programmes. United Nations (UN) and non-governmental organization (NGO) humanitarian assistance concentrates on vulnerable populations in Iraq and in the Palestinian Territories, including internally displaced people. Humanitarian access to IDPs in both areas has, however, been severely restricted. The Iraqi government has harassed and intimidated relief workers and UN personnel throughout the country for years, and it has only given permission to seven international NGOs to operate in the government-controlled area. According to several UN reports, Israeli authorities have been blocking delivery of basic food items, medicines and fuel to the Gaza Strip, and UN humanitarian access to the West Bank was being delayed by bureaucratic procedures as of May 2002.

Iraq

Iraq is host to the highest number of internally displaced people in the Middle East. Between 700,000 and 1 million people were estimated to be internally displaced there as of 2002.[1] Ethnic Kurds, Assyrians and Turkmen have suffered from several waves of displacement over the past two decades, mainly due to repression by the Iraqi government and, to a lesser extent, to inter-ethnic Kurdish fighting. Shia Arab populations in the south of Iraq have also been displaced from their homes due to government actions, particularly since 1991.

Historical Background

In the aftermath of the 1991 Gulf War, an uprising against the regime of President Saddam Hussein in the north and south of the country was rapidly crushed by government troops. In April 1991, the UN Security Council (UNSC) adopted Resolution 688, which called for the government to end the repression of its civilian population and to allow international humanitarian agencies immediate access to the country (UNSC, 5 April 1991). The same month, the UN established a 'safe haven' in the north of the country to protect the Kurdish population from Baghdad's actions. Following a US order to end all military activity in the north, the Iraqi government withdrew its troops and administrative personnel from that area. Since then, the northern governorates of Arbil, Sulaymaniah and Dahuk have been under the control of the two major Kurdish parties and enjoy de facto autonomy.

As of mid 2002, the UN sanctions imposed on Iraq in 1991 were still in place, mainly due to Iraq's refusal to allow international inspection of its weapons industry. Since 1996 the 'oil-for-food' programme has allowed Iraq to import essential goods to alleviate some of the needs of its people and to mitigate the impact of the sanctions. The oil-for-food programme has also been implemented in the region under Kurdish administration. Many international observers have criticized the dire humanitarian impact of the sanctions despite the oil-for-food programme. In May 2002, UN Security Council members agreed on revised sanctions in order to ease their humanitarian impact.

Displacement of Ethnic Kurds, Turkmen and Assyrians

The Iraqi government caused the massive displacement of Iraqi Kurds from their towns and villages during the 1970s and late 1980s. Since the mid 1970s, Baghdad has also forcibly displaced nearly 200,000 of the ethnically non-Arab citizens from the oil-rich region of Kirkuk. This displacement continued in 2002.

During the mid and late 1970s, the Iraqi regime destroyed Kurdish villages and forcibly displaced hundreds of thousands of ethnic Kurds living close to the borders with Iran and Turkey, relocating them in settlements controlled by the army. In 1988, at the end of the Iran–Iraq war, Baghdad's forces launched the Anfal campaign, destroying thousands of Kurdish villages and towns, killing between 50,000 and 100,000 civilians, and forcibly displacing hundreds of thousands of villagers. According to Human Rights Watch (HRW), the campaign of destruction led by the Iraqi government against the Kurdish population can be qualified as genocide (HRW, July 1993).[2]

Since the mid 1970s, the Iraqi government has also expelled thousands of ethnic Kurdish, Assyrian and Turkmen families from the oil-rich Kirkuk area through what is known as the Arabization policy. Kirkuk has long been claimed by the Kurds as part of Iraqi Kurdistan, but lies just south of the 'Kurdistan Autonomous Region' delineated by the Iraqi government in 1974 (see Map 8.2).

Non-ethnic Arab Iraqis have been given the choice of leaving Kirkuk or signing a form 'correcting their nationality' to be considered ethnic Arabs. Measures used by the government to encourage departures and prevent the return of displaced persons have included setting up military checkpoints around Kirkuk, demolishing Kurdish sites and prohibiting Kurds from constructing or inheriting property in the area (UNCHR, 26 February 1999). Those refusing to comply have been subjected to intimidation, arrest, revocation of ration cards and, eventually, expulsion. From 1991 to 2000, the Iraqi government has been responsible for the displacement to northern Iraq of over 94,000 persons from Kirkuk and other cities under government control, such as Mosul (UNGA, 14 August 2000, para50). In 2000, five to six families were being deported to northern Iraq each day (UNHCR/ACCORD, 14 November 2000, p57). At the same time, the Iraqi government has encouraged Arab families from central and southern Iraq to resettle in Kirkuk to affirm the 'Arabic' character of the city and to prevent Kurdish claims that Kirkuk is part of its territory. Kurdish sources reported that forced displacement from the Kirkuk area had intensified in early 2002.

Displacement due to Kurdish Fighting

Another cause of displacement has been factional Kurdish in-fighting. Two major Kurdish political parties – the Kurdish Democratic Party (KDP) and the Patriotic Union of Kurdistan

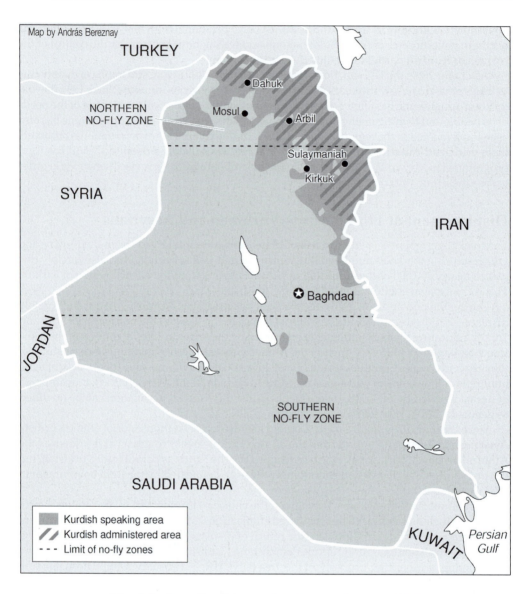

Map by András Bereznay

TURKEY

NORTHERN
NO-FLY ZONE

● Dahuk

Mosul ●

● Arbil

Sulaymaniah
●   ●
● Kirkuk

SYRIA

IRAN

✪ Baghdad

JORDAN

SOUTHERN
NO-FLY ZONE

SAUDI ARABIA

▨ Kurdish speaking area
▨ Kurdish administered area
- - - Limit of no-fly zones

KUWAIT   Persian
Gulf

Map 8.2   Iraq: Kurdish populated areas (January 2000)

Source: Rekacewicz, *Le Monde Diplomatique*, 2000

(PUK) – have been fighting over the control of the three governorates of Dahuk, Arbil and Sulaymaniah, particularly during the period from 1994 to 1997. Forcible exchange of populations took place between the parties, affecting a total of 100,000–110,000 people accused of being affiliated to the other party (UNHCR/ACCORD, 14 November 2000, p58). In 1998, both parties accepted a Washington-brokered peace agreement, which provided for the return of the people expelled from each other's territory. The implementation of the peace agreement has been slow, and the two parties were maintaining separate administrations over the region as of 2002. Hundreds of families were, nevertheless, allowed to return home in 2001. The region experienced new internal displacement in 2001 and 2002 due to clashes between the PUK and an Islamic opposition.

Internal Kurdish conflict has been exacerbated by the intervention of regional players who have all been opposed to the creation of a Kurdish state. Turkey's raids into Iraqi Kurdistan in search of PKK rebels, as well as Iranian and Iraqi government interventions and shelling from outside the Kurdish-controlled region, have all caused internal displacement.

Displacement of Shia Arabs from the Mesopotamian Marshlands

Displacement within the government-controlled area of Iraq has been caused by confrontations between the Sunni regime of President Saddam and the majority Shia Muslim population, who rebelled in the wake of the Iraqi defeat in Kuwait in 1991. Baghdad crushed the revolt and many people fled, not only to the predominantly Kurdish north but also to the Mesopotamian marshlands of the Tigris–Euphrates Delta, in the south. The Iraqi government then ordered the burning and shelling of villages in the south, and had dams built to divert water from the marshes. This allowed government forces to penetrate into formerly inaccessible areas where their Shia opponents had found refuge (USCR, 2001, p180).

Drawing on satellite images, a UN Environment Programme (UNEP) study shows that the Mesopotamian marshlands – the largest wetland in the Middle East and one of the outstanding freshwater ecosystems of the world – has now nearly vanished. Previous estimates of the population of the marsh area, the Marsh Arabs or Ma'adan, varied between 350,000 and 500,000 (Partow, 2001, p15). Following the destruction of their villages and the building of the dams, most Marsh Arabs have had to submit to compulsory resettlement within Iraq, leave the country or remain in the drained marshlands, deprived of their water-based means of livelihood.

Protection Issues

Information on human rights violations in Iraq is difficult to obtain, since the government does not allow human rights experts to travel outside of Baghdad and neighbouring countries often refuse passage to the north of Iraq. However, opposition groups based outside of Iraq have managed to gather valuable human rights information from their supporters inside government-controlled Iraq. In addition to forcible expulsions based on ethnic origin, Amnesty International (AI) reported in 2001 the execution of hundreds of people, including possible prisoners of conscience, the arrest of hundreds of suspected political opponents and widespread torture (AI, 2001).

In February 2002, the Iraqi government finally authorized the visit of the UN Special Rapporteur on the Situation of Human Rights in Iraq, after denying entry since 1992. The UN Special Rapporteur, the UN Commission on Human Rights (UNCHR), as well as national and international NGOs such as Amnesty International, have repeatedly denounced the Iraqi government's policy of forced displacement from Kirkuk and the southern marshes. The Iraqi foreign ministry has rejected allegations of forced displacement as baseless.

Living Conditions

Living conditions for the Iraqi population are often very poor regardless of whether they are displaced or not. The Gulf War severely damaged Iraq's infrastructure, interrupting the power supply and, consequently, the operation of pumping and treatment facilities. This has led to

Photo 8.1   Displaced Persons, Kurdistan, Sulaymaniah (1998)

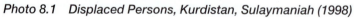

Source: Roland Sidler/ICRC

an overall deterioration in the quality and quantity of drinking water and the rapid spread of infectious diseases, such as cholera. A 1999 UN Children's Fund (UNICEF) survey reported that, in government-controlled Iraq, infant mortality increased from 47 to 108 deaths per 1000 live births, while child mortality increased from 56 to 131 deaths per 1000 live births between the 1984–1989 and 1994–1999 periods (UNICEF, 27 August 1999). It was reported in 2000 that the internally displaced persons camps, built during the 1980s, primarily in the south of Iraq, had running streams of raw sewage between housing blocks, and untreated standing sewage water with enormous potential for disease (AFSC, 21 March 2000).

A UN-Habitat survey found, in 2001, that about 40 per cent of internally displaced persons in the region under Kurdish administration lived in settlements with standards of water and electricity supplies, sanitation, drainage and road access that were below average for the area. Access to food, education and health care was, however, found acceptable (UNSC, 2 March 2001). Due to the increasing number of internally displaced in the north, several international observers reported in December 2000 that local authorities were becoming less welcoming to newcomers. The head of UN programmes in Iraq also expressed his concern about the lack of housing alternatives (Crossette, 11 December 2000). Another element adding to the difficulty in resettling the internally displaced in northern Iraq is the fact that the region is heavily mined, and clearing these minefields would reportedly take between 35 and 75 years (UNSC, 19 November 1998).

Response

The international response to humanitarian needs in Iraq and to internal displacement has been limited due to the fact that the Iraqi government severely restricts access to the UN and international NGOs. Only a handful of international NGOs have permission to operate in government-controlled Iraq. The government also reportedly harasses and intimidates relief workers and UN personnel throughout the country. In June 2000, two staff members of the UN Food and Agriculture Organization (FAO) were shot dead in Baghdad and six others wounded.

The World Food Programme (WFP) is responsible for food distribution in northern Iraq and for observing the adequacy of rations in government-controlled areas. The United Nations Human Settlements Programme (UN-Habitat) builds shelters to enable the displaced to resettle in northern Iraq on a permanent basis. Since 2001, the UN Office for Project Services (UNOPS) has been providing emergency relief items, such as tents, blankets, heaters and stoves, to internally displaced persons in the north. The European Union (EU) is the largest donor of humanitarian aid to Iraq and has focused upon the centre and south of Iraq. NGOs, the International Committee of the Red Cross (ICRC) and the International Federation of Red Cross and Red Crescent Societies (IFRC) have been providing assistance to the IDPs in Iraq, such as non-food items, housing, water and sanitation.

Endnotes

1 The Global IDP Project has established that there may be as many as 1 million IDPs in Iraq, based on various reports by the UN Secretary-General, the UN Environment Programme (UNEP), UN-Habitat and NGOs.

2 The 1988 campaign against the ethnic Kurds of Iraq has become known as 'Anfal'. *Anfal* – or the Spoils – is the name of the eight *sura* of the Koran. It is also the name given by Iraqis to a series of military actions that took place from 23 February until 6 September 1988. See HRW, July 1993.

Israel

The situation of the hundreds of thousands of Palestinians who became refugees as a result of the 1948 war between the new State of Israel and its Arab neighbours has received international exposure. However, little attention has been given to the tens of thousands of Palestinians who became displaced within Israel following the destruction of their localities at the time. The situation of the Bedouin community in Israel has been particularly difficult, as several waves of displacement have affected this group. The internally displaced people have since resettled in other parts of Israel. They now represent about one quarter of the 1 million Palestinian citizens of Israel. Many have not given up the hope of, one day, returning to their original homes.

Historical Background and Causes of Displacement

Following the UN vote on the partition of Palestine into a Jewish and an Arab state in November 1947, and the proclamation of the State of Israel in May 1948, armies from neighbouring Arab nations entered the former Mandate of Palestine and fought against Israeli military forces. At the end of the war in 1949, no general peace settlement was achieved.

Between 1948 and 1949, approximately 600,000–760,000 Arabs who had lived in the territory that became Israel were driven or fled from the country and became refugees.[1] During this period, another 46,000–48,000 Arab villagers were displaced within Israel, and today this group (including their descendants) represents about 150,000–200,000 persons.[2] The vast majority of internally displaced people were Muslim (about 90 per cent) and a minority Christian (about 10 per cent). The Druze community was spared from displacement for the most part (*Al-Haj*, September 1986, p654).

The above estimates do not include the IDPs from the Bedouin community. According to NGOs defending the rights of the internally displaced, approximately 70,000 Bedouin have been displaced as a result of the 1948 war and of subsequent forced resettlement by the Israeli authorities.[3]

In addition to the movement of populations within Israel at the time, Israel absorbed approximately 600,000 Jewish refugees, who had fled from European and Arab countries during the period of 1947–1950 (Eban, 1978).

Prospects for Return and Land Issues

In December 1948, the United Nations established the UN Relief and Works Agency for Palestine Refugees in the Near East (UNRWA). The mandate of the agency was to assist all those who were residents in Palestine in 1946 and who lost their homes and livelihood in 1948. UNRWA assisted the internally displaced within Israel from 1950 to 1952 until Israel took over this responsibility. Following the war, the UN General Assembly (UNGA) adopted Resolution 194, which affirmed that:

> . . .*the refugees wishing to return to their homes and live at peace with their neighbours should be permitted to do so at the earliest practicable date, and that compensation should be paid for the property of those choosing not to return and for loss of or damage to property which, under principles of international law or in equity, should be made good by the governments or authorities responsible (UNGA, 11 December 1948, para11).*

Over 50 years later, many people displaced from their villages in Israel and resettled in other towns are still waiting for their situation to be resolved. In some instances, destroyed villages have been labelled closed security zones by the Israeli authorities, and their former inhabitants have petitioned Israeli courts to be allowed to return. But in many cases the former land of the displaced has been built on and is now occupied by new houses and roads. While some IDPs have accepted compensation offered by the government for their lost property, others have considered the amount too low.

The Israeli government created an institutional and legal land regime by which most properties of IDPs and refugees were appropriated by the state. One of the cornerstones of this system was the Absentee Property Law of 1950. According to this law, the state acquired control of all property left by people who had fled their homes between 29 November 1947 and 19 May 1948, even if they had stayed in the country. As a result, most of the internally displaced were then declared 'present absentees' and the government acquired their properties (*Schechla*, October 2001, p22).

In 1949, the Israeli government decided to rent land to the displaced. IDPs in poor economic circumstances were to be the primary beneficiaries of land allocation, especially those from villages that had surrendered to the Israeli army. The government believed that by renting land at the locations of their resettlement, the displaced would think less about their lost villages. While in some cases the displaced did rent land without a problem, in many other cases they faced opposition from their Jewish neighbours or pressure from the Arab host communities and refused to rent abandoned land. Sometimes IDPs feared that renting land in the area of displacement would compromise their claims to their original property (Cohen, Hillel, December 2000, pp53–56).

Following the creation of the State of Israel, the IDPs lived under Israeli military administration like the vast majority of the Arab population in Israel; as a result, their freedom of movement was severely limited. The lifting of the military administration in 1966 improved their situation but did not allow them to regain their lost properties.

Today most of the displaced live, like the rest of the Arab population in Israel, in Arab towns with little or no Jewish population, where they have usually set up their own separate neighbourhoods. Alternatively they live in 'mixed' Arab–Jewish towns.

Specific land issues for the Bedouin

While many displaced still had land titles to their properties, this was not the case of the Bedouin, since traditionally their property had never been registered. In addition, the State of Israel enacted a series of laws and regulations facilitating confiscation of Bedouin land. These laws were also accompanied by several waves of displacement. In 1949, many Bedouin in the south of the country were ordered to move into a closed area under military administration. Following the cancellation of military rule in 1966, most of them continued living in the former closed area (Abu-Rabia, November 1994, p15). Since that time, many have settled in 'unrecognized villages': villages that were declared illegal by the National Planning and Building Law of 1965 and which usually do not receive municipal services.

From the 1970s to the 1990s, the Israeli government planned and built seven conventional towns for the Bedouin. It reported to the UN Human Rights Committee in 1998 that it had tried to accommodate the traditional Bedouin way of life (UN Human Rights Committee, 9 April 1998). Nevertheless, advocates for the Bedouin say the community has not been sufficiently involved in the planning of the towns and not enough consideration has been paid to their lifestyle and traditions. Furthermore, the compensation received for giving up their land in exchange for a new house in the towns is viewed as too low by many observers. While

---

Box 8.1 *NGOs promoting the rights of the internally displaced in Israel*

Many local NGOs promote the rights of the Palestinian Arab minority in Israel, including those of the internally displaced. The main organization, the **National Council for the Defense of the Rights of Displaced Persons in Israel**, was created in 1995 to advance the goal of internally displaced people to return to their villages of origin since their situation was not addressed within the framework of the Oslo peace process. The National Council is an umbrella organization uniting 30 local committees of displaced people.

Other organizations advocating on behalf on the internally displaced in Israel include:

Association for Civil Rights in Israel (ACRI)
Has projects to promote the rights of Palestinian Arab citizens of Israel, including land rights.
Website: http://www.nif.org/acri/

Adalah (Legal Center for Arab Minority Rights in Israel)
Prepares court cases related to discrimination against the internally displaced and others to be heard by the Israeli Supreme Court.
Website: http://www.adalah.org/

Arab Association for Human Rights (HRA)
Promotes the rights of the Palestinian Arab minority in Israel through advocacy. Examines issues such as land, property and the situation of the Bedouin community in the Negev.
Website: http://www.arabhra.org/

Association 40
Aims for the recognition of the unrecognized Arab villages in Israel.
Website: http://www.assoc40.org/

Committee for the Uprooted of Kafar Birem
Supports internally displaced persons wishing to return to Kafar Birem in northern Galilee.
Website: http://www.birem.org/

Regional Council for the Unrecognized Villages in the Negev
Promotes the rights of Bedouin populations living in unrecognized villages through the development of social and economic services.
Website: http://www.arabhra.org/rcuv/help.htm

Sikkuy (Equality)
Advocates for equality of Jewish and Arab citizens in Israel, including the internally displaced.
Website: http://www.sikkuy.org.il

---

the seven towns built for the Bedouin community do offer better access to services than in the traditional Bedouin settlements, the quality and level of services is still considered inferior to those in Jewish towns.

Government Response

Many displaced have appealed to Israeli courts against land confiscation; but the process is slow and the level of compensation often not considered sufficient by the recipients. Israeli Supreme Court decisions to allow the villagers of Kafar Bir'em, Ikrit and others to return to their villages were not implemented. Alternative government proposals of compensation and land exchanges have not met the demands of the displaced who want to return to their former homes. On 25 November 2001, an Israeli High Court order gave the Israeli government three months to submit a detailed plan for compensating the displaced villagers of Birem and Ikrit (*Benvenisti*, 29 November 2001). As of April 2002, the government had apparently not submitted the requested plan to the Israeli High Court. The intensification of violence in the region in 2002 did nothing to bring closer a durable solution for these internally displaced persons.

Photo 8.2   Bedouin camp of Jahalin destroyed by the Israeli army, Valley of Wadi Abu Hindi, near Jerusalem (1997)

Source: Thierry Gassmann/ICRC

Endnotes

1 See Middle East Research and Information Project (MERIP), 2001, and Bligh, 1998, p124.
2 For 1948–1949 estimates, see National Committee for the Rights of the Internally Displaced in Israel, February 2000, and Bligh, 1998, p124; for current estimates, see Nir, 8 January 2001.
3 See National Committee for the Rights of the Internally Displaced in Israel, February 2000, and BADIL Resource Centre for Palestinian Residency and Refugee Rights, 23 April 2001, p27.

Lebanon

During the Lebanese civil war of 1975–1990, almost one third of the country's population was displaced. By 1990 when the war ended, in addition to the hundreds of thousands of people who had found refuge abroad, about 450,000 people remained internally displaced in Lebanon (UNDP, 1997). Fewer than one third of them had returned home by mid 2002.

At the war's end, the south of the country remained in the hands of a Christian militia, the South Lebanese Army (SLA), and Israeli troops for another ten years. Former residents of the south finally started to return home when Israeli troops withdrew in May 2000. In June 2000, the UN confirmed that Israel had completed the withdrawal in accordance with UN Security Council (UNSC) Resolution 425 (1978). The region remained unstable, however, due to violent clashes between the Lebanese guerrilla movement Hezbollah and Israeli security forces. The point of discord for the more recent fighting has centred on the Shebaa farms, an area taken from Syria by Israel in 1967 but now claimed by Lebanon with Syria's approval. In mid 2002, cross-border incidents were occurring frequently.

Causes and Patterns of Displacement

At the beginning of the civil war in 1975, displacement of Muslims by Christian militias and of Christians by the Palestine Liberation Organization (PLO) and the Lebanese National Movement (LNM) took place in and around Beirut.[1] The capital was divided into Christian and Muslim sectors. The largest wave of displacement took place in 1985 around Mount Lebanon. Further displacement – both temporary and long term – was caused by Israeli interventions in Lebanon in 1978 and 1982. In 1989, violent fighting erupted between Christian militias and Syrian troops, and between the militias themselves, due to a disagreement over modalities for peace, leading to further displacement. In 1996, following Hezbollah rocket attacks on northern Israel, Israel launched extensive air raids and rocket attacks on Beirut and villages in southern Lebanon, which caused the temporary displacement of still hundreds of thousands more people.

Overall, the displacement has resulted in resettlement along religious lines, exacerbated economic imbalances and contributed to the disintegration of social ties. Most of the displacement has been to urban areas, particularly Beirut.

Living Conditions

Living conditions for the displaced remained poor in 2002. Many people had their homes destroyed during the war and have moved into overcrowded houses with friends or have occupied houses illegally. Overcrowding has reportedly increased the spread of disease. Some internally displaced people who had occupied houses have had to vacate properties and have received compensation; but they have not always been resettled properly. IDPs living in makeshift shelters around Beirut have been described as the poorest of Lebanese society (USCR, 2001, p189). This said, the economic, social, and security conditions of the displaced are reportedly often better in their current location than if they were to return to their communities of origin.

Factors Slowing Return and Reintegration

Since the end of the civil war, the Lebanese government has put the reintegration of the displaced high on its agenda. Already in 1989, the Charter of National Reconciliation, or Taif Agreement, declared the return of the displaced necessary for reconciliation and sustainable peace. The agreement also acknowledged the right of every Lebanese citizen displaced since 1975 to go back to the place from where she or he was displaced, and pledged financial support to enable the displaced to reconstruct their homes and villages (Government of Lebanon, 1989).

Furthermore, two main government structures were created in 1993 to implement the return of the displaced:

- The Lebanese Ministry for the Displaced was established in order to rehabilitate infrastructure and housing, improve the economic sector and to achieve national reconciliation.
- The Central Fund for the Displaced was created to finance the return of the displaced.

The government has offered compensation to internally displaced people, including their children, to rebuild homes; but the vast majority of the displaced have not reclaimed their properties. The government set the end of 2002 as the target for the return of all displaced; but there were still at least 300,000 IDPs in Lebanon as of mid 2002.

Return has been slow due to several factors apart from security. They include corruption and political rivalries between government officials, budgetary problems, and economic and social considerations. According to the Lebanese Institute for Human Rights, the implementation of the return process has been characterized by coordination problems and inconsistencies. The Lebanese Ministry for the Displaced has faced serious budgetary problems and has been accused of mismanaging the allocation of funds (Assaf and El-Fil, 7 April 2000). The Central Fund for the Displaced had to discontinue payments to the displaced in November 2001 due to a lack of funds.

Many internally displaced people have little reason to return to their villages of origin. Infrastructure has been severely damaged during the war. The villages have few schools and do not offer many employment opportunities. The director of the Central Fund for the Displaced acknowledged in 2001 that, after 25 years, many displaced persons had become part of a new social context and did not want to go back to their homes of origin (Ibrahim, 7 February 2001). This is particularly the case for children whose parents were displaced years ago and who lack strong childhood ties with the original villages and towns of their parents. Security considerations have played a role, as well. Former neighbours of different religious backgrounds have found it difficult to live together due to mistrust exacerbated by 15 years of conflict.

While return to the former security zone occupied by Israel finally started in mid 2000, it met serious obstacles. Many villages had been partly or totally destroyed, employment options were limited and physical security was inadequate. Several hundred thousand land mines located in the south caused death and injury (ICBL, 2001, p1021). In addition, violent cross-border incidents between Israeli forces and Hezbollah occurred despite the withdrawal of Israeli troops from southern Lebanon.

International Response

The international community has supported the government's efforts to reintegrate the internally displaced. The UN Development Programme (UNDP) has strengthened the government's capacity to assist the displaced and has promoted reconciliation between the different religious communities. The Lebanese government, as well as non-governmental organizations, such as the Lebanon Conflict Resolution Network and the US-based Institute of World Affairs, have organized informal discussions between members of different religious communities to promote return and reconciliation. The Lebanese NGO Forum (LNF) has provided legal aid to IDPs and promoted their rights. Many other NGOs, such as the Middle East Council of Churches (MECC) and Caritas–Lebanon, implemented programmes to assist returnees through 1999.

The Lebanese government, the UN and international donors have recently made a special effort in favour of the south. The government has taken measures to make it easier for owners to rebuild their houses in the region, while the EU has begun work with NGO partners to support the reintegration of the displaced. The UN, in cooperation with the Lebanese national de-mining office, has set up a regional mine action cell to help clear mines and unexploded ordnance. Large-scale outside investment to rebuild the south is unlikely, however, as long as instability remains in the region.

Endnotes

1   The constituency of the Lebanese National Movement (LNM) was largely made up of Lebanese Muslims and Druze.

Palestinian Territories

Since Israel occupied the Gaza Strip and the West Bank in 1967, several thousand Palestinian inhabitants have been internally displaced. The Israeli government, for what it says are security and administrative reasons, has ordered the demolition of thousands of homes in the Palestinian Territories and has confiscated land, such as in East Jerusalem. According to many human rights organizations, these demolitions have often been carried out in an illegal or discriminatory manner. House demolitions have been more frequent since the renewal of the Israeli–Palestinian conflict in September 2000 (the second Intifada). Since that time, over 9000 Palestinians have been displaced in the Palestinian Territories (UNCHR, 6 March 2002, p13; HRW, May 2002, p4)

The Conflict

Until the end of World War II, the West Bank and the Gaza Strip were part of the British Mandate of Palestine. UN General Assembly (UNGA) Resolution 181 of November 1947 recommended the partition of the mandate into a Jewish state and an Arab state. The subsequent proclamation of the State of Israel in May 1948 was rejected by the Arab states. A war followed between Arab and Israeli armies, during which between 600,000 and 760,000 people fled or were driven from Israel and became refugees.[1]

At the end of the 1948 war, Israel controlled the area which became the State of Israel, Egypt controlled the Gaza Strip, Jordan annexed the West Bank, and Jerusalem was divided between Israel and Jordan. The UN Relief and Works Agency for Palestine Refugees in the Near East (UNRWA) was created in 1950 to provide assistance to the Palestinian refugees throughout the whole of the region.

Further hostilities in June 1967 between Israel, on one side, and Egypt, Syria and Jordan, on the other, resulted in Israel's occupation of East Jerusalem, the West Bank, the Gaza Strip, Syria's Golan Heights and the Sinai Peninsula (later returned to Egypt). East Jerusalem and the Golan Heights were annexed by Israel at this time; but this was never internationally recognized. As a result of the 1967 war, as well as evictions that took place soon afterwards, several thousand Palestinians left Jerusalem for other parts of the Palestinian territories and elsewhere in the world.

From 1987 to 1993, a popular uprising against the Israeli occupation, called the Intifada, gained momentum in the Palestinian Territories. A political process of reconciliation between Israel and the Palestinians was begun with the Madrid Conference in 1991 and continued with the September 1993 signing of the Israeli–Palestinian Declaration of Principles. Several agreements were later signed between the Israelis and the Palestinians, giving a certain degree of control and jurisdiction over the Gaza Strip and the West Bank to the Palestinian Authority.

Some issues, such as border demarcation and the return of refugees, have remained outstanding for decades. Talks in the summer of 2000 in Camp David failed to solve them. Clashes between Israelis and Palestinians later in the same year brought a complete stop to the peace process. Over 1150 Palestinians and 400 Israelis, many of them civilians, were killed between September 2000 and March 2002 (RI, 5 April 2002).

Box 8.2   *Who is an IDP in Israel and in the Palestinian Territories?*

The lack of permanent, uncontested state boundaries between Israel and the Palestinian Territories makes the identification of IDPs in these areas difficult. Based on the IDP definition developed by the United Nations, and on the reasoning noted below, the Global IDP Project considers IDPs to be those people who were displaced and remain within the State of Israel and those displaced within the Palestinian Territories where they habitually resided, but not those who fled or were driven from Israel to the Palestinian Territories.

According to the UN Guiding Principles on Internal Displacement, 'internally displaced persons are persons or groups of persons who have been forced or obliged to flee or to leave their homes or places of habitual residence, in particular as a result of or in order to avoid the effects of armed conflict, situations of generalized violence, violations of human rights or natural or human-made disasters, and who have not crossed an internationally recognized State border'.

While the 'internationally recognized border' element of the above definition is useful in distinguishing between IDPs and refugees in most situations of conflict, it is problematic in the case of Israel and its neighbours. There is no internationally recognized border between Israel and Lebanon, nor between Israel and Syria. But the persons who fled or were driven from Israel in 1948 to those countries are clearly not internally displaced. Similarly, the people who left the State of Israel for Gaza and the West Bank in 1948–1949 went to an entity that was never under Israeli sovereignty and is currently under partial Palestinian sovereignty. While there is no agreed border, it is widely understood that they are not in their country of origin.

Although the legal status of the Palestinian Territories is as yet undefined, even the Israeli government does not claim that these territories are part of the State of Israel, except for East Jerusalem. Israel occupies Gaza and the West Bank which are for a great part under its military jurisdiction, but has not annexed them. The Israeli government has not extended citizenship to the Arab inhabitants of the Territories, except to residents of East Jerusalem. Finally, while the Palestinian State has not yet materialized, the right of the Palestinian people to a state has been recognized by the international community for some time.

Housing Demolition for Declared Security Reasons

From 1987 to 1993, during the first Intifada, the Israeli government destroyed hundreds of houses. If anyone who had been living in a house committed, or was suspected of having committed, an attack against an Israeli, or if shooting had come from a particular house, that house could be destroyed. Human rights organizations have criticized the punitive character of this measure.

From 1992 to mid 2000, few cases of house demolitions were reported; but since the beginning of the second Intifada, in September 2000, several large collective housing demolitions have taken place. In 2001 and 2002, the Israeli army reportedly destroyed the houses of several thousand Palestinians in East Jerusalem, the Gaza Strip and the West Bank. In the Gaza Strip alone, over 400 houses were completely destroyed and 200 seriously damaged, leaving over 5000 persons homeless (UNCHR, 6 March 2002, p13).

In April 2002, following a series of suicide bombings against Israeli civilians, the Israeli Defence Forces (IDF) launched a major operation in the Jenin refugee camp in the West Bank. According to Human Rights Watch (HRW), at least 52 people died, half of whom were civilians, and approximately 4000 people were rendered homeless (HRW, May 2002). The Israeli government has stated that the objectives of the operations in the Palestinian Territories were to arrest or kill Palestinian militants and seize their weapons. Many civilians have, however, been killed and injured during these operations. The UN decided to send a fact-finding mission to Jenin; but the mandate of the mission was rejected by Israel and ultimately disbanded.

Housing Demolition for Lack of a Building Permit

The Israeli government restricts construction by Palestinians in East Jerusalem and in the West Bank. It grants few building permits to Palestinians, and many people have built their homes without them. Two-thirds of all existing construction in East Jerusalem was reportedly undertaken without permit (Shragai, 5 June 2000). Houses built without authorization can be subject to demolition. According to Amnesty International (AI) and to B'Tselem, these demolitions are based on a discriminatory policy that has consistently refused planning permission to Palestinians while giving Israelis permission to set up settlements.

Many of these house demolitions have been linked to land confiscation. According to Amnesty International, for the last 20 years, the Israeli government has acquired land in the West Bank on the premise that this land was not officially registered or under continuous cultivation. However, the confiscated land is usually privately owned by individuals or families, or is for the collective use of a particular village. The confiscation of Palestinian property has occurred with frequency in the eastern areas of Jerusalem. The presumed aim of property confiscation has been to facilitate the expansion of the Jewish population and to secure Israeli control of the area. In order to achieve this goal, Israeli authorities have also confiscated the identity cards of several thousand residents of East Jerusalem, rendering the holders' continued presence in their native city illegal. Since 1967, the government of Israel has expropriated over 30 per cent of the area of East Jerusalem, mostly from Palestinian owners (AI, December 1999, p29).

Despite Palestinian demands, Israel has not compensated the displaced for the loss of their homes and property. The Israeli government's argument is that the house demolitions merely enforce the Israeli building laws. It has claimed that neither Palestinian nor Israeli construction is allowed on agricultural land. It has also asserted that the Municipality of Jerusalem can issue a demolition order when the construction of illegally constructed buildings interferes with plans for public facilities, such as schools or roads, or with the city's historical heritage (UNECOSOC, 14 May 2001).

Living Conditions and Protection Issues

The situation for the people of the Palestinian Territories, whether displaced or not, is distressing. In 1998, poverty affected nearly one in every four Palestinians. Following suicide bombings, the areas of the West Bank and Gaza under Palestinian Authority jurisdiction have been subject to tight security, preventing the free movement of persons and goods, which has undoubtedly aggravated poverty levels (World Bank, January 2001, p7).

The human rights and humanitarian situation worsened still further during the first half of 2002. Human rights organizations reported violations committed by the IDF, such as unlawful killings and the destruction of property of unarmed refugees. People whose homes have been destroyed have been forced to find refuge with relatives or in makeshift tents. Lack of access to medical care and services is also a major issue. According to the UN Children's Fund (UNICEF), the current violence has resulted in serious food and water shortages, an increasing threat to the well-being of the children there (UNICEF, 5 April 2002).

International Political and Humanitarian Response

The UN has repeatedly deplored the practice of demolishing Palestinian homes.[2] According to the UN Special Rapporteur on the situation of human rights in the occupied territories, the demolition of houses in Palestinian territory, either for security purposes or for administrative reasons, is difficult to reconcile with Article 53 of the Fourth Geneva Convention, which allows demolition of houses and property during armed conflict or occupation only if 'rendered absolutely necessary by military operations'. The UN Special Rapporteur has pointed out that:

> While there are doubtless instances in which houses have been demolished for genuine security reasons, the extent of the damage and the evidence of witnesses suggests that the destruction of houses in many instances is not 'rendered absolutely necessary by military operations' (UNCHR, 6 March 2002, pp13–14).

Since the beginning of the second Intifada, the UNRWA has issued several emergency appeals for humanitarian assistance to Palestinian refugees, who account for 31 per cent of the population of the West Bank and 80.6 per cent of the Gaza Strip. UNRWA also assists those who have lost their homes due to destruction.

The International Committee of the Red Cross (ICRC) has been providing tents and basic household items to families whose homes have been partially or completely destroyed. NGOs such as Caritas, Save the Children and Oxfam, as well as local organizations, have provided food and non-food items to war-affected populations.

Endnotes

1 Middle East Research and Information Project (MERIP), 2001, and Bligh, 1998, p124.
2 The UN Special Rapporteur on the Situation of Human Rights, the UN Committee against Torture, the UN Human Rights Committee and the UN Committee on the Elimination of Racial Discrimination have denounced Israeli policies on Palestinian house demolitions.

Syria

Despite the international focus on the Middle East, little attention has been given to the tens of thousands of people displaced from the Syrian territory of the Golan Heights 35 years ago. The displacement occurred during the Six Day War in 1967 when Israel seized the Heights, a strategic narrow stretch of land overlooking the Jordan Valley and the Sea of Galilee.

Causes of Displacement and Figures

Reports of the number of people displaced from the Golan Heights during the Six Day War vary depending upon the source. Israel puts it at 70,000 (USCR, 2001, p192). Syria says it was 130,000 and that those displaced and their descendants now number nearly half a million (Mission of the Syrian Arab Republic to the UN, 1997; UNGA, 31 October 2000). Syrian and Israeli accounts of the circumstances of the displacement also differ widely. According to the Syrian government, the inhabitants of the Golan were physically expelled by Israeli forces, while the Israeli government says they fled following reports of violence (UN Human Rights Committee, 25 August 2000; Arnold, 1 February 2000).

UN Response to the Conflict

Following the 1967 war, the UN Security Council (UNSC) passed Resolution 242 calling for the withdrawal of Israeli armed forces from occupied territories and for the respect and acknowledgement of the sovereignty of every state in the area. During the 1973 war, UNSC Resolution 338 urged Israel, on the one side, and Syria and Egypt, on the other, to agree to a ceasefire, to the implementation of UN Resolution 242 and to further political negotiations. An Israeli–Syrian disengagement agreement was then signed, which allowed Syria to regain Kuneitra, a town in the Golan Heights emptied of its 50,000 inhabitants and left in ruins by the Israeli army. Kuneitra was never rebuilt by the Syrian government and remains empty to this day. In 1974, the UNSC established a UN Disengagement Observer Force (UNDOF) to supervise the disengagement of Israeli and Syrian forces on the Golan Heights and to monitor the ceasefire.[1] In the absence of a peace agreement between Israel and Syria, the mandate of UNDOF has, since then, been renewed every six months.

Since December 1981, the Golan Heights have been administered under Israeli law. Despite this fact, people displaced from the Golan are considered internally displaced persons since the de facto border between the Israel-occupied Golan and Syria is not an internationally recognized border. In 1981, the UNSC said that 'the Israeli decision to impose its laws, jurisdiction and administration on the occupied Syrian Golan was null and void and without international legal effect' (UNSC, 17 December 1981). The UN has since reaffirmed this principle on numerous occasions and has regularly urged Israel to allow the internally displaced to return to their former homes and repossess their properties.

Living Conditions of the Internally Displaced

There is little information available on the living conditions of the internally displaced in Syria. Many of them have apparently been resettled in ten new villages close to the Golan and in housing projects in the suburbs of Damascus, Dara and Homs (USCR, 2001, p192). More than 30 years after the construction of villages and housing projects for the internally displaced, the Syrian government continues to define these settlements as 'temporary camps'. The displaced are apparently well treated by the Syrian government. According to an American journalist who interviewed some of the displaced in 2000 in 'new Bteha' – a village mirroring the old Bteha in the Golan – the displaced are given priority for public service jobs and universities by the Syrian government (Fecci, June 2000).

Prospects for Return

The return of the displaced population cannot be envisaged before a conclusion of negotiations between Israel and Syria on the future of the Golan Heights. Negotiations have been at a deadlock since January 2000. Syria will only discuss security arrangements after Israel agrees unconditionally to withdraw from the Golan to the 4 June 1967 line, which would give Syria access to the Sea of Galilee. In turn, Israel wants its security concerns addressed before agreeing to withdraw and has taken as a basis for negotiation the 1923 border, which would preclude Syrian access to the Sea of Galilee. Syrian President Bashar Al-Asad stated in February 2001 that Syria's position on the Golan was the same as his father's, which made any prospect for peace very difficult. Indeed, with the increasing violence in the Middle East in 2002, it would appear that any political settlement of the Golan Heights issue is unlikely in the foreseeable future.[2]

Endnotes

1 United Nations Security Council (UNSC), 22 November 1967, Resolution 242; United Nations Security Council (UNSC), 22 October 1973, Resolution 338; United Nations Security Council (UNSC), 31 May 1974, Resolution 350.
2 For the position of the Syrian government, see MEMRI, 23 January 2000, and MEMRI, 16 February 2001. For the Israeli position, see Ben-Nahum, 19 December 1995, pp2–3, and MEMRI, 24 March 2000.

UN Guiding Principles on Internal Displacement

In response to a request of the UN Commission on Human Rights (UNCHR) to develop an appropriate normative framework for the protection and assistance of the internally displaced, the Representative of the UN Secretary-General on Internally Displaced Persons prepared these Guiding Principles on Internal Displacement, in collaboration with international legal experts and in consultation with UN agencies and other organizations, international and regional, inter-governmental and non-governmental. The Guiding Principles were submitted by the Representative to the Commission on Human Rights at its fifty-fourth session.

Source: UN document E/CN.4/1998/53/Add.2

Guiding Principles on Internal Displacement

Introduction: scope and purpose

1. These Guiding Principles address the specific needs of internally displaced persons worldwide. They identify rights and guarantees relevant to the protection of persons from forced displacement and to their protection and assistance during displacement, as well as during return or resettlement and reintegration.
2. For the purposes of these Principles, internally displaced persons are persons or groups of persons who have been forced or obliged to flee or to leave their homes or places of habitual residence, in particular as a result of or in order to avoid the effects of armed conflict, situations of generalized violence, violations of human rights or natural or human-made disasters, and who have not crossed an internationally recognized State border.
3. These Principles reflect and are consistent with international human rights law and international humanitarian law. They provide guidance to:
   (a) The Representative of the Secretary-General on internally displaced persons in carrying out his mandate;
   (b) States when faced with the phenomenon of internal displacement;
   (c) All other authorities, groups and persons in their relations with internally displaced persons; and
   (d) Intergovernmental and non-governmental organizations when addressing internal displacement.
4. These Guiding Principles should be disseminated and applied as widely as possible.

Section I: General Principles

Principle 1

1. Internally displaced persons shall enjoy, in full equality, the same rights and freedoms under international and domestic law as do other persons in their country. They shall not be discriminated against in the enjoyment of any rights and freedoms on the ground that they are internally displaced.
2. These Principles are without prejudice to individual criminal responsibility under international law, in particular relating to genocide, crimes against humanity and war crimes.

Principle 2

1. These Principles shall be observed by all authorities, groups and persons irrespective of their legal status and applied without any adverse distinction. The observance of these Principles shall not affect the legal status of any authorities, groups or persons involved.
2. These Principles shall not be interpreted as restricting, modifying or impairing the provisions of any international human rights or international humanitarian law instrument or rights granted to persons under domestic law. In particular, these Principles are without prejudice to the right to seek and enjoy asylum in other countries.

Principle 3

1. National authorities have the primary duty and responsibility to provide protection and humanitarian assistance to internally displaced persons within their jurisdiction.
2. Internally displaced persons have the right to request and to receive protection and humanitarian assistance from these authorities. They shall not be persecuted or punished for making such a request.

Principle 4

1. These Principles shall be applied without discrimination of any kind, such as race, colour, sex, language, religion or belief, political or other opinion, national, ethnic or social origin, legal or social status, age, disability, property, birth, or on any other similar criteria.
2. Certain internally displaced persons, such as children, especially unaccompanied minors, expectant mothers, mothers with young children, female heads of household, persons with disabilities and elderly persons, shall be entitled to protection and assistance required by their condition and to treatment which takes into account their special needs.

Section II: Principles Relating to Protection from Displacement

Principle 5
All authorities and international actors shall respect and ensure respect for their obligations under international law, including human rights and humanitarian law, in all circumstances, so as to prevent and avoid conditions that might lead to displacement of persons.

Principle 6

1. Every human being shall have the right to be protected against being arbitrarily displaced from his or her home or place of habitual residence.
2. The prohibition of arbitrary displacement includes displacement:
    (a) When it is based on policies of apartheid, 'ethnic cleansing' or similar practices aimed at/or resulting in altering the ethnic, religious or racial composition of the affected population;
    (b) In situations of armed conflict, unless the security of the civilians involved or imperative military reasons so demand;
    (c) In cases of large-scale development projects, which are not justified by compelling and overriding public interests;
    (d) In cases of disasters, unless the safety and health of those affected requires their evacuation; and
    (e) When it is used as a collective punishment.
3. Displacement shall last no longer than required by the circumstances.

Principle 7

1. Prior to any decision requiring the displacement of persons, the authorities concerned shall ensure that all feasible alternatives are explored in order to avoid displacement altogether. Where no alternatives exist, all measures shall be taken to minimize displacement and its adverse effects.
2. The authorities undertaking such displacement shall ensure, to the greatest practicable extent, that proper accommodation is provided to the displaced persons, that such displacements are effected in satisfactory conditions of safety, nutrition, health and hygiene, and that members of the same family are not separated.
3. If displacement occurs in situations other than during the emergency stages of armed conflicts and disasters, the following guarantees shall be complied with:
    (a) A specific decision shall be taken by a State authority empowered by law to order such measures;
    (b) Adequate measures shall be taken to guarantee to those to be displaced full information on the reasons and procedures for their displacement and, where applicable, on compensation and relocation;
    (c) The free and informed consent of those to be displaced shall be sought;
    (d) The authorities concerned shall endeavour to involve those affected, particularly women, in the planning and management of their relocation;
    (e) Law enforcement measures, where required, shall be carried out by competent legal authorities; and
    (f) The right to an effective remedy, including the review of such decisions by appropriate judicial authorities, shall be respected.

Principle 8
Displacement shall not be carried out in a manner that violates the rights to life, dignity, liberty and security of those affected.

Principle 9
States are under a particular obligation to protect against the displacement of indigenous peoples, minorities, peasants, pastoralists and other groups with a special dependency on and attachment to their lands.

Section III: Principles Relating to Protection During Displacement

Principle 10

1. Every human being has the inherent right to life which shall be protected by law. No one shall be arbitrarily deprived of his or her life. Internally displaced persons shall be protected in particular against:
    (a) Genocide;
    (b) Murder;
    (c) Summary or arbitrary executions; and
    (d) Enforced disappearances, including abduction or unacknowledged detention, threatening or resulting in death.

Threats and incitement to commit any of the foregoing acts shall be prohibited.

2. Attacks or other acts of violence against internally displaced persons who do not or no longer participate in hostilities are prohibited in all circumstances. Internally displaced persons shall be protected, in particular, against:
    (a) Direct or indiscriminate attacks or other acts of violence, including the creation of areas wherein attacks on civilians are permitted;
    (b) Starvation as a method of combat;
    (c) Their use to shield military objectives from attack or to shield, favour or impede military operations;
    (d) Attacks against their camps or settlements; and
    (e) The use of anti-personnel landmines.

Principle 11

1. Every human being has the right to dignity and physical, mental and moral integrity.
2. Internally displaced persons, whether or not their liberty has been restricted, shall be protected in particular against:
    (a) Rape, mutilation, torture, cruel, inhuman or degrading treatment or punishment, and other outrages upon personal dignity, such as acts of gender-specific violence, forced prostitution and any form of indecent assault;
    (b) Slavery or any contemporary form of slavery, such as sale into marriage, sexual exploitation, or forced labour of children; and
    (c) Acts of violence intended to spread terror among internally displaced persons.

Threats and incitement to commit any of the foregoing acts shall be prohibited.

Principle 12

1. Every human being has the right to liberty and security of person. No one shall be subjected to arbitrary arrest or detention.
2. To give effect to this right for internally displaced persons, they shall not be interned in or confined to a camp. If in exceptional circumstances such internment or confinement is absolutely necessary, it shall not last longer than required by the circumstances.
3. Internally displaced persons shall be protected from discriminatory arrest and detention as a result of their displacement.
4. In no case shall internally displaced persons be taken hostage.

Principle 13

1. In no circumstances shall displaced children be recruited nor be required or permitted to take part in hostilities.
2. Internally displaced persons shall be protected against discriminatory practices of recruitment into any armed forces or groups as a result of their displacement. In particular any cruel, inhuman or degrading practices that compel compliance or punish non-compliance with recruitment are prohibited in all circumstances.

Principle 14

1. Every internally displaced person has the right to liberty of movement and freedom to choose his or her residence.
2. In particular, internally displaced persons have the right to move freely in and out of camps or other settlements.

Principle 15

Internally displaced persons have:

    (a) The right to seek safety in another part of the country;
    (b) The right to leave their country;
    (c) The right to seek asylum in another country; and
    (d) The right to be protected against forcible return to or resettlement in any place where their life, safety, liberty and/or health would be at risk.

Principle 16

1. All internally displaced persons have the right to know the fate and whereabouts of missing relatives.
2. The authorities concerned shall endeavour to establish the fate and whereabouts of internally displaced persons reported missing, and cooperate with relevant international organizations engaged in this task. They shall inform the next of kin on the progress of the investigation and notify them of any result.
3. The authorities concerned shall endeavour to collect and identify the mortal remains of those deceased, prevent their despoliation or mutilation, and facilitate the return of those remains to the next of kin or dispose of them respectfully.
4. Grave sites of internally displaced persons should be protected and respected in all circumstances. Internally displaced persons should have the right of access to the grave sites of their deceased relatives.

Principle 17

1. Every human being has the right to respect of his or her family life.
2. To give effect to this right for internally displaced persons, family members who wish to remain together shall be allowed to do so.
3. Families which are separated by displacement should be reunited as quickly as possible. All appropriate steps shall be taken to expedite the reunion of such families, particularly when children are involved. The responsible authorities shall facilitate inquiries made by family members and encourage and cooperate with the work of humanitarian organizations engaged in the task of family reunification.

4. Members of internally displaced families whose personal liberty has been restricted by internment or confinement in camps shall have the right to remain together.

Principle 18

1. All internally displaced persons have the right to an adequate standard of living.
2. At the minimum, regardless of the circumstances, and without discrimination, competent authorities shall provide internally displaced persons with and ensure safe access to:
    (a) Essential food and potable water;
    (b) Basic shelter and housing;
    (c) Appropriate clothing; and
    (d) Essential medical services and sanitation.
3. Special efforts should be made to ensure the full participation of women in the planning and distribution of these basic supplies.

Principle 19

1. All wounded and sick internally displaced persons as well as those with disabilities shall receive to the fullest extent practicable and with the least possible delay, the medical care and attention they require, without distinction on any grounds other than medical ones. When necessary, internally displaced persons shall have access to psychological and social services.
2. Special attention should be paid to the health needs of women, including access to female health care providers and services, such as reproductive health care, as well as appropriate counselling for victims of sexual and other abuses.
3. Special attention should also be given to the prevention of contagious and infectious diseases, including AIDS, among internally displaced persons.

Principle 20

1. Every human being has the right to recognition everywhere as a person before the law.
2. To give effect to this right for internally displaced persons, the authorities concerned shall issue to them all documents necessary for the enjoyment and exercise of their legal rights, such as passports, personal identification documents, birth certificates and marriage certificates. In particular, the authorities shall facilitate the issuance of new documents or the replacement of documents lost in the course of displacement, without imposing unreasonable conditions, such as requiring the return to one's area of habitual residence in order to obtain these or other required documents.
3. Women and men shall have equal rights to obtain such necessary documents and shall have the right to have such documentation issued in their own names.

Principle 21

1. No one shall be arbitrarily deprived of property and possessions.
2. The property and possessions of internally displaced persons shall in all circumstances be protected, in particular, against the following acts:
    (a) Pillage;
    (b) Direct or indiscriminate attacks or other acts of violence;
    (c) Being used to shield military operations or objectives;

   (d) Being made the object of reprisal; and
   (e) Being destroyed or appropriated as a form of collective punishment.
3. Property and possessions left behind by internally displaced persons should be protected against destruction and arbitrary and illegal appropriation, occupation or use.

Principle 22

1. Internally displaced persons, whether or not they are living in camps, shall not be discriminated against as a result of their displacement in the enjoyment of the following rights:
   (a) The rights to freedom of thought, conscience, religion or belief, opinion and expression;
   (b) The right to seek freely opportunities for employment and to participate in economic activities;
   (c) The right to associate freely and participate equally in community affairs;
   (d) The right to vote and to participate in governmental and public affairs, including the right to have access to the means necessary to exercise this right; and
   (e) The right to communicate in a language they understand.

Principle 23

1. Every human being has the right to education.
2. To give effect to this right for internally displaced persons, the authorities concerned shall ensure that such persons, in particular displaced children, receive education which shall be free and compulsory at the primary level. Education should respect their cultural identity, language and religion.
3. Special efforts should be made to ensure the full and equal participation of women and girls in educational programmes.
4. Education and training facilities shall be made available to internally displaced persons, in particular adolescents and women, whether or not living in camps, as soon as conditions permit.

Section IV: Principles Relating to Humanitarian Assistance

Principle 24

1. All humanitarian assistance shall be carried out in accordance with the principles of humanity and impartiality and without discrimination.
2. Humanitarian assistance to internally displaced persons shall not be diverted, in particular for political or military reasons.

Principle 25

1. The primary duty and responsibility for providing humanitarian assistance to internally displaced persons lies with national authorities.
2. International humanitarian organizations and other appropriate actors have the right to offer their services in support of the internally displaced. Such an offer shall not be regarded as an unfriendly act or an interference in a State's internal affairs and shall be considered in good faith. Consent thereto shall not be arbitrarily withheld, particularly when

authorities concerned are unable or unwilling to provide the required humanitarian assistance.

3. All authorities concerned shall grant and facilitate the free passage of humanitarian assistance and grant persons engaged in the provision of such assistance rapid and unimpeded access to the internally displaced.

Principle 26

Persons engaged in humanitarian assistance, their transport and supplies shall be respected and protected. They shall not be the object of attack or other acts of violence.

Principle 27

1. International humanitarian organizations and other appropriate actors when providing assistance should give due regard to the protection needs and human rights of internally displaced persons and take appropriate measures in this regard. In so doing, these organizations and actors should respect relevant international standards and codes of conduct.
2. The preceding paragraph is without prejudice to the protection responsibilities of international organizations mandated for this purpose, whose services may be offered or requested by States.

Section V: Principles Relating to Return, Resettlement and Reintegration

Principle 28

1. Competent authorities have the primary duty and responsibility to establish conditions, as well as provide the means, which allow internally displaced persons to return voluntarily, in safety and with dignity, to their homes or places of habitual residence, or to resettle voluntarily in another part of the country. Such authorities shall endeavour to facilitate the reintegration of returned or resettled internally displaced persons.
2. Special efforts should be made to ensure the full participation of internally displaced persons in the planning and management of their return or resettlement and reintegration.

Principle 29

1. Internally displaced persons who have returned to their homes or places of habitual residence or who have resettled in another part of the country shall not be discriminated against as a result of their having been displaced. They shall have the right to participate fully and equally in public affairs at all levels and have equal access to public services.
2. Competent authorities have the duty and responsibility to assist returned and/or resettled internally displaced persons to recover, to the extent possible, their property and possessions which they left behind or were dispossessed of upon their displacement. When recovery of such property and possessions is not possible, competent authorities shall provide or assist these persons in obtaining appropriate compensation or another form of just reparation.

Principle 30

All authorities concerned shall grant and facilitate for international humanitarian organizations and other appropriate actors, in the exercise of their respective mandates, rapid and unimpeded access to internally displaced persons to assist in their return or resettlement and reintegration.

References

The sources noted in the References are organized by chapter and country section. General reference material that is used repeatedly throughout the *Global Survey* is listed below under General. The Global IDP Database is indebted to the annual reports of various human rights and humanitarian agencies, as well as the information services provided by UN ReliefWeb and the UN Integrated Information Networks (UNIRIN) in the compilation of its country profiles.

General

Amnesty International (AI) (2001) *Annual Report 2001*, POL 10/001/2001, AI, London

Cohen, Roberta, and Deng, Francis M (1998) *Masses in Flight, The Global Crisis of Internal Displacement*, Brookings Institution press, Washington, DC

Cohen, Roberta, and Deng, Francis M (eds) (1998) *The Forsaken People – Case Studies of the Internally Displaced*, Earthscan, London

Hampton, Janie (ed) (1998) *Internally Displaced People, A Global Survey*, Earthscan, London

Human Rights Watch (HRW) (2002) *World Report 2002*, HRW, New York

—— (2001) *World Report 2001*, HRW, New York

—— (2000) *World Report 2000*, HRW, New York

—— (1999) *World Report 1999*, HRW, New York

International Committee of the Red Cross (ICRC) (2001) *Annual Report 2000*, ICRC, Geneva

ICRC (2000) *Annual Report 1999*, ICRC, Geneva

Käilin, Walter (2000) *Guiding Principles on Internal Displacement: Annotations, Studies in Transnational Legal Policy, No 32*, The American Society of International Law/The Brookings Institution Project on Internal Displacement, Washington, DC

US Department of State (USDOS), Bureau of Democracy, Human Rights and Labour (2002) *Country Report on Human Rights Practices 2001*, USDOS, Washington, DC

—— Bureau of Democracy, Human Rights and Labour (2001) *Country Report on Human Rights Practices 2000*, vol I and II, USDOS, Washington, DC

—— Bureau of Democracy, Human Rights and Labour (2000) *Country Report on Human Rights Practices 1999*, vol I and II, USDOS, Washington, DC

—— Bureau of Democracy, Human Rights and Labour (1999) *Country Report on Human Rights Practices 1998*, USDOS, Washington, DC

—— Bureau of Democracy, Human Rights and Labour (1998) *Country Report on Human Rights Practices 1997*, USDOS, Washington, DC

US Committee for Refugees (USCR) (2001) *World Refugee Survey 2001*, USCR, Washington, DC

—— (2000) *World Refugee Survey 2000*, USCR, Washington, DC

—— (1999) *World Refugee Survey 1999*, USCR, Washington, DC

USCR (1998) *World Refugee Survey 1998*, USCR, Washington, DC
USCR (1997) *World Refugee Survey 1997*, USCR, Washington, DC
Vincent, Marc, and Refslund, Birgit (eds) (2001) *Caught Between Borders, Response Strategies of the Internally Displaced*, Earthscan, London

Introduction

Coalition to Stop the Use of Child Soldiers (2001) *Child Soldiers Global Report*, Coalition to Stop the Use of Child Soldiers, London, 2001
Käilin, Walter (2000) *Guiding Principles on Internal Displacement: Annotations, Studies in Transnational Legal Policy, No 32*, The American Society of International Law / The Brookings Institution Project on Internal Displacement, Washington, DC
Overseas Development Institute (ODI) (2002) *Briefing Paper, International Humanitarian Action: A Review of Policy Trends*, ODI, London, April
Save the Children UK (SCF-UK) (2000) *War Brought Us Here: Protecting Children Displaced within Their Own Countries*, SCF, London
Schmeidl, Susanne (1998) 'Comparative trends in forced displacement: IDPs and refugees, 1964–96' in Hampton, Janie (ed) *Internally Displaced People: A Global Survey*, Earthscan, London
United Nations Office for the Coordination of Humanitarian Affairs (UNOCHA) (2002) *UN Consolidated Inter-Agency Humanitarian Assistance Appeals (Summary of Requirements and Contributions by affected country/region as of 17 May 2002)*, UNOCHA, Geneva, 17 May
United Nations Population Fund (UNFPA) (2001) *The State of the World Population 2001: Demographic, Social and Economic Indicators*, UNFPA website: www.unfpa.org/swp/2001/english/indicators/indicators2.html
United Nations High Commission for Refugees (UNHCR) (2002) *2001 UNHCR Population Statistics (Provisional)*, UNHCR, Geneva, 16 May

Africa

Regional overview

Amnesty International (AI) (2001) *Guinea, Liberia and Sierra Leone, A human rights crisis for refugees and the internally displaced*, AFR 05/005/2001, AI, London, 25 June
UN (2001) *Consolidated Inter-Agency Appeal 2002, Angola*, UNOCHA, New York and Geneva, November
UNICEF (2001) *A Humanitarian Appeal for Children and Women (Angola) January – December 2001*, UNICEF, New York
UNHCR/ SC-UK (2002) *Note for Implementing and Operational Partners on Sexual Violence and Exploitation: The Experience of Refugee Children in Liberia, Guinea and Sierra Leone*, UNHCR and Save the Children UK, Geneva and London

Algeria

Amnesty International (AI) (2000) *Algeria: Lack of concrete progress on outstanding concerns is disappointing*, MDE 28/016/2000, AI, London, 21 November
British Broadcasting Corporation (BBC) World Service, Newsroom (2001) 'Family of five massacred in Algeria', World: Middle East, *BBC News* website, 1 April, www.news.bbc.co.uk/hi/english/world/middle_east/newsid_1238000/1238393.stm
Cohen, Roberta (1999) 'Hard cases: internal displacement in Turkey, Burma (Myanmar) and Algeria', in *Forced Migration Review*, vol 6, 6 December, pp25–28

Dammers, Chris (1998) 'Algeria' in Hampton, Janie (ed) *Internally Displaced People: A Global Survey*, Earthscan, London

International Federation of Human Rights (FIDH) (2001) *A Vulnerable Population*, Algeria, FIDH website, 15 November, www.fidh.org/communiq/2001/dz1211a.htm

International Crisis Group (ICG) (2000) *Algeria: Project Overview*, Programs, ICG website, www.intl-crisis-group.org/projects/project.cfm?subtypeid=2

—— (2000), 'The Algerian Crisis: Not Over Yet', in *ICG Africa Report*, no 24, ICG, Algiers, Paris, London, and Brussels, October

International Federation of Red Cross and Red Crescent Societies (IFRC) (2002) *Algeria: Storms and floods appeal*, no 35/01, operations update no 2, IFRC, Geneva, 10 January 2002

Angola

Action for Southern Africa (ACTSA) (2001) *Angola Peace Monitor*, vol VIII, no 1, Angola Peace Monitor, ACSTA website, 5 October, www.actsa.org/Angola/apm/apm0801.htm

—— (2001) *Angola Peace Monitor*, vol VII, no 12, Angola Peace Monitor, ACSTA website, 5 September, www.actsa.org/Angola/apm/apm0712.htm

Global Witness (2002) 'Blair and Chirac must require transparency of resource revenues as a key to African development', Press Releases, Global Witness website, 8 February, www.globalwitness.org/press_releases/display2.php?id=91

Human Rights Watch (HRW) (2002) *Angola briefing under the Arria formula to the United Nations Security Council*, HRW, New York, 5 March

Médecins Sans Frontières (MSF) (2002) *MSF briefing to UN Security Council: The humanitarian situation in Angola*, MSF, Luanda, 5 March

Pearce, Justin (2002) 'Angola to end civil war', World: Africa, *BBC News* website, 4 April, www.news.bbc.co.uk/hi/english/world/africa/newsid_1910000/1910017.stm

United Nations (UN) (2001) *Consolidated Inter-Agency Appeal 2002, Angola*, UNOCHA, New York and Geneva, November

UN News Service (2002) 'UN Envoy meets with Angolan President to discuss proposed peace plan', UN News Centre website, 8 April, www0.un.org/apps/news/story.asp?NewsID=3318&Cr=gambari&Cr1

United Nations Office for the Coordination of Humanitarian Affairs (UNOCHA) (2002) *Humanitarian Situation in Angola*, UNOCHA, Luanda, 8 February

—— (2001) *Mid-Year Review of the 2001 United Nations Consolidated Inter-Agency Appeal for Angola (January–May 2001)*, UNOCHA, New York and Geneva, 22 May

United Nations Security Council (UNSC) (2001) *Supplementary Report of the Monitoring Mechanism on Sanctions against UNITA*, S/2001/966, UN, New York, 12 October

United Nations Children's Fund (UNICEF) (2001) *UNICEF 2001 Appeal for Children and Women*, UNICEF, New York

World Food Programme (WFP) (2001) 'Caught in the crossfire: Plight of Angola's "single-parent mothers"', Newsroom: in depth, WFP website, 12 July, www.wfp.org/newsroom/in_depth/angola.html

Burundi

Coalition to Stop the Use of Child Soldiers (2001) 'Burundi', in *Child Soldiers Global Report 2001*, Coalition to Stop the Use of Child Soldiers, London

Food and Agriculture Organization (FAO) Global Information and Early Warning System (GIEWS) (2001) *Food supply situation and crop prospects in sub-Saharan Africa*, no 3, FAO, Rome, December

—— (2001) 'Crop Prospects and Food Supply Position in Individual Countries: Burundi', in *Africa Report*, no 2, FAO, Rome, August

Human Rights Watch (HRW) (2000) 'Emptying the Hills: Regroupment in Burundi', in *Reports by Country*, vol 12, no 4, HRW, New York, June

International Medical Corps (IMC) (2002) 'Burundi: IMC combats malaria among children', Our Programs, IMC website, 25 March, www.imc-la.com/programs/Articles/Burundi/031402-HopeInAction.html#malaria

United Nations (UN) (2001) *Consolidated Inter-Agency Appeal 2002, Burundi*, UNOCHA, New York and Geneva, November

United Nations Commission for Human Rights (UNCHR) (2001) *Rapport sur la situation des droits de l'homme au Burundi soumis par le Rapporteur spécial, Mme Marie-Thérèse A. Keita Bocoum, conformément à la résolution 2000/20 de la Commission*, E/CN.4/2001/44, UN, Geneva, 19 March

—— (2000) *Specific Groups and Individuals: Report of the Representative of the Secretary-General, Mr. Francis Deng, submitted pursuant to Commission on Human Rights resolution 2000/53. Addendum, Profiles in displacement: Forced relocation in Burundi*, E/CN.4/2001/5/Add.1, UN, Geneva, 6 March

United Nations Office for the Coordination of Humanitarian Affairs (UNOCHA) (2002) *Affected Populations in the Great Lakes Region*, UNOCHA, Nairobi, 28 February

—— (2002) *Burundi, Affected Populations by Province Refugees and Internally Displaced (January 2002)*, UNOCHA, Nairobi, 15 January

—— (2000) *Affected Populations in the Great Lakes Region*, UNOCHA, Nairobi, 8 June

United Nations Senior Inter-Agency Network on Internal Displacement (2000) *Mission to Burundi 18-22 December 2000*, UN, Geneva, 23 December

United Nations Children's Fund (UNICEF) (2001) *UNICEF Humanitarian Action: Burundi Donor Update*, UNICEF, New York, 1 March

United States Agency for International Development (USAID)/BHR/OFDA (2001) *Burundi, Complex Emergency Information Bulletin #1*, USAID/BHR/OFDA, Washington, DC, 3 July

Democratic Republic of Congo

Amnesty International (AI) (2001) *Rwandese-controlled eastern DRC: Devastating human toll*, AFR 62/011/2001, AI, London, 19 June

International Rescue Committee (IRC) (2001), Mortality Study, eastern Democratic Republic of Congo (February-April 2001), DR Congo page, IRC website, April, www.intranet.theirc.org/docs/morII_exec.pdf

Oxfam (2002) *Oxfam update from the field: Goma volcano*, Emergencies, Oxfam website, 2 February, www.oxfam.org.uk/atwork/emerg/drcvolcano/update0202.html

—— (2001) *No End in Sight: The human tragedy of the conflict in the Democratic Republic of Congo, Aug 2001*, Policy, Oxfam website, 6 August, www.oxfam.org.uk/policy/papers/drc/drc2.htm

Refugees International (RI) (2001) 'Notes from the field: Congo', RI, Washington, DC, 4 September

United Nations (UN) (2001) *Consolidated Inter-Agency Appeal 2002, Democratic Republic of the Congo*, UNOCHA, New York and Geneva, November

United Nations Office for the Coordination of Humanitarian Affairs (UNOCHA) (2002) *Affected Populations in the Great Lakes Region*, UNOCHA, Nairobi, 28 February

—— (2001) *Flash OCHA: RDC situation humanitaire au 30 septembre 2001*, UNOCHA, Kinshasa, 30 September

—— (2000) *Affected Populations in the Great Lakes Region*, UNOCHA, Nairobi, 31 December

—— (2000) *DRC Monthly Humanitarian Bulletin, May–June 2000*, UNOCHA, Kinshasa, 11 July

—— (1999) *DRC Monthly Humanitarian Bulletin, 15 June–15 July 1999*, UNOCHA, Kinshasa, 15 July

United Nations Security Council (UNSC) (2002) Tenth report of the Secretary-General on the United Nations Organization Mission in the Democratic Republic of the Congo, S/2002/169, UN, New York, 15 February

—— (2001) *Addendum to the report of the Panel of Experts on the Illegal Exploitation of Natural Resources and Other Forms of Wealth of DR Congo*, S/2001/1072, UN, New York, 13 November

—— (2001) *Ninth report of the Secretary-General on the United Nations Organization Mission in Democratic Republic of the Congo*, S/2001/970, UN, New York, 16 October

—— (2001) *Eighth report of the Secretary-General on the United Nations Organization Mission in the Democratic Republic of the Congo*, S/2001/572, UN, New York, 8 June

—— (2001) *Report of the Panel of Experts on the Illegal Exploitation of Natural Resources and Other Forms of Wealth of the Democratic Republic of the Congo*, S/2001/357, UN, New York, 12 April

Eritrea

International Federation of Red Cross and Red Crescent Societies (IFRC) (2002) *Eritrea Appeal 2002–2003*, IFRC, Geneva

State of Eritrea Ministry of Health/Save the Children UK/ECHO (2001) *Nutrition Survey Report in Gash Barka Region. Lalai Gash, Shambuko and Gonge Sub-Zones*, Government of Eritrea, Save the Children UK, ECHO, Asmara, August

United Nations (UN) (2001) *Consolidated Inter-Agency Appeal 2002, Eritrea*, UNOCHA, New York and Geneva

—— (2000) UN Country Team Appeal: Humanitarian Assistance to Eritrea, UNCT, Asmara, January

United Nations Integrated Regional Information Networks (UNIRIN) (2002) 'Eritrea-Ethiopia: Tigray official seeks clarification over Badme', Eritrea, *IRIN News* website, 22 April, www.irinnews.org/report.asp?ReportID=27393&SelectRegion=Horn_of_Africa&SelectCountry=ERITREA-ETHIOPIA

United Nations Security Council (UNSC) (2002) *Progress report of the Secretary-General on Ethiopia and Eritrea*, S/2002/245, UN, New York, 8 March

United Nations High Commission for Refugees (UNHCR) (2000) *Special Funding Appeal for UNHCR's supplementary programme to provide emergency assistance to Eritrean Refugees in Sudan, Djibouti and Yemen and to IDPs and returnees in Eritrea*, UNHCR, Geneva, July

Famine Early Warning System Network (FEWS Net) (2002) *FEWS Eritrea Food Security Update: 7 February*, Region and Country Centres, FEWS Net website, 25 February, www.fews.net/centers/files/Eritrea_200201en.pdf

Ethiopia

Government of Ethiopia (2000) *Ethiopia: Relief Assistance Requirements for Internally Displaced People and Deportees*, Government of Ethiopia, Addis Ababa

United Nations (UN) (2001) *Strategy Paper for Ethiopia 2002*, UNOCHA, New York and Geneva

United Nations Country Team Ethiopia (UNCTE) (2000) *Relief Action Plan and Appeal 2000*, UNCTE, Addis Ababa, 28 January

United Nations Development Programme Emergencies Unit for Ethiopia (UNDP EUE) (2002) *Current situation and progress of humanitarian assistance to vulnerable population segments affected by the border conflict in Ethiopia's Tigray Region*, UNDP EUE, Addis Ababa

—— (1999) *Situation of displaced people in Afar Region remains sketchy: Mission: 22 to 26 March 1999*, UNDP EUE, Addis Ababa

United Nations Integrated Regional Information Networks (UNIRIN) (1999) *Irin Focus on Displaced People in Rift Valley*, Archive, IRIN News website, 11 November

—— (2002) 'Eritrea-Ethiopia: Tigray official seeks clarification over Badme', Eritrea, IRIN News website, 22 April, www.irinnews.org/report.asp?ReportID=27393&SelectRegion= Horn_of_Africa&SelectCountry=ERITREA-ETHIOPIA

World Food Programme (WFP) (2002) 'Ethiopia', in *Emergency Report*, no 6, WFP, Rome

Guinea

Amnesty International (AI) (2001) *Guinea, Liberia and Sierra Leone, A human rights crisis for refugees and the internally displaced*, AFR 05/005/2001, AI, London, 25 June

Blunt, Elizabeth (2001) 'The Guinea conflict explained', World: Africa, *BBC News* website, 13 February, www.news.bbc.co.uk/hi/english/world/africa/newsid_1167000/1167811.stm

United Nations (UN) (2001) *Consolidated Inter-Agency Appeal 2001, West Africa*, UNOCHA, New York and Geneva, March

—— (2001) *Consolidated Inter-Agency Appeal 2002, West Africa*, UNOCHA, New York and Geneva

United Nations Environment Programme (UNEP) (2001) *General Map of Guinea*, UNEP, Nairobi, 11 March

United Nations Office for the Coordination of Humanitarian Affairs (UNOCHA) (2002) *Guinea: Official Map of IDPs by prefecture, 1 February 2002*, UNOCHA, Geneva, 1 February

Guinea-Bissau

Amnesty International (AI) (2001) *Guinea-Bissau, Human rights violations since the armed conflict ended in May 1999*, AFR 30/011/2001, AI, London

International Committee of the Red Cross (ICRC) (2000) *Annual Report 1999: Dakar regional delegation (covering Burkino Faso, Cape Verde, Gambia, Guinea-Bissau, Mali, Niger, Senegal)*, ICRC, Geneva, 31 August

Manley, Andrew (1998) *Guinea Bissau/Senegal: War, Civil War and the Casamance Question*, Writenet, UK, November

United Nations Security Council (UNSC) (2001) *Report of the Secretary-General on developments in Guinea-Bissau and on the activities of the UN Peace-building Support Office in that country*, S/2001/1211, UN, New York, 14 December

—— (2001) *Report of the Secretary-General on developments in Guinea-Bissau and the activities of the United Nations Peace-building Support Office in that country*, S/2001/622, UN, New York, 22 June

Kenya

Article 19 (1997) *Deadly Marionettes: State-Sponsored Violence In Africa*, Publications, Article 19 website, October, www.article19.org/docimages/477.htm#2.3

Galava, Denis (2000) 'A people scavenging for a desperate future', *East African Standard*, Nairobi, 29 October

Human Rights Watch (HRW) (1997) *Failing The Internally Displaced – the UNDP Displaced Persons Program In Kenya*, HRW, Washington, DC, June

Kathina Juma, Monica (2000) *Unveiling Women as Pillars of Peace – Peace Building in Communities Fractured by Conflict in Kenya*, UNDP/Management Development and Governance Division, New York

Mbura Kamungi, Prisca (JRS) (2001) *The Current Situation of Internally Displaced Persons In Kenya*, Resources, JRS website, March, www.jesref.org/resources/ken-idp.pdf

Owino, Opondo (2000) 'Kanu MPs block help for clashes victims', *Daily Nation*, Nairobi, 23 November

United Nations Office for the Coordination of Humanitarian Affairs (UNOCHA) (2001) *Humanitarian Update Kenya*, Issue 8, Kenya, ReliefWeb, August, www.reliefweb.int/w/ rwb.nsf/6686f45896f15dbc852567ae00530132/9cc7ad7d7784cd8885256abe004 f2a44?OpenDocument

United Nations Development Fund for Women African Women in Crisis Programme (UNIFEM/AFWIC) (2002) *The Lives and Life-Choices of Dispossessed Women in Kenya* (prepared by Prisca Mbura Kamungi), UNIFEM/AFWIC, Nairobi, January

Liberia

Amnesty International (AI) (2002) *Liberia: Civilians at risk as president calls for a state of emergency* AFR 34/001/2002, AI, London, February

—— (2001) *Liberia: Killings, torture and rape continue in Lofa County*, AFR 34/009/2001, AI, London, August

International Committee of the Red Cross (ICRC) (2002) *Update on ICRC activities in Liberia*, OP/REX 02/94, Update No 6, ICRC, Geneva, February

Tostevin, Matthew (2002) 'Rumour and plot theories bubble in tense Liberia', Reuters as found on Afghanistan page, ReliefWeb, 14 February, www.reliefweb.int/w/rwb.nsf/d2fc8ae9db883867852567cb0083a028/156f66eaeeadeb 03c1256b60005208d0?OpenDocument

United Nations (UN) (2001) *Consolidated Inter-Agency Appeal 2002, Liberia*, UNOCHA, New York and Geneva, November

Nigeria

Ibeanu, O (1998) 'Nigeria', in Hampton, Janie (ed), *Internally Displaced People: A Global Survey*, Earthscan, London

International Committee of the Red Cross (ICRC) (2001) *E-mail from ICRC Geneva to NRC Geneva*, 16 August

Marin, Cécile (1999) 'Bataille pour le pétrole au Nigeria', *Le Monde Diplomatique*, Paris, February

United Nations Integrated Regional Information Networks (UNIRIN) (2002) E-mail from IRIN Nigeria to NRC Geneva, 15 March

—— (2002) *IRIN Weekly Updates (various from 2001-2002)*, Nigeria page, IRIN website, www.irinnews.org/frontpage.asp?SelectRegion=West_Africa&SelectCountry=Nigeria

—— (2002) 'Nigeria: Hundreds flee after mob kills seven policemen', Archive, *IRIN News* website, 21 January www.irinnews.org/report.asp?ReportID=19685&SelectRegion= West_Africa&SelectCountry=NIGERIA

—— (2002) 'Nigeria: Scores reported dead in clashes over fishpond', Archive, *IRIN News website*, 11 January, www.irinnews.org/report.asp?ReportID=18941&SelectRegion=West_ Africa&SelectCountry=NIGERIA

—— (2002) 'Nigeria: Dozens reported dead in clashes between farmers, herders', Archive, *IRIN News* website, 8 January, www.irinnews.org/report.asp?ReportID=18545&Select Region=West_Africa&SelectCountry=NIGERIA

—— (2001) 'Nigeria: Up to 300,000 displaced in central region', Archive, IRIN News website, 29 October, www.irinnews.org/report.asp?ReportID=12562&SelectRegion=West_Africa& SelectCountry=NIGERIA

—— (2000) 'Nigeria: IRIN Focus on communal conflict', Archive, IRIN News website, 4 January, www.irinnews.org/report.asp?ReportID=22018&SelectRegion=West_Africa& SelectCountry=NIGERIA

United Nations Development Programme (UNDP) (2001) Fax from UNDP Resident Representative Lagos to NRC Geneva, 21 August

Republic of Congo-Brazzaville

Médecins Sans Frontières (MSF) (2000) *Health and War in Congo-Brazzaville*, Republic of Congo page, MSF website, 27 November, www.msf.org/countries/page.cfm?articleid=3A09CB3B-E42A-11D4-B2010060084A6370

United Nations (UN) (1999) *Consolidated Inter-Agency Appeal 1999, Republic of Congo*, UNOCHA, New York and Geneva, November

United Nations Development Programme (UNDP) (2001) *Mid-Term Review of the UN Plan 2001*, UN Country Team, Republic of Congo-Brazzaville, August

United Nations Children's Fund (UNICEF) (2000) *Republic of Congo Donor Update*, Republic of Congo, Emergencies, UNICEF website, 12 October, www.unicef.org/emergROC12Oct.pdf

United States Committee for Refugees (USCR) (2001) *Current Country Update, Congo-Brazzaville*, Worldwide Refugee Information, USCR website, 2 October, www.refugees.org/world/countryrpt/africa/Mid_countryrpt01/congo_brazzaville.htm

Rwanda

Human Rights Watch (HRW) (2001) *Uprooting the Rural Poor in Rwanda*, HRW, New York, May

Government of Rwanda (2001) *Brookings Initiative in Rwanda: Land and Human Settlements*, Republic of Rwanda, Kigali

United Nations (UN) (2000) *Common UN Framework for Assistance in the context of the 'Imidugudu' Policy*, UN, New York, February

United Nations Commission for Human Rights (UNCHR) (2000) *Report on the situation of human rights in Rwanda*, E/CN.4/2000/41, UN, Geneva, 25 February

—— (2001) *Situation of Human Rights in Rwanda*, E/CN.4/2001/45/Add.1, UN, Geneva, 21 March

United Nations Office for the Coordination of Humanitarian Affairs (UNOCHA) (1999) *Affected Populations in the Great Lakes Region*, UNOCHA, Nairobi, 24 December

—— (2000) *Mission Report: Displacement and Resettlement in Rwanda*, UNOCHA, New York, 18 December

United Nations Development Programme (UNDP) (2001) *Country Cooperation Frameworks and Related Matters Rwanda 2002-2006*, DP/CCF/RWA/2, UNDP, New York, 20 September

Senegal

Amnesty International (AI) (1998) *Senegal, Climate of Terror in Casamance*, AFR 49/01/98, AI, London, 17 February

Manley, Andrew (1998) *Guinea Bissau/Senegal: War, Civil War and the Casamance Question*, Writenet, UK, November

United States Committee for Refugees (USCR) (2001) *Mid-Year Country Report, Senegal*, Worldwide Refugee Information, USCR website, August, www.refugees.org/world/countryrpt/africa/Mid_countryrpt01/senegal.htm

World Food Programme (WFP) Executive Board (2001) *Country Strategy Outline – Senegal*, WFP/EB.1/2001/7/2, WFP, Rome, 2 January

Sierra Leone

Agence France-Presse (AFP) (2002) 'Sierra Leone parliament ratifies UN war crimes court', as found on Sierra Leone country page, ReliefWeb, www.reliefweb.int/w/rwb.nsf/d2fc8ae9db883867852567cb0083a028/23a827c712b37c5fc1256b8400517ea9?OpenDocument

Amnesty International (AI) (2000) *Action needed to end use of child combatants*, AFR 51/075/2000, AI, London

—— (1998) *Sierra Leone 1998, A Year of Atrocities Against Civilians*, AFR 51/022/1998, AI, London

Human Rights Watch (HRW) (2002) 'Civil War in Sierra Leone: Focus on Human Rights', Current Events, HRW website, 3 March, www.hrw.org/campaigns/sierra/index.htm

—— (2000) 'Fresh Reports of RUF Terror Tactics', Latest News, HRW website, 26 May, www.hrw.org/press/2000/05/sl0526.htm

—— (1999) 'Getting Away with Murder, Mutilation, Rape: New Testimony from Sierra Leone', *Reports by Country*, vol 11, no 3(A), HRW, New York

Médecins Sans Frontières (MSF) (2001) 'With large numbers returning, new crises are now possibilities', Sierra Leone, ReliefWeb, 24 September, www.reliefweb.int/w/rwb.nsf/f303799b16d2074285256830007fb33f/e26f4be151a32cc0c1256ad1004c2a93?OpenDocument

Physicians for Human Rights (2002) *War-related Sexual Violence in Sierra Leone: A Population-Based Assessment*, Physicians for Human Rights, Washington, DC

Save the Children UK (SCF-UK) (2000) 'Sierra Leone', in *War brought us here: protecting children displaced within their own countries by conflict*, Save the Children UK, London

United Nations (UN) (2001) *Consolidated Inter-Agency Appeal 2002, Sierra Leone*, UNOCHA, New York and Geneva, November

United Nations Office for the Coordination of Humanitarian Affairs (UNOCHA) (2000) *Sierra Leone Humanitarian Situation Report*, special issue, UNOCHA, New York and Geneva

—— (2000) *Sierra Leone Humanitarian Situation Report 14 Nov–6 Dec 2000*, UNOCHA, New York and Geneva, 6 December

United Nations Security Council (UNSC) (1999) *Resolution 1270*, UN, New York, 22 October

Somalia

Food Security Analysis Unit (FSAU) (2002) *Monthly Food Security Report for Somalia January 2002*, FSAU, Nairobi

Menkhaus, Ken (2000) *Somalia: A situation Analysis*, Weitenet Paper No 07/2000, November, UNHCR Centre for Documentation and Research, Geneva

Save the Children UK (SCF-UK) (2002) *Somalia Emergency Update*, Emergency Updates, SCF-UK website, January, www.savethechildren.org.uk/sudan/index.html

United Nations (UN) (2002) *2001 UN Consolidated Inter-Agency Humanitarian Assistance Appeal: Summary of Requirements and Contributions by affected country/region*, Financial Tracking System, ReliefWeb, 29 April, www.reliefweb.int/fts/reports/pdf/ocha_21_2002.pdf

—— (2001) *United Nations Inter-Agency Consolidated Appeals Process Strategy Paper 2002, Somalia*, March, UNOCHA, New York and Geneva, November

—— (2001) *United Nations Inter-Agency Consolidated Appeal 2002, Somalia*, November, UNOCHA, New York and Geneva, March

United Nations Integrated Regional Information Networks – Central and Eastern Africa (UNIRIN–CEA) (2002) *Somalia: Concern over escalating violence in Gedo*, Archive, IRIN News website, 8 April, www.irinnews.org/report.asp?ReportID=27345&SelectRegion=Horn_of_Africa&SelectCountry=SOMALIA

—— (2001) *Somalia: IRIN Interview with Kevin Farrell, WFP Somalia*, Somalia, ReliefWeb, 9 July, wwww.reliefweb.int/w/rwb.nsf/f303799b16d2074285256830007fb33faab70a25725d61a985256a8700529f13?OpenDocument

United Nations Children's Fund (UNICEF) (2001) *UNICEF Somalia Review August 2001*, UNICEF, Hargeisa, 7 September

United States Fund for UNICEF (2000) *Somalia Situation Report*, US Fund for UNICEF, New York, 6 September

Sudan

Christian Aid (CAID) (2001) *The regulatory void: EU company involvement in human rights violations in Sudan*, in-depth, CAID website, 17 May, www.christianaid.org.uk/indepth/0105suda/sudan.htm

Harker, John (2000) *Human Security in Sudan:The Report of a Canadian Assessment Mission. Prepared for the Minister of Foreign Affairs*, Department of Foreign Affairs and International Trade, Ottawa

International Crisis Group (ICG) (2002) 'God, Oil and Country Changing the Logic of War in Sudan', *ICG Africa Report*, no 39, ICG, Brussels

Jaspars, S (1999) Targeting and Distribution of Food Aid in SPLM Controlled Areas of South Sudan, WFP, Rome

Operation Lifeline Sudan (OLS) (1999) *Agreement on the Implementation of Principles Governing the Protection and Provision of Humanitarian Assistance to War Affected Civilian Populations*, UN, Geneva, 15 December

Pérouse de Montclos, Marc-Antoine (2001) 'Migrations Forcees et Urbanisation: Le Cas de Khartoum', *Les Dossiers du CEPED*, no 63, CEPED, Paris

Sudan People's Liberation Movement/United Nations Operation Lifeline Sudan (SPLM/UN OLS) (1998) *SPLM/SRRA – OLS Joint Targeting and Vulnerabilities Task Force in SPLM Controlled Areas of Bahr el Ghazal: Final Report*, SPLM/UN OLS, Nairobi, 27 August

United Nations (UN) (2001) *Consolidated Inter-Agency Appeal for Sudan 2002*, UNOCHA, New York and Geneva, November

—— (2000) *Consolidated Inter-Agency Appeal for Sudan 2001*, UNOCHA, New York and Geneva, November

United Nations Commission for Human Rights (UNCHR) (2002) *Specific Groups and Individuals: Mass Exoduses and Displaced Persons Report of the Representative of the Secretary-General on Internally Displaced Persons, Mr Francis Deng, Submitted Pursuant to Commission on Human Rights Resolution 2001/54 Addendum Report on the Mission to the Sudan*, E/CN.4/2002/95/Add.1, UN, Geneva, 5 February

—— (1999) *Question of the violation of human rights and fundamental freedoms in any part of the world: Situation of human rights in the Sudan*, E/CN.4/1999/38/Add.1, UN, Geneva

United Nations International Advisory Committee (UNIAC) Sudan (2001) *Background Note, Meeting at Palais des Nations, Geneva*, UNIAC, Geneva, 14 December

United Nations Integrated Regional Information Networks – Central and Eastern Africa (UNIRIN–CEA) (2002) *SUDAN: UN attempts to reverse flight bans*, Archive, UNIRIN website, 4 March, www.irinnews.orgreport.asp?ReportID=23599&SelectRegion=East_Africa&SelectCountry=SUDAN

—— (2001) *Horn of Africa Update*, Sudan, ReliefWeb, 23 July, www.reliefweb.int/w/rwb.nsf/6686f45896f15dbc852567ae00530132/e0c861531301a6fb85256a9200625610?OpendDocument

—— (2001) *Horn of Africa Update*, Sudan, ReliefWeb, 12 July, www.reliefweb.int/w/rwb.nsf/f303799b16d2074285256830007fb33f/3fd65224c39b005f85256a87006ea126?OpenDocument

United Nations Operation Lifeline Sudan (UNOLS) (1999) *Agreement on the Implementation of Principles Governing the Protection and Provision of Humanitarian Assistance to War Affected Civilian Populations*, UNOLS, Geneva, 15 December

United Nations Children's Fund (UNICEF) (2001) *Unicef returns former child soldiers home*, Press Releases, Sudan, Emergency Updates, UNICEF website, 29 August, www.unicef.org/newsline/01pr71.htm

United States Committee for Refugees (USCR) (2001) *USCR mid-year update on Sudan Sept 2001*, Current Country Update, Sudan, USCR website, 2 October, www.refugees.org/world/countryrpt/africa/Mid_countryrpt01/sudan.htm

World Food Programme (WFP) (2002) *WFP condemns air attack at food distribution site in Southern Sudan*, Press Releases, Sudan, WFP website, 13 February, www.wfp.org/index.asp?section=2

Uganda

Katwikirize, Stuart (2001) *Understanding Resettlement Capacities and Vulnerabilities of Displaced Male and Female Headed Households: A Case of Three Camps in Northern Uganda*, World Vision and Cranfield University, Kampala, December

Oxfam (2002) *The Challenges and Hopes for Protection and Resettlement of Internally Displaced People in the Rwenzori Region*, Oxfam/Kabarole/DED-Uganda, Kampala, 8 February

United Nations (UN) (2001) *Consolidated Inter-Agency Appeal for Uganda 2002*, UNOCHA, New York and Geneva, November

United Nations Integrated Regional Information Networks (UNIRIN) (2002) 'Uganda-Sudan: Focus on missing child abductees', IRIN Africa, IRIN website, 5 April, www.irinnews.org/report.asp?ReportID=27126&SelectRegion=East_Africa&SelectCountry=UGANDA-SUDAN

United Nations Office for the Coordination of Humanitarian Affairs (UNOCHA) (2002) *Humanitarian Update Uganda*, vol 4, issue 3, Uganda, ReliefWeb website, 31 March, www.reliefweb.int/w/Rwb.nsf/480fa8736b88bbc3c12564f6004c8ad5/1341acf5ea09f411c1256b95004a7c93?OpenDocument

—— (2002) *Affected Populations in the Great Lakes Region*, UNOCHA, Nairobi, 28 February

World Food Programme (WFP) (2001) *Protracted Relief and Recovery Operation, Uganda (10121.0): Targeted Food Assistance for Relief and Recovery of Refugees, Displaced Persons and Vulnerable Groups in Uganda*, WFP/EB.1/2002/8/2, WFP, Rome, December

Women's Commission for Refugee Women and Children (WCRWC) (2001) *Against All Odds: Surviving The War On Adolescents: Promoting The Protection and Capacity of Ugandan and Sudanese Adolescents in Northern Uganda*, WCRWC, New York

The Americas

Regional overview

United Nations Commission for Human Rights (UNCHR) (1999) *Report of the United Nations High Commissioner for Human Rights on the Office in Colombia*, E/CN.4/1999/8, UN, Geneva, 16 March

Cohen, Roberta, and Sanchez-Garzoli, Gimena (2001) *Internal Displacement in the Americas: Some Distinctive Features, an Occasional Paper*, May, The Brookings-CUNY Project on Internal Displacement, Washington, DC

Colombia

British Broadcasting Corporation (BBC) Monitoring International Reports via NewsEdge Corporation (2002) 'Colombia: Outgoing UN official highlights "scourge" of displacement', *El Espectador*, Bogotá, 24 March

Consultoría para los Derechos Humanos y el Desplazamiento (CODHES) (2002) *Codhes Informa, no 40*, CODHES, Bogotá, 15 February

—— (2002) *Estimativo de Personas Desplazadas Año 2001, Según Departamento de Llegada 341.927*, CODHES, Bogotá, 5 February

—— (2001) *Codhes Informa, no 35*, CODHES, Bogotá, 1 January

Consultoría para los Derechos Humanos y el Desplazamiento – Sistema de Información sobre Desplazamieuto Forzado y Derechos Humanos en Colombia (CODHES–SISDES) (2001) *Desplazamiento en Colombia departamentos de llegada de enero a septiembre año 2001*, CODHES, Bogotá, 21 November

González Bustelo, Mabel (2001) 'Desterrados. Despazamiento forzado en Colombia', *Cuadernos para el debate, no 12*, MSF, Barcelona

Inter-American Commission on Human Rights (IACHR) (2000) 'Chapter IV: Colombia', in *Annual Report 2000*, IACHR, Washington, DC

Solivida/International Organization for Migration (IOM)/Defensoría del Pueblo (2002) *Informe sobre el Estado de la niñez en Colombia 2001*, Defensoría del Pueblo website, March, www.defensoria.org.co/web/ninez_movie.htm

United Nations Commission for Human Rights (UNCHR) (2001) *Report of the Special Rapporteur on Violence Against Women, Its Causes and Consequences, Ms Radhika Coomaraswamy, Submitted in Accordance with Commission on Human Rights Resolution 2001/49, Addendum*, E/CN.4/2002/83/Add. 3, UN, Geneva, 11 March

United Nations (UN) Resident Coordinator (2001) *Departamentos que Requieren Atencion Prioritaria en Relacion al Deplazamiento (al 1°de Enero del 2001)*, UN Resident Coordinator, Bogotá, 19 January

World Food Programme (WFP) (1999) *Protracted Relief and Recovery Operation in Colombia (6139.00): Assistance to Persons Displaced by Violence in Colombia*, WFP/EB.3/7-B/3, WFP, Rome, 8 September

Guatemala

Bailliet, Cecilia (2001) E-mail to NRC Geneva, 10 December

Commission for Historical Clarification (CEH) (1998) *Guatemala Memory of Silence, Conclusions and Recommendations*, Guatemala, Science and Human Rights Data Centre website: www.hrdata.aaas.org/ceh/report/english/toc.html

Inter-American Commission on Human Rights (IACHR) (2001) 'Chapter XIV: The Human Rights of those Uprooted by the Armed Conflict', in *Fifth Report on the Situation of Human Rights in Guatemala*, OEA/Ser.L/V/II.111, doc 21 rev, IACHR, Washington, DC, 6 April

Loughna, Sean, and Vicente, Gema (2000) *Population issues and the situation of women in post-conflict Guatemala*, ILO, Geneva

United Nations Human Rights Verification Mission in Guatemala (MINUGUA) (2001) *Sexto Informe del Secretario General de las Naciones Unidas sobre la Verificación de los Acuerdos de Paz de Guatemala*, Informes Cronograma, MINUGUA website, June, www.minugua.guate.net/informes/SEXTOINFORME.pdf

MINUGUA (2000) *The situation in Central America: procedures for the establishment of a firm and lasting peace and progress in fashioning a region of peace, freedom, democracy and development*, A/55/174, UNHCHR, Geneva, 26 July

United Nations Development Programme/United Nations High Commission for Refugees (UNDP/UNHCR) (1995) *CIREFA: an Opportunity and Challenge for Inter-Agency Cooperation*, UNDP/UNHCR, May

Mexico

Amnesty International (AI) (2001) 'Mexico', in *Annual Report 2001*, POL 10/001/2001, AI, London

Centro de Derechos Humanos Fray Bartolomé de Las Casas (CDHFBC), AC (1999) *Executive Summary of the report: Presumed Justice*, CBHBC, Mexico, March

Centro de Investigaciones Economicas y Politicas de Accion Comunitaria (CIEPAC) (1999) 'The Internally Displaced of the War in Chiapas', *Chiapas al Dia*, no 168, CIEPAC, Chiapas, 28 August

Cohen, Roberta, and Sanchez-Garzoli, Gimena (2001) *Internal Displacement in the Americas: Some Distinctive Features, an Occasional Paper*, The Brookings-CUNY Project on Internal Displacement, Washington, DC, May

Human Rights Watch (HRW) (2001) 'Military Injustice, Mexico's Failure to Punish Army Abuses', *Reports by Country*, vol 13, no 4(B), HRW, New York

Schwartz, Janet Leslie, and Saliba, Armando (2002) 'Indian group denounces gov't plans for violent displacement in Chiapas', Campaigns: Current Campaigns: Chiapas, Global Exchange website, 28 February, www.globalexchange.org/campaigns/mexico/chiapas/newsMexico022802.html

International Service for Peace (SIPAZ) (2001) *SIPAZ Quarterly Reports*, vol VI, no 4, 4 December, SIPAZ, Santa Cruz

Peru

Cohen, Roberta, and Sanchez-Garzoli, Gimena (2001) *Internal Displacement in the Americas: Some Distinctive Features*, Displacement, Foreign Policy: Featured Research, The Brookings Institution website, May, www.brookings.org/dybdocroot/fp/projects/idp/articles/idamericas.htm

Coordinadora Nacional de Derechos Humanos (CNDDHH) (2002) 'Informe Annual' 2001, Lima, June

Mesa Nacional sobre Desplazamiento y Afectados por Violencia Politica (MENADES) (2000) *Propuesta de MENADES al Ministerio de Promocion de la Mujer y Desarrollo Humano (PROMUDEH) sobre el Tema de la Poblacion Afectada por Violencia Política*, Government of Peru, Lima, December

Asia

Regional overview

Cohen, Roberta (2000) *Addressing Internal Displacement in Asia: A Role for Regional Organizations*, Foreign Policy Studies: Internally Displaced Persons: Articles and Papers, Brookings Institution website, www.brook.edu/dybdocroot/views/papers/cohenr/2000IDASia.htm

Conetta, Carl (2002) 'Operation Enduring Freedom: Why a Higher Rate of Civilian Bombing Casualties', *Briefing Report #11*, Cambridge, MA, Commonwealth Institute, Project on Defense Alternatives, Cambridge, January

Herold, Marc W (2001) *A Dossier on Civilian Victims of United States' Aerial Bombing of Afghanistan: A Comprehensive Accounting*, Departments of Economics and Women's Studies, McConnell Hall, Whittemore School of Business and Economics

University of New Hampshire, Cursor homepage, December, www.cursor.org/stories/civilian_deaths.htm

Afghanistan

Afghanistan Information Management Service (AIMS) (2002) *Afghanistan, Internally displaced Persons (IDPs) (Aggregated to Province Divisions) as of 20 February*, AIMS, Islamabad, 20 February

Associated Press (AP) (2002) 'Some Afghans survive by selling kids', News Archive, *Afghan News Network Services* website, 8 February, www.qxsn.com/news/allnews2002/article_2002_02_8_4346.html

Conetta, Carl (2002) 'Operation Enduring Freedom: Why a Higher Rate of Civilian Bombing Casualties', *Briefing Report #11*, Cambridge, MA, Commonwealth Institute, Project on Defence Alternatives, Cambridge, January

Farr, Grant (2001) 'Afghanistan: Displaced in a Devastated Country', in Vincent, Marc and Refslund, Birgit (eds) *Caught Between Borders – Response Strategies of the Internally Displaced*, Earthscan, London

Herold, Marc W (2001) *A Dossier on Civilian Victims of United States' Aerial Bombing of Afghanistan: A Comprehensive Accounting*, Departments of Economics and Women's Studies, McConnell Hall, Whittemore School of Business and Economics

University of New Hampshire, Cursor homepage, December, www.cursor.org/stories/civilian_deaths.htm

Human Rights Watch (HRW) (2002) 'Paying for the Taliban's crimes', *Reports by Country*, vol 14, no 2(C), New York, April

International Committee of the Red Cross (ICRC) (2001) 'Afghanistan: Concern about growing mine threat', Afghanistan, ICRC website, 4 October, www.icrc.org/icrceng.nsf/Index/6AF491BD995F51ECC1256ADB00514AF5?OpenDocument

Marshall, Andrew (2002) 'Aid agencies face dilemma over displaced Afghans', Reuters , Afghanistan page, ReliefWeb, 25 February, http://wwww.reliefweb.int/w/rwb.nsf/ 3a81e21068ec1871c1256633003c1c6f/a1b52a5ec7e65913c1256b6b005fd33b?OpenDocument

Médecins Sans Frontières (MSF) (2002) 'Severe increase in malnutrition in Mazlakh camp, Afghanistan', Press Room, MSF US website, 6 February, www.doctorswithoutborders.org/ pr/2002/02-06-2002_pf.html

—— (2002) 'Cluster bombs the legacy to Afghan population', Afghanistan, MSF website, 18 January, www.msf.org/countries/page.cfm?articleid=E755D9DB-D547-42F5-888C17 D60135AE38

Refugees International (RI) (2002) *A Recovery Investment for Afghanistan's Refugees and Displaced People*, Bulletins, RI website, 8 January, www.refintl.org/cgi-bin/ri/bulletin?bc=00359

Schenkenberg van Mierop (ed) (2002) NGO Coordination and Some Other Relevant Issues in the Context of Afghanistan from an NGO Perspective, ICVA, Geneva, 9 April

United Nations (UN) (2002) *Immediate and Transitional Assistance Programme for the Afghan People 2002*, UN Coordination Office for Afghanistan, Kabul and Islamabad, January

United Nations Office for the Coordination of Humanitarian Affairs (UNOCHA) Internal Displacement Unit (2002) *The IDP Situation in Afghanistan: Report of a mission by the Internal Displacement Unit*, UNOCHA, Geneva, 28 March

—— (2002) *Afghanistan OCHA Situation Report*, no 37, UNOCHA, New York and Geneva, 29 January

United States Agency for International Development /United States Bureau for Democracy/ United States Office of US Foreign Disaster Assistance (USAID/USDCHA/USOFDA) (2002) *Central Asia Region, Complex Emergency Situation Report # 28*, USAID/USDCHA/USOFDA, Washington, DC, 12 April

Bangladesh

Chittagong Hill Tracts Commission (CHTC) (2000) *'Life Is Not Ours' – Land and Human Rights in the Chittagong Hill Tracts*, Bangladesh, update 4, CHTC, Amsterdam

Feeny, Thomas (2001) 'The Fragility of Peace in the Chittagong Hill Tracts', in *Forced Migration Review*, vol 11, October, pp25–27

Burma/Myanmar

Amnesty International (AI) (2001) *Myanmar: Ethnic Minorities, Targets of Repression*, ASA 16/ 014/2001, June, AI, London

Burma Ethnic Research Group (BERG) (2000) 'Internal Displacement in Burma', in *Disasters* vol 24, no 3, September, pp228–239

Burmese Border Consortium (2002) *Relief Programme: July to December 2001*, Burmese Border Consortium, Bangkok

—— (2001) *Programme report January to June 2001, Funding Appeal for 2002*, Burmese Border Consortium, Bangkok, June

—— (2001) *Burmeese Border Refugee Sites with Population Figures (map)*, Bangkok

Christian Solidarity Worldwide (CSW) (2000) *Trip Report – Thailand and Burma*, November, CSW, Hong Kong

Cusano, Chris (2001) 'Burma: Displaced Karens. Like water on the Khu Leaf', in Vincent, Marc, and Refslund, Birgit (eds) *Caught Between Borders, Response Strategies of the Internally Displaced*, Earthscan, London

EarthRights International (2000) *Total Denial Continues*, EarthRights International, Washington, DC

International Labour Organization (ILO) (2002) *Developments concerning the question of the observance by the Government of Myanmar of the Forced Labour Convention, 1930 (No. 29)*, GB.283/5, ILO, Geneva, March

—— (1998) *Report of the Commission of Inquiry appointed under article 26 of the Constitution of the International Labour Organization to examine the observance by Myanmar of the Forced Labour Convention, 1930 (No 29): Part V, Conclusions and recommendations*, ILO, Geneva, 2 July

Médecins Sans Frontières (MSF) (2002) *10 Years for the Rohingya Refugees in Bangladesh: Past, Present and Future*, MSF in Bangladesh, MSF website, March 2002, www.msf.org/source/downloads/2002/rohingya.doc

United Nations Commission for Human Rights (UNCHR) (2002) *Report on the Situation of Human Rights in Myanmar, Prepared by Mr Paulo Sergio Pinheiro, Special Rapporteur of the Commission on Human Rights, in Accordance with Commission Resolution 2001/15*, E/CN.4/2002/45, UN, Geneva, 10 January

India

Agence France-Presse (AFP) (2001) '60,000 Flee Kashmir Border Amid India-Pakistan Military Build-up, Shelling', Headlines, *Common Dreams News Centre* website, 30 December, www.commondreams.org/headlines01/1230-03.htm

Amnesty International (AI) (2002) *India: Memorandum to the Government of Gujarat*, ASA 20/004/2002, AI, London, 28 March

AI (2001) *India: Call for restraint in Kashmir*, ASA 20/046/2001, AI, London

Human Rights Watch (HRW) (2002) *Prevent Further Communal Violence in India*, News Archive, HRW website, 13 March, http://hrw.org/press/2002/03/india0313.htm

Lama, Mahendra P (2000) 'Internal displacement in India: causes, protection and dilemmas' *Forced Migration*, vol 8, August, pp24–29

Naga Peoples Movement for Human Rights (NPMHR) (2002) *Summary Report on the Conditions of the Internally Displaced Peoples (IDPs) from the Imphal Valley to the Naga Hills Areas of Manipur – a Repercussion of the Indo-Naga Cease*, Features, NPMHR website, 5 January, www.kuknalim.net/features/NPMHRReportOnIDPs.PDF

Permanent Mission of India to the United Nations Office, Geneva (2000) *Statement at the 56th Session of the Commission on Human Rights* (Agenda Item 14), Geneva

Pettersson, Bjorn (2002) 'Development-induced displacement: internal affair or international human rights issue?' in *Forced Migration Review*, vol 12, January, pp16–19

Roy, Arundhati (1999) *The Cost of Living*, Flamingo, London

South Asia Human Rights Documentation Centre (SAHRDC) (2001) *No Refuge: The Plight of Conflict-Induced Internally Displaced Persons in India*, HRF/33/01, Human Rights Features, HRDC website, 16 March, www.hrdc.net/sahrdc/hrfeatures/HRF33.htm

United States Committee for Refugees (USCR) (2000) *Displacement from Kashmir*, Worldwide Refugee Information, USCR website, www.refugees.org/world/articleskashmir_displaced_india.htm

Indonesia

Aceh Child Rights Alliance Directory (ACRA) (2001) *Song of the exiled, sad story of the Aceh refugee*, News Analysis, ACRA website, www.acra.ws/acra/Analisys/SongofTheExiled.html

Action Contre la Faim (ACF) (2001) *Post Distribution Monitoring*, ACF, Ambon, May

Action by Churches Together (ACT) (2001) *ACT Appeal Indonesia: Assistance to displaced in Sulawesi: ASID-13*, 6 August, ACT, Geneva

Human Rights Watch (HRW) (2001) 'Indonesia: The war in Aceh', in *Reports by Country*, vol 13, no 4(C), HRW, New York, August

Indonesian Observer (2001) 'Muslim, Christian IDPs return to North Maluku', Jakarta. 20 April

United Nations (UN) (2001) *Consolidated Inter-Agency Appeal for Internally Displaced Persons in Indonesia 2002*, UNOCHA, New York and Geneva, November

United Nations Office for the Coordination of Humanitarian Affairs (UNOCHA) (2002) *Inter-agency mission to Central Sulawesi 28 January–1 February 2002*, UN OCHA, Jakarta, February

United Nations Children's Fund (UNICEF) (2002) *UNICEF humanitarian appeal for children and women Jan–Dec 2002*, UNICEF, New York, 11 February

World Food Programme (WFP) (2002) *Internally displaced in Indonesia suffer from high rates of poverty, poor health: WFP survey*, WFP, Jakarta, 7 May

—— (2001) *WFP Mission to Madura, March 10-11*, March, WFP, Jakarta

—— (2000) *Joint UN Agency Humanitarian Mission to Central Sulawesi*, Food Sector Report, WFP, Jakarta, 22 August

World Food Programme Vulnerability Analysis and Mapping Unit (WFP VAM) (2002*) IDP Source and Recipient Regions*, WFP, Jakarta, 24 April

—— (2001) *IDP Source and Recipient Regions*, WFP, Jakarta, 17 July

Pakistan

International Committee of the Red Cross (ICRC) (2001) Email from ICRC Geneva to NRC Geneva, 31 August

—— (2001) *The ICRC in Pakistan: Summary of ICRC activities in 2000*, ICRC, Geneva, 1 June

Institute for Multi-Track Diplomacy (IMTD) (2001) *Pakistani Kashmir Refugee Camps*, Diplomacy/Conflict ResolutionTraining, IMTD website, www.imtd.org/initiatives-kashmir-refugee.htm

The Philippines

Balay Rehabilitation Centre (2002) *Notes on the phenomenon of internal displacement in the Philippines 2001*, Human Rights Monitor, Human Rights Network on the Web, 26 February, www.hrnow.org/monitor.htm

Balay Research, Documentation and Information Programme (2000) *Internally displaced Persons: Collateral damage or victims of human right violations*, Resources, Human Rights Now, 23 November, www.hrnow.org/resources.htm

Community and Family Services International (CFSI) (2001) *Promoting the Transition From Conflict to Peace and Development at the Community Level, Progress Report Number One*, CFSI, Pasay City, October

Ecumenical Commission for Displaced Families and Communities (ECDFC) (2001) *Recorded Armed Conflict Related Displacement Incidents*, The Philippines: Sources, Global IDP Database, 10 December, www.db.idpproject.org/Sites/idpSurvey.nsf/052E569F7C11651CC1256 B9C005A2FF2/$file/ECDFC_displacement_incidents_Dec01.pdf

Human Rights Network on the Web (2000) *Documented human rights violations that resulted from the intensified military operations in Maguindanao and North Cotabato by the armed forces of The Philippines*, Human Rights Monitor: Archive, Mindano Alert, Human Rights Now, 9 May, www.hrnow.org/monitor.htm

International Campaign to Ban Land Mines (ICBL) (2001) *Land Mine Monitor Report 2001*, HRW, New York, August

Oxfam (2001), *Reaching for the gun: the humanitarian impact of small arms in Central Mindanao*, Oxfam, London, January

—— (2000) *Anthropometric and Household Food Security Survey among Displaced Families in Central Mindanao*, Philippines: Sources, Global IDP Project website, November, www.db.idpproject.org/Sites/idpSurvey.nsf/E4AECACDFE8F7D8C1256A0D005A1D7F/$file/SURVEY+REPORT+.pdf

United Nations Development Programme (UNDP) (2001) *Surrendering to Peace*, News and Events, UNDP in The Philippines website, 6 September, www.undp.org.ph/neLatest%20News/readnew.asp?id=43

United Nations (UN) Resident Coordinator (UNRC) (2000) *Situation Update on Peace and Development in Mindanao*, Manila, 7 August

—— (2000) *Situation Update on Peace and Development in Mindanao*, Manila, 6 June

—— (2000) *Situation Update on Peace and Development in Mindanao*, Manila, 8 May

—— (2000) *Situation Update on Peace and Development in Mindanao*, Manila, 31 May

Solomon Islands

Amnesty International (AI) (2000) *Solomon Islands: A black day for human rights*, ASA 43/013/2000, AI, London, 19 December

—— (2000) *Solomon Islands: A forgotten conflict*, ASA 43/05/00, AI, London, 7 September

European Union (EU) (2002) *Country strategy paper and national indicative programme for the period 2002-2007*, I:\CSP\Sol\CSS27septRev.gm.doc, EU, Brussels, 19 March

Kudu, Donald (2000) *Impact of the ethnic unrest on social development and disadvantaged groups in Solomon Islands*, Annex E-3 of the Experts Group Meeting on the Post-Conflict Situation in Solomon Islands, UNDP, University of Queensland and ILO, Brisbane, October

Rarawa, Denton H (2000) *The impact of the social unrest on Guadalcanal on the Solomon Islands economy*, Annex E-2 of the Experts Group Meeting on the Post-Conflict Situation in Solomon Islands, UNDP, University of Queensland and ILO, Brisbane, October

Roughan, John (2000) *A second look at the ethnic crisis in Solomons*, Annex E-1 of the Experts Group Meeting on the Post-Conflict Situation in Solomon Islands, UNDP, University of Queensland and ILO, Brisbane

Saemane, George (2000) *Relief and rehabilitation: current situation and future directions*, Annex E-6 of the Experts Group Meeting on the Post-Conflict Situation in Solomon Islands, UNDP, University of Queensland and ILO, Brisbane, October

Schoorl, J J and Friesen, W (2002) 'Migration and displacement', in de Bruijn, B (ed) *Report on the 1999 Solomon Islands population and housing census: analysis, 2002*, Solomon Islands Government Statistics Office, Honiara

Solomon Islands Government (2000) *The Townsville Peace Agreement*, Solomon Islands Government, Honiara

United Nations Children's Fund (UNICEF) (2001) *UNICEF Humanitarian Action: Solomon Islands Donor Update*, UNICEF, New York, 21 December

Sri Lanka

Amnesty International (AI) (2002) *Sri Lanka: Rape in custody*, ASA 37/001/2002, AI, London, 28 January

—— (2000) *New Emergency Regulations – erosion of human rights protection*, ASA 37/019/2000, AI, London, 1 July

Commissioner General of Essential Services (CGES) (2002) *Commissioner of General Essential Services issue of dry rations assistance*, Government of Sri Lanka, Sri Jayewardenepura Kotte, January

Centre for Policy Alternatives (CPA) (2001) *Human Rights Violations of Internally Displaced Persons and Government Policies classified by reference to the UN Guiding Principles on Internal Displacement*, Research Papers, Centre for Policy Alternatives website, CPA, Colombo, October

International Campaign to Ban Land Mines (ICBL) (2001) *Land Mine Monitor Report 2001*, HRW, New York, August

International Committee of the Red Cross (ICRC) (2001) *Sri Lanka: Mounting violence highlights protection needs*, ICRC, Geneva, 4 December

Jesuit Refugee Service (JRS) (2000) *Restricting freedom of movement: the 'pass system'*, Resources, JRS website, December, www.jesref.org/inf/lka-spcl/pass-sys.htm

Médecins Sans Frontières (MSF) (2002) 'Sri Lanka's health service is a casualty of 20 years of war', Afghanistan, MSF website, 9 February, www.msf.org/countries/page.cfm?articleid= 333E1035-03EF-4C36-9BE1443DFD83044B

—— (2001) *Assessing Trauma in Sri Lanka, Psycho-Social Questionnaire, Vavuniya*, MSF, Amsterdam, 31 May

Refugees International (RI) (2002) *A chance to invest in peace*, Bulletins, RI website, 4 March, www.refintl.org/cgi-bin/ri/bulletin?bc=00375

United Nations High Commission for Refugees (UNHCR) (2000) *Internal Displacement in Sri Lanka, Contribution to the IDP Project of the Norwegian Refugee Council*, UNHCR, Geneva, November

——/Consortium of Humanitarian Agencies (2000) *Internally displaced persons in government welfare centres in Sri Lanka, workshop results and proposals for action*, UNHCR, Geneva, September

United Nations Mine Action Service (UNMAS) (2001) *Mission Report, Sri Lanka*, 4 June, Sri Lanka, UN Mine Action website, UNMAS, Geneva

World Food Programme (WFP) (2002) 'WFP urges aid for forgotten victims of strife in Sri Lanka', Newsroom, WFP website, 28 February, www.wfp.org/index.asp?section=2

Uzbekistan

Amnesty International (AI) (2001) *Uzbekistan, The Rhetoric of Human Rights Protection: Briefing for the United Nations Human Rights Committee*, EUR 62/006/2001, AI, London, June

International Crisis Group (ICG) (2001) 'Uzbekistan at Ten – Repression and Instability', *ICG Asia Reports*, no 21, ICG, Osh/Brussels, 21 August

International Helsinki Federation of Human Rights (IHF) (2001) *Mission to Central Asia (Kazakhstan, Kyrgystan and Uzbekistan) 7–16 June*, IHF, Vienna, 18 July

—— (2001) *Human Rights in the OSCE Region: The Balkans, the Caucasus, Europe, Central Asia and North America, Report 2001(events of 2000)*, IHF, Vienna, May, pp352–362

United States Mission to the Organization for Security and Cooperation in Europe (2001) *US Statement to the OSCE*, US Mission to the OSCE, Vienna, 22 February

Europe

Regional overview

Bagshaw, Simon (2000) *Internally Displaced Persons and Political Participation: The OSCE Region, an Occasional Paper*, Brookings Institution Project on Internal Displacement, Washington, DC

International Organization for Migration/United Nations High Commission for Refugees (IOM/UNHCR) (2000) *Regional Conference to Address the Problems of Refugees, Displaced Persons, Other Forms of Involuntary Displacement and Returnees in the Countries of the Commonwealth of Independent States and Relevant Neighbouring States, Assessment Report of the Conference Process (1996-2000)*, IOM/UNHCR, Geneva

Organization for Security and Cooperation in Europe (OSCE) (2000) *Supplementary Human Dimension Meeting, Migration and Internal Displacement, Final Report*, OSCE, Vienna, 25 September

OSCE Office for Democratic Institutions and Human Rights/Brookings Institution Project on Internal Displacement/NRC (2000) *Regional Workshop on Internal Displacement in the South Caucasus (Armenia, Azerbaijan, Georgia) 10–12 May*, OSCE ODIHR/Brookings Institution Project on Internal Displacement/NRC, Tbilisi

Special Coordinator of the Stability Pact for South Eastern Europe (2001) *Regional Return Initiative for Refugees and Displaced Persons, Agenda for Regional Action (AREA) 2001–2003, Croatia – Bosnia and Herzegovina – Federal Republic of Yugoslavia*, Special Coordinator of the Stability Pact for South Eastern Europe, Brussels, 20 June

United Nations High Commission for Refugees (UNHCR) (2002) 'Refugees and Others of Concern to UNHCR', *2001 UNHCR Population Statistics (Provisional)*, UNHCR, Geneva, 16 May

Armenia

Darbinyan, Armenak (1999) *Armenia Residual Humanitarian Needs, Independent Report*, UN Resident Coordinator's System in Armenia, Yerevan

Government of Armenia, Department of Migration and Refugees (2000) *Project – Post-Conflict Rehabilitation of Bordering Territories of the ROA*, Government of Armenia, Yerevan

Greene, Thomas (1998) 'Internal Displacement in the North Caucasus, Azerbaijan, Armenia and, Georgia' in Cohen, Roberta and Deng, Francis (eds) *The Forsaken People – Case Studies of the Internally Displaced*, Earthscan, London

International Organization for Migration (IOM) (1999) *Migration Trends Among Internally Displaced Persons in Border Regions of the Republic of Armenia*, IOM, Yerevan, January

United Nations Commission for Human Rights (UNCHR) (2000) *Report of the Representative of the Secretary-General on internally displaced persons, Mr. Francis Deng, submitted pursuant to Commission on Human Rights resolution 2000/53, Addendum, Profiles in displacement: Armenia*, E/CN.4/2001/5/Add.3, UN, Geneva, 6 November

World Food Programme (WFP) (2001) *Protracted Relief and Recovery Operation – Armenia 10053.0 (former WIS no 6120.02) – Relief and Recovery Assistance for Vulnerable Groups*, WFP/EB.2/2001/6-b, WFP, Rome, 5 April

Azerbaijan

Azerbaijan State Committee of Statistics (2002) *Regional Distribution of the IDP Population (as of 1 January 2002)*, State Committee of Statistics, Baku

International Federation of Red Cross and Red Crescent Societies (IFRC) (2001) *The Caucasus: Armenia, Azerbaijan, Georgia, Programme Update No 3, period covered April–June 2001*, IFRC, Geneva, 7 September

International Medical Corps (IMC) (2000) *Population Health Needs and Health Service Utilization in Southern Azerbaijan*, Technical Report, IMC, Los Angeles, November

Mercy Corps International (MCI) (2001) *Azerbaijan Humanitarian Assistance Program, Program Overview*, MCI, Baku, May

Radio Free Europe/Radio Liberty (RFE/RL) (2002) 'Fronts harden on eve of Minsk Group Co-Chairs' visit', in *Caucasus Report*, vol 5, no 9, *Reports*, Radio Free Europe/Radio Liberty website, 7 March, www.rferl.org/caucasus-report/2002/03/9-070302.html

United Nations Commission for Human Rights (UNCHR) (1999) *Report of the Representative of the Secretary-General on Internally Displaced Persons, Mr Francis M Deng, Profiles in Displacement: Azerbaijan*, E/CN.4/1999/79/Add.1, UN, Geneva, 25 January

United Nations Development Programme (UNDP) (2000) *Azerbaijan Human Development Report 1999*, UNDP, Baku

—— (1999) *Azerbaijan Human Development Report 1999*, UNDP, Baku

World Food Programme (WFP) (2002) *Protracted Relief and Recovery Operation – Azerbaijan 19168.0, Targeted Food Assistance for Relief and Recovery of Displaced Persons and Vulnerable Groups in Azerbaijan*, WFP/EB.2/2002/6/3, WFP, Rome, 3 April

—— (1999) *WFP Assistance to Internally Displaced Persons, Country Case Study on Internal Displacement, Azerbaijan, Internal Displacement Issues, Final Draft*, WFP, Rome, November

—— (1999) *Protracted Relief and Recovery Operation – Azerbaijan 6121.00, Relief and Recovery Assistance for Vulnerable Groups*, WFP/EB.2/99/5-B/2, WFP, Rome, 28 April

Bosnia and Herzegovina

Amnesty International (AI) (2000) *Bosnia-Herzegovina, Waiting on the doorstep: minority returns to eastern Republika Srpska*, EUR 63/07/00, AI, London

Human Rights Watch (HRW) (2000) 'Unfinished Business: Return of Displaced Persons and Other Human Rights Issues in Bijeljina', *Reports by Country*, vol 12, no 7(D)

International Crisis Group (ICG) (2001) 'The Wages of Sin: Confronting Bosnia's Republika Srpska', *Balkans Report*, no 118, ICG, Sarajevo and Brussels

—— (2000) *Bosnia's Refugee Logjam Breaks: Is the International Community Ready?* Programmes, ICG website, 31 May, www.crisisweb.org/projects/showreport.cfm?reportid=61

Ministry for Human Rights and Refugees (2001) *Implementation of Annex VII; General Framework for Agreement on Peace in B & H*, Government of Bosnia and Herzegovina, Sarajevo

Office of the High Representative of Bosnia and Herzegovina (OHR) (2002) *21st Report by the High Representative for Implementation of the Peace Agreement to the Secretary-General of the United Nations*, Office of the High Representative, Sarajevo, 5 March

United Nations (UN) (2001) *Consolidated Appeal 2002, South-Eastern Europe*, UNOCHA, New York and Geneva

United Nations Commission for Human Rights (UNCHR) (2002) *Situation of human rights in parts of South-Eastern Europe, Report of the Special Representative of the Commission on Human Rights on the situation of human rights in Bosnia and Herzegovina and the Federal Republic of Yugoslavia, Jose Cutileiro*, E/CN.4/2002/41, UN, Geneva

—— (2001) *UNHCR's Position on Categories of Persons from Bosnia and Herzegovina in Continued Need of International Protection*, UNHCR Sarajevo Protection Unit, Sarajevo

—— Sarajevo Protection Unit (2001) *Health Care in Bosnia and Herzegovina in the Context of the Return of Refugees and Displaced Persons*, UNHCR, Sarajevo

United Nations High Commission for Refugees/United Nations High Commissioner for Human Rights (UNHCR/UNHCHR) (2000) *Daunting Prospects - Minority Women: Obstacles to their Return and Integration*, UNHCR, Sarajevo

World Food Programme (WFP) (2000) *WFP Assistance to Internally Displaced Persons, Country Case Study on Internal Displacement, Displacement in Bosnia-Herzegovina, Final Draft*, WFP, Rome

Croatia

Government of Croatia (2002) *Action Plan for Implementation of Repossession of Property end of 2002*, Government of Croatia, Zagreb

Government of Croatia Ministry of Public Works, Reconstruction and Construction (2002) *Total of Returns to the Republic of Croatia and Displaced Persons and Refugees Awaiting Solutions*, Government of Croatia, Zagreb, April

—— (2002) *Implementation of the Repossession of Property until 1 April 2002 According to the Action Plan for Repossession of Property by the end of 2002*, Government of Croatia, Zagreb

Norwegian Refugee Council (NRC) (2002) *Question of the Violation of Human Rights and Fundamental Freedoms in any Part of the World, Written statement submitted to the UN*

Commission on Human Rights by the Norwegian Refugee Council, E/CN.4/2002/NGO/154, UN, Geneva

Organization for Security and Cooperation in Europe (OSCE) (2002) *Supporting the return of refugees and displaced persons*, OSCE Activities: OSCE Mission to Croatia: Return and Reintegration, OSCE website, www.osce.org/croatia/return/

Cyprus

Council of Europe (CoE) Parliamentary Assembly (2001) *Situation in Cyprus, Rapporteur: Mr. Andras, Bársony, Hungary, Socialist Group, Political Affairs Committee*, Doc 9302, CoE, Strasbourg

European Court of Human Rights (ECHR) (2001) *Cyprus v. Turkey*, Rec. 2001-IV (10.05.01), ECHR, Strasbourg

—— (1996) *Loizidou v. Turkey*, rec 1996-VI, fasc 26 (18.12.96), ECHR, Strasbourg

Kyle, Keith (1997) *Cyprus: In Search of Peace*, Minority Rights Group, London

United Nations Commission for Human Rights (UNCHR) (2002) *Questions of the Violation of Human Rights and Fundamental Freedoms in any Part of the World, Including the Question of Human Rights in Cyprus*, E/CN.4/2002/33, UN, Geneva, 4 March

United Nations Security Council (UNSC) (2001) *Report of the Secretary-General on the United Nations operations in Cyprus*, S/2001/1122, UN, New York, 30 November

United Nations High Commission for Refugees (UNHCR) (1999) 'Refugees and Others of Concern to UNHCR', *1998 Statistical Overview*, UNHCR, Geneva, July

Wilkinson, M James (1999) *Moving Beyond Conflict Prevention to Reconciliation – Tackling Greek–Turkish Hostility*, Carnegie Corporation, New York

Federal Republic of Yugoslavia

European Council on Refugees and Exiles/ International Council of Voluntary Agencies (ECRE/ICVA) (2000) *The Protection of Refugees and IDPs in Serbia, March–May 2000*, ECRE and ICVA, London and Geneva

Humanitarian Community Information Centre (HCIC) (2000) *Kosovo: Minorities, Minority Communities in and around Kosovo*, HCIC, Kosovo

HelpAge International (2001) *Building a Better Future, Older People in Serbia*, Help Age International, London, November

Institute of Public Health of Serbia, Dr Milan Jovanovic Batut (2001) *Health status, health needs and utilization of health services in 2002, Report on the analysis for adult population in Serbia: Differences between domicile population, refugees and internally displaced persons*, Institute of Public Health of Serbia, Belgrade

Norwegian Refugee Council (NRC) (2001) *Update on Issues of Concern to IDPs from Kosovo Currently Residing in Serbia Proper*, NRC, Belgrade

Organization for Security and Cooperation in Europe (OSCE) (1999) *Human Rights in Kosovo: As Seen, As Told, An analysis of the human rights findings of the OSCE Kosovo Verification Mission October 1998 to June 1999*, OSCE, Warsaw

OSCE Mission in Kosovo/United Nations Interim Administration Mission in Kosovo (2002) *Property Rights in Kosovo*, OSCE Mission in Kosovo and UNMIK, Pristina

United Nations (UN) (2001) *Consolidated Inter-Agency Appeal 2002, South-Eastern Europe*, UNOCHA, New York and Geneva, November

United Nations Office for the Coordination of Humanitarian Affairs (UNOCHA) (2002) *Humanitarian Situation, Protection and Assistance: Internally Displaced Persons in Serbia and Montenegro*, Humanitarian Risk Analysis No 18, UNOCHA, Belgrade, 26 April

—— (2002) *UN Interagency progress report and recommendations on the situation in Southern Serbia, FRY*, UNOCHA, New York and Geneva, 29 January

United Nations Security Council (UNSC) (2002) *Report of the Secretary-General on the United Nations Interim Administration Mission in Kosovo*, S/2002/62, UN, New York
—— (2001) *Letter dated 23 October 2001, from the Secretary-General addressed to the President of the Security Council, Monthly Report to the United Nations on KFOR Operations*, S/2001/1002, UN, New York, 23 October
United Nations High Commission for Refugees (UNHCR) Commissioner for Refugees of the Republic of Serbia (2001) *Registration of Internally Displaced Persons From Kosovo and Metohija*, UNHCR, Belgrade
United Nations High Commission for Refugees/Organization for Security and Cooperation in Europe (UNHCR/OSCE) (2001) *Assessment of the Situation of Ethnic Minorities in Kosovo (Period covering March 2001 through August 2001)*, UNHCR and OSCE, Pristina, October
US Committee for Refugees (USCR) (2000) *Serbia, Reversal of Fortune: Yugoslavia's Refugee Crisis since the Ethnic Albanian Return to Kosovo*, USCR, Washington, DC

Former Yugoslav Republic of Macedonia
Human Rights Watch (HRW) (2001) 'Macedonian police abuses documented ethnic Albanian men separated, tortured at police stations', News Archive, HRW website, 31 May, www.hrw.org/press/2001/05/macedonia0530.htm
International Federation of Red Cross and Red Crescent Societies (IFRC) (2001) Email from IFRC Macedonia to NRC Geneva, 7 December
International Helsinki Federation of Human Rights (IHF) (2001) *Report: Fact-finding missions regarding the ongoing crisis and human rights violations in the Republic of Macedonia*, IHF, Vienna, 8 June
Macedonian Centre for International Cooperation (MCIC) (2002) *MCIC Situation report in Macedonia*, various, MCIC, Skopje, www.aidmacedonia.org
United Nations High Commission for Refugees (UNHCR) (2001) 'Former Yugoslav Republic of Macedonia (FYROM)', in *Briefing Notes: Afghanistan, FYR of Macedonia, UNHCR Staff Memorial*, UNHCR, Geneva, 25 September
United States Committee for Refugees (USCR) (2001) *Mid-Year Country Report: Macedonia*, Worldwide Refugee Information, USCR website, September, www.refugees.org/world/countryrpt/europe/mid_countryrpt01/macedonia.htm
World Food Programme (WFP) (2001) *WFP Emergency Report No 52 of 2001*, Newsroom, Emergency Reports, WFP website, 28 December, www.wfp.org/index2.html

Georgia
Cohen, Jonathan (ed) (1999) 'A Question of Sovereignty – the Georgia-Abkhazia Peace Process', *Accord – An International Review of Peace Initiatives*, Issue 7, London
Dale, Catherine (1997) 'The Dynamics and Challenges of Ethnic Cleansing: The Georgia-Abkhazia Case', *Refugee Survey Quarterly*, vol 16, issue 3, pp77–109
Georgian Young Lawyers' Association (1999) *Monitoring of Legal and Actual Status of Internally Displaced Persons in Georgia*, Georgian Young Lawyers' Association, Tbilisi
International Committee of the Red Cross (ICRC) (2001) *Special Report Georgia: Paradise Lost*, ICRC, Geneva, May
International Federation of Red Cross and Red Crescent Societies (IFRC) (2000) *Internally Displaced Persons: A Socio-Economic Survey*, IFRC, Tbilisi, November
International Helsinki Federation for Human Rights (IHF) (2001) *Human Rights in the OSCE Region: The Balkans, the Caucasus, Europe, Central Asia and North America Report 2001 (Events of 2000)*, IHF, Vienna, September

Kharashvili, Julia, 'Georgia: Coping by Organising. Displaced Georgians from Abkhazia', in Marc Vincent and Birgitte Refslund Sorensen (eds) (2001) *Caught Between Borders – Response Strategies of the Internally Displaced*, Pluto Press (London, Sterling, Virginia), pp227–249

United Nations Commission for Human Rights (UNCHR) (2001) *Report of the Representative of the Secretary-General on Internally Displaced persons, Mr Francis Deng, Submitted Pursuant to Commission on Human Rights Resolution 2000/53, Addendum, Profiles in Displacement: Georgia*, E/CN.4/2001/5/Add.4, UN, Geneva, 25 January

United Nations Office for the Coordination of Humanitarian Affairs (UNOCHA) (2001) 'Georgia Briefing Notes on Samegrelo/Imereti', UNOCHA, Tbilisi, 9 November

—— (2001) 'Georgia Briefing Notes on South Ossetia', UNOCHA, Tbilisi, 15 March

United Nations Security Council (UNSC) (2002) *Report of the Secretary-General concerning the situation in Abkhazia, Georgia*, S/2002/88, UN, New York, 18 January

—— (2001) *Report of the Secretary-General concerning the situation in Abkhazia, Georgia*, S/2001/1008, UN, New York, 24 October

—— (2001) *Report of the Secretary-General concerning the situation in Abkhazia, Georgia*, S/2001/59, UN, New York, 18 January

Republic of Moldova
For Confidence Building Association (2000) *Evaluation of the real number of Internally Displaced Persons in the Republic of Moldova (July–October 2000)*, UNHCR, Chisinau

Nantoi, Oazu (1999) *Report on the Problem of Internally Displaced Persons in the Republic of Moldova*, UNHCR, Chisinau

Organization for Security and Cooperation in Europe (OSCE) (2002) Telephone conversation between OSCE Mission to Moldova and NRC Geneva, 30 May

United Nations High Commission for Refugees (UNHCR) (2002) Telephone conversation between UNHCR Moldova and NRC Geneva, 29 May

—— (2002) 'Refugees and Others of Concern to UNHCR', *2001 UNHCR Population Statistics (Provisional)*, UNHCR, Geneva, 16 May

Russian Federation
Funch Hansen, Lars, and Krag, Helen (1998) *On the Situation in the Prigorodny District (Republic of North Ossetia–Alania, Russian Federation)*, UNHCR, Geneva

Human Rights Watch (HRW) (2002) 'Swept Under: Torture, Forced Disappearances, and Extrajudicial Killings During Sweep Operations in Chechnya', *Reports by Country*, vol 14, no 2(D), HRW, New York

HRW (2002) *Memorandum to the United Nations Commission on Human Rights on the Human Rights Situation in Chechnya*, HRW, New York

Human Rights Centre 'Memorial' (2001) *Situation of Internally Displaced Persons in the Republic of Ingushetia, spring 2001*, Human Rights: HR News, Memorial Website, 13 June, www.memo.ru/eng/memhrc/texts/spring2001.shtml

International Committee of the Red Cross (ICRC) (2002) *Internally Displaced Persons in Ingushetia, Economic Security Review, 14 January–15 February 2002*, ICRC, Geneva and Moscow, February

Médecins Sans Frontières (MSF) (2002) Chechnya/Ingushetia: Vulnerable Persons Denied Assistance, MSF, Brussels

Trier, Tom, and Deniev, Kharon (2000) *Chechnya in Figures, Survey of the Population of the Republic of Chechnya, Russian Federation, as an Instrument for Providing Targeted Humanitarian Assistance, Interim Report, Final Version*, Danish Refugee Council, ASF, Danish People's Aid, Narzan, Stavropol, October

United Nations (UN) (2001) *Consolidated Inter-Agency Appeal 2002, North Caucasus*, UNOCHA, New York and Geneva, November

United Nations High Commissioner for Human Rights (UNHCHR) (2002) *Situation in the Republic of Chechnya of the Russian Federation, Report of the High Commissioner for Human Rights submitted in accordance with Commission resolution 2001/24*, E/CN.4/2002/38, UNHCHR, Geneva

United Nations High Commission for Refugees (UNHCR) (2002) *Paper on Asylum Seekers from the Russian Federation in the context of the situation in Chechnya*, UNHCR, Geneva, January

Turkey

Atreya, Navita, McDowall, David, and Ozbolat, Perihan (2001) *A Report to Asylum Aid, Asylum Seekers from Turkey: the Dangers They Flee (Report of a mission to Turkey, 4-17 October 2000)*, Asylum Aid, London, 28 February

Commission of the European Community (CEC) (2001) *Regular Report on Turkey's Progress towards Accession*, SEC(2001) 1756, CEC, Brussels

Council of Europe (CoE) PA Committee on Migration, Refugees and Demography (2002) *Humanitarian situation of the displaced Kurdish population in Turkey, Committee on Migration, Refugees and Demography*, Rapporteur: Mr John Connor, Ireland, Group of the European People's Party, Doc 9391, CoE, Strasbourg

Export Credits Guarantee Department (ECGD) (2000) *Stakeholders' Attitudes to Involuntary Resettlement in the context of the Ilisu Dam Project, Turkey*, UK government, Turkey, ECGD, UK government site, www.ecgd.gov.uk/downloads/ILISUfinal.pdf

Human Rights Foundation of Turkey (HRTF) (2001) *Monthly Report of Human Rights in Turkey May 2001*, HRTF Documentation Centre, Ankara, May

—— (2001) *Monthly Report of Human Rights in Turkey February 2001*, HRFT Documentation Centre, Ankara, February

—— (2001) *Monthly Report of Human Rights in Turkey January 2001*, HRFT Documentation Centre, Ankara, January

Human Rights Foundation of Turkey/Union of the Chambers of Turkish Engineers and Architects/Immigrants Association for Social Cooperation and Culture/Social Law Research Foundation/Freedom and Solidarity Party/People's Democracy Party (2001) *Joint Press Release*, Press Releases, HRFT website, 31 May, www.tihv.org.tr/press/press20010531.html

Info-Türk (2001), 'EU report: Turkey must do more for EU membership', Info-Türk website, November, www.info-turk.be/279.htm

Turkish Daily News (2001) *Displaced children resorting to crime*, News Articles, Turkish Daily News website, 7 August, www.turkishdailynews.com/old_editions/08_07_01/dom2.htm#d22

Turkish Daily News (2001) *Women are part of the South-Eastern landscape*, News Articles, Turkish Daily News website, 5 April, www.turkishdailynews.com/old_editions/04_05_01/feature.htm#f1

United States Committee for Refugees (USCR) (1999) *The Wall of Denial: Internal Displacement in Turkey*, USCR Washington, DC

Middle East

Regional overview

Cohen, Roberta, and Deng, Francis M (1998) *Masses in Flight, The Global Crisis of Internal Displacement*, Brookings Institution Press, Washington, DC

Iraq

American Friends Service Committee (AFSC) (2000) *Congressional Staffers' Iraq Trip Report*, AFSC, Philadelphia, 21 March

Crossette, Barbara (2000) 'Iraq is Forcing Kurds from their Homes, the UN Reports', *New York Times*, New York, 11 December

Human Rights Watch (HRW) (1993) *Genocide in Iraq: The Anfal Campaign Against the Kurds*, HRW, New York, July

Rekacewicz, Philippe (2000) 'L'Irak, neuf ans après la Guerre du Golfe', *Le Monde Diplomatique*, Paris, January

United Nations Commission for Human Rights (UNCHR) (1999) *Situation of human rights in Iraq, Report submitted by the Special Rapporteur, Mr. Max van der Stoel, in accordance with Commission resolution 1998/65*, E/CN.4/1999/37, UN, Geneva, 26 February

United Nations General Assembly (UNGA) (2000) *Situation of human rights in Iraq, Note by the Secretary-General*, A/55/294, UN, Geneva, 14 August

United Nations Security Council (UNSC) (2001) *Report of the Secretary-General pursuant to paragraph 5 of resolution 1330 (2000)*, S/2001/186, UN, New York, 2 March

—— (1991) *Resolution 688*, S/RES/0688, UN, New York, April

—— (1998) *UN Secretary General Report pursuant to paragraph 10 of Security Council resolution 1153*, S/1998/1100, UN, New York, 19 November

Partow, Hassan (2001) 'The Mesopotamian Marshlands: Demise of an Ecosystem', *Early Warning and Assessment Technical Report*, Division of Early Warning and Assessment Technical Report, UNEP/DEWA/TR.01-3 Rev 1, UNEP, Nairobi

United Nations High Commission for Refugees/Australian Centre for Country of Origin Asylum Research and Documentation (UNHCR/ACCORD) (2000) 'Iraq Country Report', in *Final Report of the 6th European Country of Origin Information Seminar, Vienna*, UNHCR and Accord, Vienna, 14 November

United Nations Children's Fund (UNICEF) (1999) *Results of the 1999 Iraq Child and Maternal Mortality Surveys, Preliminary Report*, UNICEF, Baghdad, 21 August

Israel

Abu–Rabia, Aref (1994) 'The Bedouin Refugees in the Negev', *Refuge*, vol 14, no 6, Centre for Refugee Studies, Toronto, pp15–17

Al–Haj, Majid (1986) 'Adjustment Patterns of the Arab Internal Refugees in Israel', *Internal Migration*, vol 24, no 3, September, pp651–673

BADIL Resource Centre for Palestinian Residency and Refugee Rights (2001) *Report to the Committee on Economic, Social and Cultural Rights, 25th Session, General Item: Follow–Up Procedure (Israel)*, BADIL, Bethlehem, 23 April, p27

Benvenisti, Meron (2001) 'No connection to the right of return', *Ha'aretz Daily Newspaper*, Tel Aviv, 29 November

Bligh, Alexander (1998) 'Israel and the Refugee Problem: From Exodus to Resettlement, 1948–52', *Middle Eastern Studies*, vol 34, no 1, p124

Cohen, Hillel (2000) 'Années 50: Israël loue leurs terres aux Arabes', *Revue d'Etudes Palestiniennes*, vol 22, December, pp48–64

Eban, Abba (1978) *An Autobiography*, Weidenfeld and Nicolson, London

Middle East Research and Information Project (MERIP) (2001) *Palestine, Israel and the Arab–Israeli Conflict, The Palestinian Arab Refugees*, MERIP, Washington, DC

National Committee for the Rights of the Internally Displaced in Israel (2000) *Presentation of the Organization*, National Committee for the Rights of the Internally Displaced in Israel, Shefar-Amr, February

Nir, Ori (2001) 'Focus "Internal refugees" demand their rights too', *Ha'aretz Daily Newspaper*, Tel Aviv, 8 January

Schechla, Joseph (2001) 'The Invisible People Come to Light: Israel's "Internally Displaced" and the "Unrecognized Villages"', *Journal of Palestine Studies*, vol 31, no 1, issue 121, University of California Press for the Institute for Palestine Studies, October, pp20–31

United Nations General Assembly (UNGA) (1948) *Palestine - Progress Report of the United Nations Mediator*, A/RES/194(III), Question of Palestine, UN, New York, 11 December

United Nations Human Rights Committee (1998) *Initial report of States parties due in 1993: Israel*, CCPR/C81/Add.13, UN, Geneva, 9 April

Lebanon

Assaf, Georges, and El-Fil, Rana (2000) 'Resolving the issue of war displacement in Lebanon', *Forced Migration Review*, vol 7, 7 April, pp31–33

Government of Lebanon (1989) *National Reconciliation Charter of Lebanon*, Government of Lebanon, Beirut

Ibrahim, Alia (2001) 'Children of displaced offered compensation to return', *Daily Star*, Beirut, 2 March

—— (2001) 'Help for displaced nears end', *Daily Star*, Beirut, 7 February

International Campaign to Ban Land Mines (ICBL) (2001) *Land Mine Monitor Report 2001*, HRW, New York

United Nations Development Programme (UNDP) (1997) 'Chapter 3k: The Displaced and Development', in *A profile of sustainable human development in Lebanon*, UNDP, New York

Palestinian Territories

Amnesty International (AI) (2001) *Broken Lives – a Year of Intifada*, MDE 15/083/2001, AI, Oxford

—— (ed) (1999) *Israel and the Occupied Territories, Demolition and dispossession: the destruction of Palestinian homes*, MDE 15/059/1999, AI, London, December

Bligh, Alexander (1998) 'Israel and the Refugee Problem: From Exodus to Resettlement, 1948–52,' *Middle Eastern Studies*, vol 34, no 1, p124

B'Tselem (2002) *The Israeli Information Centre for Human Rights in the Occupied Territories*, Statistics, B'Tselem website, www.btselem.org/English/Statistics/index.asp

Human Rights Watch (HRW) (2002) *Israel, the Occupied West Bank and Gaza Strip, and the Palestinian Authority Territories, Jenin: IDF Military Operations*, HRW, New York, May

Middle East Research and Information Project (MERIP) (2001) *Palestine, Israel and the Arab–Israeli Conflict, The Palestinian Arab Refugees*, MERIP, Washington, DC

Refugees International (RI) (2002) Palestinian Refugees Face Humanitarian Crisis as Violence Continues, Bulletins, RI website, 5 April, www.refintl.org/cgi-bin/ri/bulletin?bc=00389

Shragai, Nadav (2000) 'How the Palestinians built their own Jerusalem', *Ha'aretz Daily Newspaper*, Tel Aviv, 5 June

United Nations Commission for Human Rights (UNCHR) (2002) *Report of the Special Rapporteur of the Commission on Human Rights, Mr John Dugard, on the Situation of Human Rights in the Palestinian Territories Occupied by Israel Since 1967*, E/CN.4/2002/32, UN, Geneva, 6 March

United Nations Economic and Social Council (UNECOSOC) (2001) *Implementation of the International Covenant on Economic, Social and Cultural Rights, Addendum, Israel*, E/1989/5/Add.14, UN, New York, 14 May

United Nations General Assembly (UNGA) (1947) *Resolution 181*, A/RES/181(II)(A-B), UN, New York, November

United Nations Children's Fund (UNICEF) (2002) *Occupied Palestinian Territories, Donor Alert*, UNICEF, New York, 5 April

World Bank (2001) *Poverty in the West Bank and Gaza*, World Bank, Washington, DC, January

Syria

Arnold, Michael S (2000) 'The Golan capture', *Jerusalem Post,* Jerusalem, 1 February

Ben-Nahum, Yonatan (1995) 'The Border That Has Not Stopped Moving', *Davar Rishon,* Supplement, 19 December, pp2-3

Fecci, JoMarie (2000) 'A View from Damascus: Internal Refugees From Golan's 244 Destroyed Syrian Villages', *Washington Report on Middle East Affairs,* American Educational Trust (AET), Washington, DC, June, pp10–12

Middle East Media and Research Institute (MEMRI) (2001) *An Interview with Syria's President, Bashar Assad,* MEMRI, Washington, DC, 16 February

—— (2000) 'Leading Israeli Author Skeptical of Peace with Syria', *Special Dispatch No 81 – Israel,* MEMRI, Washington, DC, 24 March

—— (2000) 'An Account of the Syrian-Israeli Negotiations', *Special Dispatch, No 68 – Syria,* MEMRI, Washington, DC

Mission of the Syrian Arab Republic to the United Nations in Geneva (1997) *Position Paper,* Government of Syria, Geneva

United Nations General Assembly (UNGA) (2000) *Implementation of the outcome of the World Summit for Social Development and of the special session of the General Assembly in this regard,* A/55/PV.46, UN, New York, 31 October

United Nations Human Rights Committee (2000) *Syrian Arab Republic,* CCPR/C/SYR/2000/2, UN, Geneva, 25 August

United Nations Security Council (UNSC) (1981) *Israel–Syrian Arab Republic,* Resolution 497, UN, New York, 17 December

Index